Praise for *Mentor*

"I can't think of anyone in American letters other than Frank Conroy whose teaching of writing matched the power of his brilliant prose. His dictums still echo with me, twenty years after being in his workshop. Frank could be dogmatic, brilliant, erratic, and inspired in the space of two hours. Intensely personal, moving, powerful, and insightful, *Mentor* is a must read for people who write and for every reader who has wondered about the mysterious alchemy that produces a writer."

—ABRAHAM VERGHESE, author of *Cutting for Stone*

"*Mentor* is a touching memoir about one of those rare encounters in life where the deep connection between two human beings transcends time and death. It is about artists and their arts, fathers and sons, families and friends, and, above all, love that allows each generation of artists to dream and create on the shoulders of its mentors."

—YIYUN LI, author of *The Vagrants*

"Tom Grimes has written a most affecting book. Part memoir and part homage to his mentor, Frank Conroy, it is also an extremely candid meditation on the writing life, both its joys and its pains. Anyone who has ever been on either side of the mentor-student relationship will catch glimpses of himself in this remarkable memoir."

—SCOTT ANDERSON, author of *Triage*

"*Mentor* is a tender, tough, and appropriately bewildered look into the heart of the Iowa Writers' Workshop—indeed, into what it means to be a writer of ambition altogether. It is also a magnificent double portrait of two fiction writers, rendered in fine, piercing, fond, and ruthless prose—and, above all, a love letter to a teacher."

—ELIZABETH McCRACKEN, author of *An Exact Replica of a Figment of My Imagination*

MENTOR

a memoir

MENTOR

a memoir

TOM GRIMES

Tin House Books
Portland, Oregon & New York, New York

Published by Tin House Books, Portland, Oregon, and New York, New York
Distributed to the trade by Publishers Group West, 1700 Fourth St., Berkeley, CA 94710, www.pgw.com

Library of Congress Cataloging-in-Publication Data
Grimes, Tom, 1954-
Mentor : a memoir / Tom Grimes.
     p. cm.
Includes bibliographical references and index.
ISBN 978-0-9825048-8-8 (alk. paper) — ISBN 978-0-9825048-9-5 (pbk. : alk. paper)
1. Grimes, Tom, 1954- 2. Conroy, Frank, 1936-2005. 3. Authors, American—20th century—Biography. 4. Authorship. 5. Mentoring of authors—United States. 6. Creative writing (Higher education)—United States. I. Title.
PS3557.R489985Z46 2010
813'.54—dc22
[B]
                          2010007124

First U.S. edition 2010

An excerpt from this work appeared in *Narrative Magazine.*

Printed in Canada

Interior design by Diane Chonette

www.tinhouse.com

The publisher is grateful for permission to reproduce excerpts of Frank Conroy's work from *Stop-Time,* Viking Penguin; *Body & Soul* and *Dogs Bark, but the Caravan Rolls On,* Houghton Mifflin Harcourt; *Time and Tide,* Crown Publishers; as well as Fritz McDonald for his essay that appeared in *The Workshop: Seven Decades from the Iowa Writers' Workshop,* edited by Tom Grimes; Brady Udall for his introduction to "Buckeye the Elder," which appeared in *The Workshop: Seven Decades from the Iowa Writers' Workshop,* edited by Tom Grimes; e-mail from Neil Olson; and, with the author's deepest gratitude, letters written to him by Will Conroy.

For the Conroys

Maggie, Dan, Will, and Tim

PART ONE

CHAPTER ONE

I was living in Key West and working as a waiter the first time I saw Frank Conroy. Each January, a literary seminar brought two dozen famous writers to the island. Panels featuring them took place in a large auditorium at the community college. On opening day at nine o'clock in the morning, the year's keynote speaker addressed everyone in attendance. Given that my restaurant shift ended sometime after midnight and I invariably closed the After Deck bar several hours later, 9:00 AM had a middle-of-the-night feel to me. The bar's wooden planks, white tables, and white chairs were suspended several feet above the Atlantic's shallow inlet and overlooked what, as a young writer, I knew to be Sam Lawrence's house. As an editor, he'd published Kurt Vonnegut, Tim O'Brien, and Thomas McGuane, idols to me at the time. Occasionally, I'd spot a cocktail party under way on his deck and wonder who was there sipping a scotch and if, someday, I might be one of them.

When my alarm rang at eight thirty, I rose, splashed water on my face, brushed my teeth, then biked across the island from the clapboard house where I lived to the hall where Frank Conroy was

scheduled to speak. I took a seat in the dim balcony, far from the stage.
I'd been writing for more than a decade, and during the past year my
first stories had found homes in nationally respected literary journals.
Nevertheless, the chasm between the podium and myself seemed
unbridgeable. It was as if the writers who would occupy the stage's
empty chairs had pierced a literary dimension in space-time and had
returned simply to pass along wisdom, be applauded, and collect an
honorarium. I feared that I would never join their ranks. I'd grown
up in a bookless house, raised by a father who'd quit school after the
eighth grade and mocked the novels I toted to the mediocre junior
college in New York that had granted me admission. And although I'd
managed two successful businesses in Manhattan—one of which sold
expensive stationery, the other housewares and antiques—before my
wife, Jody, and I moved to Key West two years earlier, I felt condemned
to lead a waiter's life, not a writer's. That my station would climb no
higher seemed apparent. Each winter, during high season, town was
packed with tourists, and the job's relentless, exhausting labor made
composing an aesthetically coherent sentence, one with the rhythm,
tempo, and music of a distinctive voice, as impossible for me as it was
impossible for a physicist to snatch an electron from space while it
orbited the nucleus of an atom. Clearly, I needed to change my life, but
I didn't know what life would replace the one I'd created. Like a novelist who never outlines a book, I'd never plotted my future. Instead, I
trusted my intuition. Sometimes the results were good; other times,
disastrous. Only one constant existed: I wrote. Writing was my center of gravity. If I quit, I'd implode. All my notebooks would become
worthless. All my unfinished drafts, orphaned. The million words I'd
written, however, insisted that I not give up. And since I couldn't allow
my doubt to overwhelm my work, at times I needed to glimpse the life
I'd envisioned for myself. So I went to hear Frank Conroy speak.

I also went because, when I'd recently mentioned applying to law
school, Jody stunned me by suggesting that I apply to writing programs instead. In New York, we'd lived four blocks from NYU and ten
subway stops from Columbia University, each of which had a notable

creative writing program, but never once had we discussed submitting my work to either of them. Nor had I ever had an impulse to join a writers' group. I had no writer friends. I pursued my work in a vacuum. What existed were books, a typewriter, notepads, pencils, erasers, and I. Plus, the rejection letters I plucked out of our narrow metal mailbox, which I dreaded and revered for its power either to obliterate my expectations or, rarely, to deliver word of my infinitesimal success. Beyond these monkish concerns, a palpable literary world didn't exist for me. But, with several stories in print and no other prospects, I decided to take Jody's advice, although I still half believed that creative writing programs had nothing to teach anyone and was suddenly terrified of being rejected. I selected four programs: Iowa because it was Iowa; Syracuse because Raymond Carver had taught there, and it was in New York; Boston University because I could graduate in a year; and the University of Florida at Gainesville because it was near Key West and so second rate that it would probably accept me without hesitation. I assembled an application that included the beginning of a novel—not the slim, semiautobiographical novel I'd written in my midtwenties, but a new, more ambitious one. I dropped four copies off at the Key West post office and then did what most young writers do—I waited.

In the auditorium, roughly three hundred people, most in their fifties or sixties, waited for Frank Conroy to appear. In 1987, he'd become the director of the Iowa Writers' Workshop, and by the time he arrived in Key West in January 1989, he'd become as renowned for his new position as he'd been celebrated for his memoir, *Stop-Time*, twenty years earlier. Now, the raked rows of cushioned chairs and the velvet maroon drape, which hung several feet behind the dais, reinforced the event's theatricality. A program listing the seminar's events had been handed out. Around me, audience members studied each author's biographical note, or circled the day and time of a panel they didn't want to miss. A few men wore Hawaiian shirts, and the smooth face of the woman seated beside me gleamed with lotion. She smelled like a freshly peeled mango, and I wondered if she was, or hoped to be, a writer. Her long, glossy fingernails would have made typing difficult, and it was too dark to see if, like me, she had a calloused groove near the upper knuckle of her middle finger from holding a pencil while scribbling in a notebook. A slender gold bracelet circled her tanned left wrist, and her arms, bare to the shoulder, had the lean, sculpted look of a fortysomething woman who excelled in yoga and ran a charity marathon once a year. I imagined her sitting, freshly showered, at a walnut-stained, Colonial-style, lemon-waxed desk with brass handles on each of its six drawers. Already, the woman had become a character to me. Then the lights dimmed and a spotlight illuminated the podium. Frank Conroy emerged from the shadows and, in a gait neither hurried nor languid but at the deliberate pace of someone accustomed to having audiences await his arrival, he made his way to the microphone. He carried several sheets of white eight-and-a-half-by-eleven-inch paper in one hand. He parted his silvery-gray hair on the left like a schoolboy, yet the comfortable way he moved in his slightly baggy blazer and khaki pants lent him a patrician style. It seemed as if he'd boarded at a preparatory academy during his early teens and dated girls who wore plaid skirts and kneesocks before enrolling at Wellesley or Bard, when in fact he'd been educated at a New York City public high school. He approached my height, six foot, perhaps an inch more. He raised his head just enough for the audience at the rear of the hall to get a glimpse of his face as he adjusted the microphone. For an instant, his eyeglass lenses reflected the light. Then he lowered his head and, without acknowledging anyone's presence, began to read. I'd planned to approach him to ask one question when he finished speaking. How that encounter would play out dominated my thoughts and numbed most of my senses. I no longer noticed the woman's scent or felt the chair supporting me. If acid burned my throat, I didn't taste it. I don't remember a single syllable formed by his tongue and palate; to me, they composed a series of incomprehensible sounds. For twenty minutes, watching him stand at the podium constituted my entire universe. Then his address ended and he walked off the stage, ignoring what I recognized as applause.

I'd sat at the end of a row so I wouldn't have to say "Excuse me" to anyone as I left the hall. A carpeted stairwell led to the ground floor and I scurried down it, my footsteps muffled. I found the broad, high-ceilinged lobby empty except for a service counter, which sold coffee and pastries. He may have exited through a rear door, or remained backstage to talk with friends. He couldn't have been avoiding me because he didn't know I was pursuing him. So I waited and, while waiting, revised the latest draft of what I would say. First, a greeting; then an introductory statement followed by, if permitted, a question I'd honed to the minimum number of words. I decided to say: "Excuse me, Mr. Conroy. I've applied for admission to the Iowa Writers' Workshop. *If accepted* at thirty-two, do you think I'm too old to attend?" Settling on this, I felt like I'd made a publication deadline, for three seconds later, out from behind a wall leading backstage stepped Frank Conroy. He wore scuffed running shoes and was slightly pigeon-toed. He reached into one blazer pocket and retrieved a crumpled handkerchief, which placed him in another era. I thought handkerchiefs, like fedoras, had gone out of style. He made his way toward me, which lifted my hopes, but intensified my anxiety. Then I understood the purpose of his direction: he was headed my way because I stood between the coffee counter and him. I judged five feet to be a respectful distance from which to launch a question. Any farther I would have to shout, any closer I would have to whisper. So I said, "Mr. Conroy, I enjoyed your talk and wonder if I could ask you one question?"

He wiped the tip of his nose, bunched his handkerchief, and slipped it into his pocket.

"I've applied to the Writers' Workshop."

"Yeah, you and eight hundred others."

He didn't look at me, or stop walking, as he said it. Instead, he cruised by the way an ocean liner steams past a small, deserted island. His quick and impersonal brushback caught me off guard, and I started to ask question two before question one had been answered.

"Just one question, five seconds," I said, improvising.

"Let me get a cup of tea," he said.

I watched him stroll to the counter, place his order, search an incredibly long time for a fistful of coins, pay, pour a line of sugar as white and long as an unfiltered cigarette into his cardboard cup, then turn and once again head my way. When he was about five yards away, he ceased stirring his tea, looked up, and smiled. His impatience had been momentary. He had a cold, and now, tea in hand, he would happily answer my question. He arched his eyebrows, elongating his face, which made him seem ten years younger as he shouted, "Hi!" Surprised, I extended my hand when he extended his. Then he walked right past me. He'd spotted an old friend. Shoulder to shoulder, their backs to me, they sauntered off.

Outside, my hands shook as I tried to fit the key into my bike's lock. I cursed the lock, its chain, my hands, and my stupid fucking bike, which I rode across town, at times standing on the pedals, like a kid, pumping harder in order to move faster. At home, I kicked open the front gate, chained the bike to the front porch, unlocked the front door, slammed it shut behind me, bounded up the uncarpeted stairs I'd painted battleship gray on one of my days off, then slowed at the top of them, where two floor-to-ceiling bookcases made of one-by-six pine wood planks stood. I'd never alphabetized my library. The three hundred or more books I owned had tattered spines. Most were paperbacks. Some were taller than others, making the collection look craggy and disheveled. I spotted *Stop-Time* on a high shelf and reached for it, tipping it forward and grabbing it. Jody had heard me swearing in the hallway as I looked for the book. Alarmed, she'd come to find me.

"What's wrong?"

"Nothing."

I opened the book to its center.

"What are you doing?"

Without answering, I struggled to tear it in half. When I failed, I ripped out pages by the handful until I'd gutted the thing, splitting in two the author's name and the book's title. Then I carried the shredded mess into the kitchen and flung it at the trash bin, railing at pages that fluttered away. I collected them, maddest at the ones that insisted on slipping out of my fingers. Once I'd crushed every page by jamming my foot into the trash bin and stomping on the pile with one foot, I turned and said, "Fuck Frank Conroy."

* * *

Gainesville turned me down. The writing program's director wrote a letter in which he explained that I would thrive in a different environment. Jody interpreted the letter generously.

"He's saying you belong in a better program."

"He's saying I'm rejected." I closed my fist around the sheet of stationery and dropped the paper ball into the trash.

Our mail arrived at 3:00 PM. By that time, I had laid one of my five pink button-down shirts on our ironing board to press it before doing the same to one of the white aprons I tied around my waist each evening. I owned two pairs of tan, permanently creased, stain-resistant, polyester-blend pants and a pair of brown shoes with leather tops and spongy rubber soles to cushion my feet. Once I began to prep for work, I refused to collect the day's mail. Even if a tall magazine or an envelope propped open the wooden mailbox's lid, I ignored it. I closed the gate, swung my right leg over my bike seat, and pedaled to work. I didn't want to know if another story had been rejected. Being a servant required supreme detachment, a buffer between myself and the nightly anger, frustration, and humiliation guaranteed by the job. To survive psychologically, I practiced "empty mind," a state in which Zen masters experience the world as simultaneously substantial and empty. It's there, yet it isn't. From my shift's beginning until its end, the world was nothing and I was no one. If I knew that a story had been rejected, maintaining this state was impossible. My ego remained attached to my failure. Then, rather than basking in emptiness, I heard customers' complaints, resented their demands, and bitched if I received a lousy tip. But if I didn't open a rejection letter before work, it didn't exist until I was home, where, after midnight and after I'd had several beers, my reaction to bad news was muted, my pain dulled. Also, the best palliative for rejection was immediately available. I would file the letter, print a fresh copy of the story, and change the heading of my "Dear Editor" cover letter. The next morning, I would mail out the package, along with a stamped, self-addressed envelope in which an editor could place a rejection letter. Fresh hope negated past failure. My story had three to six months to live, and I could forget it, as I had trained myself to do.

Syracuse turned me down next. But rather than simply sending a letter, the program's staff returned my application manuscript, upon which someone had scrawled and then partially erased the words *B-, boring*. This may have been due to laziness. After all, someone could have used Wite-Out to mask the handwriting, made a copy of the original page, and replaced it with an innocent replica. Not only would this have been kind, it also would have been postmodern: a copy of a copy of a copy, like a Warhol lithograph of soup cans or Marilyn Monroe. Classic rejection letters lie to minimize an author's pain: "We regret." "We wish we could." "We're sorry but due to space limitations." But editors never regret, wish, or feel sorry: they simply avoid being cruel, and the staff at Syracuse hadn't. At best, its response was careless, at worst, mocking and sadistic.

I recall being furious about the rejection, and so, one frustrated afternoon, I violated every waiter's cardinal rule: on your day off, never answer your phone an hour before service begins unless you want to listen to a sick or hungover colleague beg you to work his or her shift. But as I was in the mood to punish myself for continuing to be a failure, I picked up the receiver and said, "Hello."

The man's voice, slightly hoarse from smoking cigarettes, was several octaves higher that it had been the first time I'd heard it. Now, it sounded confident, coolly eager. And rather than callously avoiding me, the man speaking was searching for me.

"This is Frank Conroy from the Iowa Writers' Workshop," the voice said. "I'd like to speak to Tom Grimes."

My hand trembling as if I'd done something wrong, I answered, "Speaking."

"I never call anyone," he said, "but I've read your manuscript."

I don't remember what Frank said next. I do remember flashing on an image of our kitchen trash can crammed with *Stop-Time*'s torn pages. Nevertheless, my pages had bridged the chasm between "Fuck Frank Conroy" and the fact that Frank Conroy was speaking to me. He praised, in words I can't articulate, the excerpt of my unfinished novel. Attempting to write the book terrified me. A premonition that I may have been setting myself up for a literary failure from which I'd never recover stalked every word I wrote. Perhaps I'd taken on too large a subject, but within a minute of half hearing Frank's voice, I trusted his interest in my work and I said, "I don't know if I can finish the novel without help."

He said, "Well, when you're here, you'll get it."

I muttered, "Thanks." And then there was a pause before he spoke again.

"Your file says you're a waiter at Louie's Backyard in Key West. Is that the place on the water?"

"Yes, it is."

Instantly forgetting literature and sounding like a boy recounting a day at an amusement park, he said, "They make the best meat-loaf sandwich I've ever had!"

Wanting to somehow return his generosity, I said, "I'll get the recipe for you, if you want it."

Then Frank did what, as I would later come to understand, Frank always did. He said, "Give it to Connie when she calls you. You're getting our top scholarship." In his mind, no misgivings existed; I'd take it. "See you in August." He hung up before I could say, "Okay."

I can't say what happened after I returned the phone to its cradle. In a creative writing workshop, this is when the famous writer overseeing the conversation (I'll call him Frank) says, "First off, don't be vague. Don't just have the character wander around the apartment, dazed. Give the reader concrete details. You have five senses at your disposal: touch, sight, scent, taste, and hearing. Use them. As in, 'I heard the front door close. The loud crackle of a brown paper grocery bag drifted up the stairwell.' (Is *drifted* the best verb?) 'My wife was home, and the ceiling fan whirred as I stood in the living room, waiting for her.' We know she's going to walk through the living room doorway moments later, so don't write, 'moments later.' It's redundant and stupid. These characters have cats. Have one cat stroll toward the staircase. Or the other one raise its head from the seat cushion it's lounging on. Don't just have the narrator say—and why is the author using first person, anyway? Third would distance the writer from the main character. That way the author doesn't risk self-indulgence. Follow? The character's life has suddenly—never use the word *suddenly*— the character's life has been altered in a manner he doesn't yet fully comprehend. But, in addition to excitement, the situation requires a touch of gravitas. I'm not saying describe a funeral. Just don't have the main character leap up and yell, 'Yippee!' Above all, avoid melodrama. Understate the narrator's emotional reaction. What the author withholds, the reader supplies. Establish and maintain the story's cocreation; it's essential. Have the character do something he'd normally do. Open a beer. Put the can in a rubber holder so the can doesn't sweat. And if you risk having him recall the shredded pages of *Stop-Time* as he drops the flip top into the trash, don't linger on it. One sentence. At that point, his wife walks into the kitchen, carrying groceries. It's probably best if she doesn't say anything. And when he speaks, leaving out 'he said' depersonalizes his statement. Remember, the reader knows what's coming. Nothing in the narrator's life will ever be the same. So capture his astonishment in unadorned dialogue. 'Frank Conroy called. I got into Iowa.' End of scene. End of chapter. Any questions?"

No.

CHAPTER TWO

The day after my conversation with Frank, I pedaled to the local bookstore where I often spent hot afternoons among its deserted stacks, skimming and then purchasing dusty, inexpensive editions of used books. I rarely could afford to buy new, expensive books, which the owner refused to discount. He was a thin man with dark red hair and a mustache I found pretentious. He sat near the cash register, adjacent to the front door. Since he also refused to air-condition the shop, a six-foot-high fan spun above his head as he perched on a wooden stool, leafing through a book. He never said hello to me, not when I walked in, not when I set books on the counter for him to ring up, and definitely not when I left the store empty-handed. Even when a book was published by a writer so important to me that I couldn't wait a year for it to appear in paperback and spent $12.95 for the hardcover, he still refused to acknowledge me. Occasionally, I'd see him at a literary event in town—a reading, a talk. Afterward, he would always make his way through the exiting crowd to shake the celebrated author's hand and smile throughout their discussion, starstruck and fawning. Then he'd hand the writer his business card and the following day autographed copies of the writer's books were on display in the bookstore's window.

After chaining my bike to a parking meter, I walked into the store, worried that a copy of *Stop-Time* wouldn't be in stock. But in the alphabetically organized fiction section, I found several editions. Some had brittle yellow pages; others were damp from Key West's humidity. A few were water-stained, the typeface distorted by the book's bloated pages. Among the group stood three recent Viking Penguin paperbacks. The words "Author of *Midair*," the title of Frank's story collection, were printed beneath his name. Between its appearance and *Stop-Time*'s, eighteen years had passed, and, as Frank's initial celebrity faded, he'd become a largely forgotten writer. *Stop-Time* had been a 1968 National Book Award finalist for nonfiction, and despite its modest sales—seven thousand copies in hardcover—at age twenty-nine Frank's stardom was confirmed by New York's literary heavyweights. Norman Mailer called *Stop-Time*, "Unique, an autobiography with the intimate unprotected candor of a novel." William Styron praised it. Soon, *Esquire* and the *New Yorker* commissioned articles and essays. Frank swigged bourbon at Elaine's, a chic Upper East Side restaurant where Woody Allen had a reserved table. Hollywood began to send Frank five-figure checks for doctoring screenplays. With his wife and two young sons, he moved from Manhattan to Brooklyn Heights, and, on Nantucket Island, he reconstructed, with the help of a crew of hippies, an unheated barn, which would be their summer house. As a boy, Frank had been rootless and poor. Now he had two homes, two sons, and, because of his wife's trust fund and what he earned from writing, he had money, too.

"Success was an intoxicant," he later wrote about that period of his life. "Music, movies, my favorite bar, the excitement of meeting new people after my first book came out. There was a kind of forward momentum I never questioned but simply rode, night after night, a continuous social stimulation to which I became addicted. And the more my marriage weakened, the more desperately I tore around town. Much deeply foolish behavior, and I blame no one but myself for that. Years of hysteria." At thirty-five, Frank "had no job, an unpredictable income as a pianist and freelance magazine writer, no savings, and no plan." After his divorce, his time with his sons—one five, one seven—would be limited to three months each summer. Otherwise, he was absent, mimicking his own father- less childhood. He retreated to Nantucket, where he tried working on a scallop boat, but found he wasn't strong enough to keep up. Each winter, he had to crawl under his barn to deice the frozen alu- minum pipes with a blowtorch. Soon, screenwriting assignments dwindled to nothing, and magazines no longer commissioned him to write articles. He was alone and had only one means of rescuing himself: the piano. As a boy, he'd taught himself how to play. So he put together a jazz quintet, which began to perform at a club called the Roadhouse. Summer tourists filled the band's coffers, and each winter local patrons provided enough money to allow Frank to pay his mortgage and buy groceries. He'd survived without help from New York. "Once you leave, people simply forget about you," he wrote. Iowa hadn't. Just as I'd been stunned when I received Frank's call, he was astonished to receive a call from John Leggett, at the time the workshop's director. The call would change Frank's life. "Forty, broke, unemployed and in debt, I accepted an offer to come to Iowa and the well-known Writers' Workshop more from a sense of desperation than any deep conviction that I'd know what to do when faced with a roomful of young writers. I was, in fact, appre- hensive." That passed. By the time Frank called me, he'd become comfortably authoritative. Like a character out of Dickens, Frank's literary touchstone, he'd risen from debtor to the workshop's direc- tor. *Stop-Time* had survived, too. Twenty years after publication, it was still in print. I can't remember when I first read it, or recall buying my first copy—I've had several—or even squeezing it onto a shelf among the hundreds of books I owned. But, at some point,

Stop-Time appeared, like an unanticipated supernova, in my literary galaxy. And since Frank's story was similar to mine, I was drawn to it, the way gravity draws planets toward the sun. In the sweltering bookshop, I clutched an intact copy of it bearing a subtitle: *The Classic Memoir of Adolescence.* Above Frank's name, an Andrew Wyeth–like illustration depicts a black-haired boy. His age is indeterminate—he might be twelve, he might be fifteen. He leans against a building's outer wall, its color a washed-out tan, duskier than a strip of white pine. In the distance stand two leafless trees. A wintry sun casts no shadows. The boy wears a dark green, zippered jacket, visible from its collar to midarm. His head tilts toward the reader, who notices the boy's partially closed eyelids, his straight but somewhat thick nose, his graceful lips. It's a somber portrait, the boy's expression guarded, his vulnerability unmistakable. Copy in hand, I walked to the register, where the owner ignored me as I laid three one-dollar bills on his tacky countertop and then waited for change. I unchained my bike and rode home. I had several hours before I needed to prepare for the night's shift. So I sat on our apartment's small deck and began rereading *Stop-Time*, freshly curious, and absolved of my literary sin.

CHAPTER THREE

Every author is required to use only those details that advance the story. If a detail is essential, keep it. If it isn't, cut it. So I won't dwell on the elation I felt after I'd served my final customer, or describe my hellacious trip through thunderstorms, traffic jams, treacherous mountain roads, and oceans of cornfields from Key West to Iowa City in a U-Haul truck, accompanied by Jody and two sedated yet nonetheless cranky cats. Instead, I'll tell you about Connie Brothers. Connie had shoulder-length, pecan-colored hair. At forty-five, her face lacked wrinkles and crow's feet, and her round cheeks were always faintly pink, as if she'd just come in from the cold. A small, nearly undetectable mole resided above the right side of her mouth. Connie was slight, she stood about five foot six, and other than the fact that she never wore jeans, I can't recollect a single blouse or skirt from her nondescript wardrobe. In a way, this simplicity made her seem, to me, otherworldly and eternal. I've known Connie for many years, and her looks defy age. Perhaps her continual happiness keeps it at bay. I don't know. But I've never seen her upset or angry. And not once have I entered her office without her looking up to smile at me.

The day after Frank and I spoke, she called me. Her voice was slightly nasal yet softened by a perpetual whisper. At times, she sounded like an excited schoolgirl revealing a secret to a friend, and I don't believe she ever uttered my last name. From the outset it was, "Tom? It's Connie." She mentioned reading my application manuscript. Then she said, "Frank wants you to have the Maytag," a scholarship named for the washing machine company. "It's ten thousand dollars a year, and you aren't obligated to do anything but write."

"Really?"

"Yeah."

"Frank mentioned this, but can I ask you something?"

"What is it? Tell me." Her tone shifted to one of concern. She must have sensed my nervousness and the fact that I hesitated to ask what I wanted to ask, as if by doing so I'd be breaking a rule or causing trouble.

"Well, do you think I could teach instead?"

"You mean you'd rather work than have the scholarship?"

"Yes."

"Now why would you want to do that?" she said, as if she'd encountered an endangered species and wanted to know how it survived.

"I may want to teach after I graduate," I said. I'd be thirty-five by then and I'd sworn never again to utter the words "Can I tell you about our specials this evening?" I explained that I wanted to see if I liked teaching. If I did and if I was good at it, then having two years of experience would strengthen my résumé.

"No one's ever turned down the Maytag before."

"You think it's a bad idea?"

"No, no, not at all."

"Should I do it?"

"Are you sure you want to?"

I glanced at Jody, who was seated next to me at the kitchen table.

She nodded. "Yes," I said.

"Absolutely?"

"Yes."

"Okay. I'll tell Frank."

I'd neglected to consider the possibility of antagonizing him and didn't know if he was as quick-tempered as my father. "Will he be upset?"

"Of course not. He said to give you whatever you want."

"You're sure?"

"Yes."

"Positive?"

"Yes."

"Okay, then. Ask him."

At a salary that would equal the scholarship's stipend, ten thousand dollars for the year, I was assigned to teach sophomore literature courses, rather than freshman comp. I could choose the books I wanted to teach. Since I was writing a first-person novel, I decided that I would study, along with my students, first-person novels.

"And Frank's okay with this idea?"

"Actually," Connie said, "he admired it."

* * *

Jody and I found a small house with a second-floor room adjacent to our bedroom where I'd work. I assembled my makeshift desk in front of a window that looked down on a narrow dirt road and the back-yards and wooden garages bordering each side of it. It was August, and the leaves of the treetop outside the window partially obscured my view, but they left enough natural light for me to write by each morning. Before classes started, I prepared my syllabus and began to read the novels I would teach. On the first day of classes, I opened a spiral-bound, red-covered notebook. After ruling out notebooks with cerulean blue and pea green covers, I'd bought five red ones. I'm a superstitious writer. I didn't want to switch colors as I wrote the novel, and my intuition had drawn me to red, which I believed would bring me luck, as would the new pack of twelve No. 2 pencils, a thumb-sized pink eraser, and a handheld pencil sharpener with a transparent plastic casing that allowed me to see the sharpener's blade peel away thin slices of wood each time I needed to write with a finer point.

I was determined to work three to four hours per day, seven days a week. At 8:30 AM, when Jody left for her new job at a design firm, I carried a cup of milky coffee and a slice of toast lacquered with jam into my office, closed the door, and waited. The air still, the room quiet, my pencil ready, the page blank and patient. An hour passed. Then for ten minutes I watched a squirrel leap from branch to branch and occasionally pause to scratch one ear with his rear claw, or else perch on a limb, looking attentive and slightly paranoid. As cars exited garages and rolled down the dirt lane, I studied them with sniperlike concentration, noting their grimy windshields or polished hoods. Gradually, the sun crept toward its noonday peak and brightened my window. Shadows no longer slanted. Instead, they stood as erect as cadets. And I developed a layman's interest in avian life. I'd been unaware of my interest in blue jays and cardinals. Why hadn't I noticed their vibrant plumage before? Maybe I could become an ornithologist. And why were sports teams named after birds, fish, and marine mammals? The blue jays, the cardinals, the marlins, the dolphins? From time to time, I summoned the energy to focus on my novel, on the empty page, and on the words I needed to fill it. Hemingway eluded this mental blankness by stopping work midsentence. The next morning, he'd have to finish the sentence. By the time he did, he'd be into the novel again, its tempo, its rhythm, its groove, its landscape, its characters' thoughts and their actions. I had to find that first word. And I'd made a rule: I would never leave my chair until I'd pressed enough graphite onto a page to form a paragraph. I'd staked my future on this book. I either wrote it and succeeded, or I failed to and was finished.

Five years earlier, I'd begun the novel without a clue as to what, if anything, it might become. Immodestly, I wanted to rewrite *The Great Gatsby*, and for several days I mimicked its sentence rhythms, its restrained, romantic, yet morally upright cadence, which perfectly articulated Nick Carraway's view of the world. I imitated Fitzgerald's linguistic fluidity and the nuanced felicity of his prose. In an abstract way, I focused not on plot or character, but on money, and a grandiose, and no doubt naïve, insight into its place in American life. I continued this, filling perhaps twenty notebook pages, until a sentence escaped from Fitzgerald's parade of flawless sentences and became my own. I heard my narrator say, "A word of advice: Don't appear on the cover of *Sports Illustrated* when you're twenty-one." And then I listened and wrote. I wasn't taking dictation; I revised phrases and chose more accurate or appropriate words before committing them to paper. But I had a character, although I didn't have his story, only the genesis of it. I'd never expected to write about baseball. My imagination had surprised me, and so I made a decision. If baseball was to be my subject, then baseball would be the lens through which I examined America. Baseball would be my great white whale. And as I was writing the novel's initial pages, I discovered a passage in John Cheever's diaries that summed up my task. At least, I believed it did. And so, at all times, I kept it tucked in my notebook, and I reread it often, to assuage my doubts and to remind me of what I'd set out to accomplish.

Cheever had written: "I think that the task of an American writer is not to describe the misgivings of a woman taken in adultery as she looks out of a window at the rain but to describe four hundred people under the lights reaching for a foul ball. This is ceremony. The umpires in clericals, sifting out the souls of the players; the faint thunder as ten thousand people, at the bottom of the eighth, head for the exits. The sense of moral judgments embodied in a migratory vastness."

Now, at my desk, I waited. Several hours later I wrote my first sentence in Iowa City. From there, I continued. Calm, euphoric, terrified.

* * *

I met Connie in her small office. Or maybe the office only felt small because it was filled with hundreds of books written by graduates, dozens of the most recent ones stacked on her desk. Once I sat down she said, "So, tell me everything." I tried to compress the details of my life into a coherent narrative. And when I left her office an hour later she said, as if she'd adopted me, "See you, sweetie."

But I still hadn't met Frank. I'd *seen* him, along with everyone else in the program, the day preceding our first class. We'd gathered in a large classroom, many of us sitting lotus style on the floor, or with our knees pulled to our chest, once all the seats were taken. Frank stood at a podium and introduced himself. Then he introduced the faculty, some of whom had attended the meeting, and some whom hadn't. Finally, he mentioned the year's visiting writers, concluding with "And Norman Mailer is coming," his voice rising to convey our good fortune, although Mailer's strongest work, which I admired, was a decade old and younger students considered him a relic. If Frank had promised Raymond Carver, a buzz would have engulfed the room. But Carver had died a year earlier, in 1988.

In any case, I was electrified by hope. And I'd anticipated a grand setting for the workshop. Green, freshly clipped lawns, ivy-covered walls. Instead, the English-Philosophy Building was a square brick structure with few windows surrounded by a busy road, the muddy Iowa River, a parking lot, and a set of train tracks. EPB's halls were dim and boxcar straight, its tile floors scuff marked, its plaster ceiling low. Light fixtures were scarce. Room 457, which sounded like a torture cell out of Orwell's *1984*, would be where Frank held his workshop. I reached it by climbing four flights of thick metal stairs. Six or seven students loitered outside its doors. Feeling out of my depth, and by nature prone to solitude, I wandered past them. Fifty feet away, a short hallway intersected with the main one and I slid into it. A bulletin board had been nailed to one wall and I scanned the papers tacked to it. They announced fiction competitions, calls for manuscripts, and fellowship application deadlines. While I was studying the notices, a door opened, brightening the hallway. I looked to my left and saw Frank appear in its archway, holding a set of keys. He glanced up. His iciness toward would-be writers was less intense than it had been in Key West, but still noticeable. He paused to look at me. Connie must have described me to him because a moment later he said, "Are you Tom?"

"Yes."

"Come on in here." Once we were in his office, he said, "Close the door." He sat behind a wide desk. Manuscripts were everywhere. An Oxford American Dictionary was propped open on a stand behind his chair, its fine print visible from where he'd told me to take a seat. He didn't ask about me at all. To him, I was a novel incarnate. All he saw was literary promise. But being in that room with him altered my perception and I experienced a type of vertigo. I believe he said, "I'll tell you. Your manuscript. Jesus Christ." I'm certain that, an instant later, he said, "If you want, you can have the best agent in America tomorrow. I'll call her in the morning, if you want me to." *Her* being Candida Donadio, who had sold Philip Roth's *Goodbye, Columbus*, as well as Joseph Heller's *Catch-22* (which was originally entitled *Catch 18*, but another writer, Leon Uris, had published a novel called *Mila 18*, so, to avoid confusion and possibly lose sales, Candida changed 18 to 22, for October 22, her birthday. Heller received a $750 advance, and $750 on publication.) Candida had also represented Thomas Pynchon (who later married her assistant, Melanie Jackson, and became *her* client). And she peddled the work of William Gaddis, Robert Stone, Mario Puzo (an obscure literary novelist until he wrote *The Godfather*), and, of course, Frank.

Surprising myself, I hesitated. In retrospect, I believe I declined Frank's offer because I was superstitious and somewhat overwhelmed. So I said, "Thanks." Then I added, "Is it okay if I don't commit right now?"

Within an instant he raised his hands, don't-shoot-me style, and said, "Absolutely! Absolutely!" He'd made an offer I didn't seem comfortable with, and he wanted me to know that whatever I chose to do was okay with him. No reasons needed. No guilt.

I said, "I'd rather write the book without that pressure."

"I understand. Don't worry about it. You know, if I rushed you—"

"No, no, I appreciate it. I mean, thanks. But it doesn't feel, well, somehow it doesn't feel right."

"Hey, I understand. Do what you need to do. When you want me, I'm here." He checked his watch. "I guess we should get started."

Two doors led into 457. Knowing enough not to trail the program's director into class on the first day, I made sure that Frank entered through one, and I, lagging behind, entered through the other. Frank didn't take attendance. Instead, he went directly to the blackboard and picked up a piece of chalk. He wrote: *meaning, sense, clarity.*

Then he faced us. "If you don't have these, you don't have a reader." He moved sideways and drew an arc. At its two bases, he wrote: *writer, reader.* At the top of the arc he wrote: *zone.*

"The writer cocreates the text with the reader. If a writer gives the reader too much information, the reader feels forced to accept whatever the writer says and eventually stops reading. If a writer gives the reader too little information, the reader feels compelled to search for whatever the writer says and eventually stops reading. So, you want to meet the reader halfway." He circled the word zone. "That's where you want to be." He turned to the board again and sketched a rectangle. Inside it he wrote: *voice, tone, mood.*

Above that, he drew a smaller rectangle, then a smaller one, and one smaller still, as they climbed the board in the shape of a ziggurat. Beginning with the lowest of the three rectangles and then continuing upward, he wrote a word inside each of them: *subtext, metaphor, symbol.*

He waved a hand at them and said, "That's the fancy stuff. For now, worry about the basics." Then he took a seat at the square that had been formed by placing several desks adjacent to one another.

He said, "We do two stories a week. Who'll go up first?" Two of my classmates each raised a hand. "Okay," Frank said. "And the week after?" Two more. "Okay."

I surveyed the other thirteen students in the class. Those in their second year were noticeably at ease. The rest were diffident and looked a bit shell-shocked. One woman in the room was older than me. A few other students were roughly my age. Two were in their midtwenties—a long-haired girl who wore glasses appeared to be fifteen, and a short, redheaded guy, who likely had his ID checked at bars before they'd serve him alcohol.

With fingers spread and his wrists arched, Frank tapped his desktop the way he'd play a piano. He said, "We don't have any text, so there's nothing to talk about. Someone explain to the new guys what we do next."

Steve Kiernan, a second-year student, answered, "We go to a bar called the Mill." He gave us directions. Then Frank said, "Okay, that's it. See you there." And we left.

I walked to the bar alone, hiking uphill from the river plain where EPB stood to the state capitol building. From there I passed an indoor mall, a shop that sold Iowa Hawkeye football jerseys, a textbook store, a bakery, a bank, and a gas station. The ugly building beside it was the Mill. It had chocolate-brown wooden facing. An orange sign hanging from the roof announced that the restaurant served burgers, pasta, and pizza; basically, cheap food for destitute students. I opened a glass door and stepped into a dark bar. The cool air chilled my light sweat. I could see a second barroom with a restaurant area in the back. The room I'd entered seemed to be reserved for serious drinkers. I noticed someone from class, Charles D'Ambrosio. He wore work boots, black pants, a black T-shirt, and a skimpy, unlined black blazer. He had an iced drink in front of him. I settled onto the stool beside his.

"Hi."

"Hey."

I ordered tap beer because it was cheaper than bottled. When the bartender handed it to me, I raised it and Charlie and I tapped glasses. He seemed keyed up and was perspiring, sweat beading on

his forehead. Black stubble covered his round face and spread halfway
down his neck. We exchanged backstories. He had grown up in Seattle,
studied at Oberlin, later worked at a warehouse in Chicago, and then
held construction jobs in New York.

"Are you in your early thirties?" I asked him.

"Yeah."

"You think we're too old to be here?"

"Uh-uh."

"Good. What are you writing?"

"Stories. You?"

"Novel."

Others, including Frank, entered through a side door and went
directly into the back room. Charlie and I each ordered another drink,
paid our tab, and joined them. The back room's bar was long; fifty
people could lean on it. Wooden, maple-syrup-stained dining booths
pressed against the opposite wall. Seventy or eighty students from the
eight workshops that met each Tuesday had crowded a separate space
with more booths and freestanding tables. Frank made his way toward
one of them. In his right hand he held a shot glass full of bourbon, in
his left, a quart bottle of imported beer and a chilled mug. He sat on
a chair in the middle of things, then reached into his blazer pocket,
pulled out a cigarette, and lit it. When he noticed Charlie and me,
he raised his eyebrows and waved us over by tilting his head to the
side. Other students seemed to avoid Frank as if he was radioactive.
By joining him, I felt *italicized*. I'd already sensed that others regarded
me with some wariness. After an orientation meeting for new teaching assistants several days earlier, a second-year TA asked each of our
group of six over lunch what we were working on. I said a novel. He
said, "What's it about?" When I said baseball, he held his ham and
cheese sandwich several inches from his mouth and didn't take a bite.
"So you're the baseball guy," he said. I didn't know what he was referring to, but I'd encountered the same reaction several times. I felt like
a scarlet *B* for baseball had been branded onto my chest (and Charlie
was the only person not to see me that way).

Meanwhile, Frank wore a literary halo. The first chapter of his novel, *Body & Soul*, had been published in the September issue of *GQ*. Sam Lawrence had given him a six-figure advance and Candida (I later learned) told Frank, "When Sam Lawrence pays you to sit down and write a novel, you sit down and write a novel," although I believe Frank was intimidated by the idea of writing one. At the same time, his essay "Think About It" appeared in *The Best American Essays 1989*. The new publications resurrected his reputation and put him at ease. He no longer had to worry about directing the program with a relatively thin body of work. Frank had a slight overbite, and a lick of his silver hair continually fell across his right eye and he had to brush it back. His hands appeared large, his fingers long, ideal for a piano player. He smiled more than he laughed, as if he always held something back. And despite his success, I detected in him a quality (which I knew to be not entirely true) of a boy who had leapt from adolescence straight into accomplished adulthood. He, Charlie, and I talked about writers and writing in an offhand way, referring to Faulkner as if he lived down the street. As we drank, the evening slid into timelessness. At some point, Frank vanished, and Charlie and I closed the bar. The next morning, I woke with a hangover and went directly to work.

* * *

I put in seventy hours a week. Beginning at eight fifteen, I wrote for three to four hours. I taught two afternoons a week. In the evening, I graded student essays. I read a novel a week (some five hundred pages long) for a seminar. I read the hundreds of stories submitted to the *Iowa Review*, where I was an editorial assistant. And I critiqued my peers' workshop stories, stunned at how bad some were. I'd expected to read impressive and publishable work; instant and daunting classics, like the stories Flannery O'Connor had written as an Iowa student. But most (not all) of what I plucked off the shelves outside the MFA office, where each week's stories and poems

were stacked on Friday afternoons, depressed me. "Minimalist"
fiction was in vogue—this was 1989—and to me it had the effect
of making the majority of my classmates timid. Understatement,
ambiguity, minor epiphanies. Marriages collapsed because hus-
bands forgot to stop at the dry cleaners or pick up a baguette. Don
DeLillo called it "around the house and in the yard" subject matter.
Raymond Carver's plain, unadorned style seemed easy to imitate
(it wasn't). Characters were almost universally earnest, every writer
terrified of committing to the page a politically incorrect remark.
Stories became precious and, while making margin notes designed
to help a classmate—which is why we'd come to Iowa, to give support and in return to get it—I often wondered if my work was as
flimsy, unpolished, and lacking in imagination, and I feared that it
was. I doubted my ability, so I worked harder, revising pages and
erasing what I'd written in pencil repeatedly until I had rubbed
through a sheet of notebook paper. My writing improved. It gained
power and fluidity. Sentences now came rapidly, with fewer flaws.

One evening in workshop, I raised my hand when Frank asked
for the following week's submissions and he said, "You and you,"
meaning me and someone I no longer remember. (This happened a
third of my lifetime ago.) I submitted my chapter for photocopying
and then returned to work, feeling exposed and vulnerable.

I aimed for five hundred words a day, sometimes more. The
novel's momentum had increased, but I couldn't determine if the
story was good or bad. It felt right, but that didn't mean it was right.
Often what feels best reads worst. Nevertheless, I wrote seven days
a week and I stopped in midsentence—using Hemingway's trick,
which helped. Often, I would revise the previous morning's page
before continuing. Frank hadn't read a word of what I'd written
since my arrival, and, even though it had become our habit
after workshop to sit together at the Mill, he never asked about
the novel's progress. So I didn't know how he'd react to the new
chapter, which increased my anxiety. But he had a stake in what
I submitted to workshop as well. One afternoon I'd learned why

everyone but Charlie treated me oddly. At the end of an editorial meeting for the *Iowa Review*, yet another person said, "Oh, you're the baseball guy." Immediately, I turned to Fritz McDonald, a second-year student who sat beside me. I said, "Would you please tell me what's up with the baseball shit?!" He lowered his head and, even though we now were the only ones in the room, he spoke softly. "Well, last spring, Frank came out of his office holding your manuscript, shouting, 'Get me this guy's telephone number.' Some of the TWIFs [second-year teaching-writing assistants who teach creative writing classes and screen application manuscripts] read your pages and thought DeLillo had submitted his work as a goof." Later, I heard that Fritz had referred to me as "Golden Boy," but his comment didn't bother me because I had absolutely no confidence, and I worked manically, out of terror. Only Charlie understood that I was a bundle of neuroses, plagued by moods that swung from elation to despair.

I entered the next workshop as taut as a guitar string ready to snap. I'd staked my identity on my novel, and my novel's worth on Frank's opinion of it. What if my new work disappointed him? Emotionally, I was still a boy, and I'd projected my desire for a father onto him. No matter what others said about my work, the only important voice to me that day was Frank's.

As the author, I wasn't permitted to speak on my work's behalf. Instead, others spoke as if I weren't in the room. (At least, in theory.) Personal attacks weren't tolerated; we focused exclusively on the text. (Not that comments didn't sting, or, in rare instances, reduce someone to tears.) As always, Frank asked someone to begin the discussion. Then we argued about narrative grace, about a story's flaws, about what "worked" and "didn't work." People often said they "wanted more," although what "more" was wanted remained ambiguous. Some students were silent and never commented. Others suggested the existence of nonexistent problems. Initially, Frank stayed out of the conversation, but his reputation for fierce, often scathing criticism influenced what was said. To him, sentences were fiction's bedrock. If a

writer's sentences lacked aesthetic integrity, if the sentences were careless, sloppy, clichéd, or imprecise, the story failed. Also, a character's
actions had to be understood at a purely functional level, which might
involve a character simply starting a car. ("When did we learn the character was old enough to drive?! He behaves like a twelve-year-old!")
Motivation had to be irrefutable. (Why does she run off to Canada?!
All her boyfriend said was, "Can I call you back?!") Then Frank would
lower his voice and advise us to "use exclamation points infrequently."

I remember little of what was said. Mainly, my peers hated the
chapter. "I was lost." "Do people really speak this way?" "If the narrator's a baseball player, how come he's intelligent?" One exchange,
however, resonates so vividly that when I recall it I feel like I am sitting in room 457, thirty-four years old again, rather than fifty-four.

Steve Kiernan said to Frank, "There are too many metaphors."

"Where?"

"Page three, next to last paragraph."

Frank scanned the passage, along with the rest of us. "I don't see
a problem."

"Can I read the paragraph?"

"Sure."

"The next pitch glided by me with a cartoon slowness, the
drug (a cigar-sized joint) letting out the waistline of time, seconds
doing rubber-band stretches. A lost-in-space weightlessness flowed
through me as I saw the ball stop and hover, still as a hummingbird,
over the plate [my narrator was at bat], while I, insubstantial as a
movie image, slashed and chopped at it like some amphetamine-
crazed samurai."

"So?"

"So, he's in a cartoon, time's slowing down, the ball's a hummingbird, he's a movie image *and* a samurai?"

"What do you want? He's stoned!"

Earlier, Frank had read a long phrase from the text aloud. I'd written, ". . . the earth, in that drought year, as dense, hot, and parched as a
pizza stone."

"You see the image," Frank said. "It's concrete, and the relationship between object and simile is superbly balanced."

Frank's comments made me uncomfortable. Was he defending *my* work, or *his* judgment? Maybe my application manuscript *hadn't been* scholarship material. Or perhaps the new work hadn't lived up to the earlier work's promise. At one point, Charlie suggested that the novel's ambition could be found in its prose. Otherwise, no one agreed with Frank, the conversation's energy died, and class ended.

I stayed behind until the voices in the stairwell faded to silence. Then I slipped into my denim jacket and walked into the hall. Headed for the elevators, Frank stopped when he saw me. "They didn't get it," he said. He compared my wild prose to the comic anarchy of a Marx Brothers skit. "Worry about maintaining the power of the voice. Forget the rest." Then he hopped onto the elevator. I took the stairs. I wasn't eager to stop at the Mill, but I had to. Otherwise, I'd appear to be sulking, rather than confused by all I'd heard.

In the packed bar, though, students who weren't in my workshop but had read one of the copies left on the hallway's shelves said they loved the chapter. It was funny, many claimed. And they'd heard the class went well. Max Phillips disagreed with Frank on a minor issue. Frank had suggested that I change "wanna" to "want to." As in, "I don't want to hit." Max said, "But 'wanna' captures the character's infantile nature." I never made the change. To my ear, "want to" sounded stilted. As writers, debating this minutia constituted our lives.

All evening, I avoided Frank. I didn't want anyone to think I'd approached him for consolation.

At my desk the following morning, my classmates' voices rioted in my head. I couldn't hear my narrator, and if I lost his voice I'd lose the novel. I worked for six hours and composed two sentences. But I'd silenced the other voices. And they never interfered with my work again.

CHAPTER FOUR

Jody and I hadn't experienced winter in three years. "Winter," in Key West, meant a temperature plunge from 80 degrees to 60 degrees. Two days later, when the temperature reached 75, spring began. By late September in Iowa, though, the leaves had turned candle-flame yellow and apple red. Kids trick-or-treated on Halloween amid bare-limbed trees. And for the first time since I was a kid in Queens, I had to rake and bag leaves. From my desk, I could see the narrow road and the dingy garages and dying backyard grass that bordered it. The sun set at 4:30 PM, frost glazed our lawn each morning, and while pumpkins still rested on our neighborhood's front porches, I completed Book One of my novel. Instinctively, I knew I'd reached its midpoint. Its scope could no longer be enlarged, no characters added. Conflicts would now be resolved, not developed. As always, I'd tracked how long I'd worked and how many words I'd produced daily in a small, gray-covered assignment pad. In seventy-two days I'd written one hundred and fifty-three pages. Of them, Frank had read only the chapter I'd put up in workshop. One night at the Mill, where we now regularly shared a table, I told him I was burning out. "So take a break," he said. "Slow down." I received no other advice from him. But in a sense, I didn't need it. His presence was all that mattered.

Still, I couldn't decide if he was my teacher, mentor, friend, father, or a composite of these figures. By chance, a French film-maker making a documentary about America had come to Iowa City. He planned to include the workshop in his film, but baseball intrigued him as well. Foreigners can't understand the game's attraction. Why is it called our "national pastime"? And, unlike other sports, why does baseball lore and mythology exist? Frank told him that if someone could deconstruct baseball for the French, I could. "He's coming to the house to watch a World Series game," Frank said after class. "Why don't you come over?"

"Are you sure?" I said.

"Why wouldn't I be sure? We'll drink beer and watch a ball-game."

I said, "Okay," but later, at home, I began to agonize over the situation. My problem was that I didn't know who to be in my rela-tionship with Frank. "He wants to be your friend," Jody said. "So be his friend."

"But I'm his student."

"Then be both."

For me, this was difficult. I was comfortable having drinks with Frank once a week. Deepening our relationship, though, meant I had a greater chance of being rejected by him if I let him down in any way. I couldn't admit this outright, but I couldn't conceal my anxiety, either. I'm not good at that. This is why I write. It's my way of con-trolling my world and my emotions. I focus on sentences. For several hours a day, nothing else matters. I live inside language. And while I'm often frustrated by writing's difficulty, I'm also at peace.

So I set aside my novel and concentrated on composing a letter to Frank. Over the course of two days, I revised it twenty times, tossing entire drafts, tinkering with individual words, contemplating punc-tuation. Like a good passage of prose, the letter's tone and tempo had to be perfect. I was trying to express a lifetime of insecurity in two hundred words. At the same time, I didn't want to seem pathetic. I would like to read that letter, all these years later, and, occasionally, I wonder if it's tucked inside one of Frank's books, although I doubt it survived. Frank wasn't sentimental. I can't re-create precisely what I wrote, but here's the gist of the letter:

> *Frank,*
>
> *I don't quite know what to say about your invitation, other than thanks. I have to admit, though, I'm not sure where the line between teacher and friend lies, and I don't want to appear too eager to cross it, or too indifferent not to cross it. I also don't want to complicate my writing or your reading of my novel. Your critical voice already dominates my thoughts as I write. And while it would be one thing for my work to disappoint you as a teacher, it would be another matter to disappoint you as a friend. I hope you understand my confusion. Please don't interpret it as a lack of gratitude. What I feel is the exact opposite. If I didn't, I never would have written this letter.*
>
> *Sincerely,*
> *Tom*

When I laid the sealed envelope containing the letter in Frank's office mailbox, a momentary peace flooded my heart. It evaporated before I reached the mailroom door.

I thought Frank might call once he read the letter, but he didn't. Jody said, "It's fine, don't worry. The man has a life that doesn't revolve entirely around you." I wrote with my office door open, anyway, so I could hear the telephone ring. Then my concentration collapsed and the sentences I managed to write required endless revision. After five days, I'd advanced the novel by a single page.

Frank didn't say anything until we were once again at the Mill, alone at a table. He didn't lean forward, as if he were about to speak to me in confidence, but he did look at me directly when he said,

"Listen, I read your letter, and I understand. But here's the deal. You can think I'm the biggest prick in the world and it won't affect how you write your novel. The work's strong enough to find its own direction. So this other stuff"—he waved one hand over the table, as if dispersing a puff of cigarette smoke—"don't worry about it. Do what you need to do. Otherwise, you'll make yourself crazy. You follow?"

"Yes."

We never watched a World Series game together. The French filmmaker had left town unexpectedly. Shortly afterward, November arrived, and by the time we left workshop each week the temperature was in the forties, or lower. So I began to ride to the Mill with Frank. And if we happened to stand at the bar for an hour, oblivious to everyone else, I didn't fret about it. We'd become friends, which surprised no one but me.

* * *

A week later, Frank spotted me outside his office. "Come in and shut the door," he told me. I did. Then I sat across from him and slouched in the armchair I'd come to think of as mine. My compulsion to sit erect had faded. "How would you like to travel with the Mets?" he said.

"The baseball team?"

"Who else?"

During a flight to New York, Frank had been seated beside a man who dropped his pen. When Frank leaned down to retrieve it, he noticed the chapter of his novel published by *GQ* in the man's open briefcase. Its pages had been torn out of the magazine and stapled together. After sitting up and returning the pen, Frank said, "I'm Frank Conroy. I wrote the pages in your briefcase."

Frank told stories about his adventures in the same excited voice as the boy he'd described in *Stop-Time*. It was as if he still couldn't believe his good fortune.

"Then I found out who *he* was," Frank said. "Frank Cashen, the general manager of the Mets! Look, he even gave me this." Frank handed me a dark blue pen with the Mets orange logo printed on it. "And guess what? He's a *big* reader. I'm talking about good stuff, not shit. Hey, let's face it, he was reading me!" Frank laughed. He always laughed when he congratulated himself. It was his way of saying, I pulled off another trick! And nobody caught me! "Then I told him about you. If you want to spend time with the team for research, call." Frank handed me Mr. Cashen's card. "Ask for Jean."

"You're serious?"

"I sent him fifty pages of your book. He said they reminded him of early Richard Ford."

At the time, I hadn't read the "early" Richard Ford, but I was struck by the precision of Mr. Cashen's compliment. How many people would divide a writer's career like that?

"You can fly to Florida in March," Frank said, "during spring training. And if you need money to cover the trip, let me know and we'll work something out. You can pay it back after you sell your book"— something he never doubted would happen, although I did. "Come on, let's go grab lunch."

Generally, Frank preferred to eat lunch alone, before heading home to work on *Body & Soul*. He liked the act's mind-cleansing solitude. There couldn't be any other reason, given that most of Iowa City's restaurants served awful food. But a drugstore with 1940s décor had survived. Eight immovable metal stools topped with padded leather cushions faced a lunch counter manned by a soda jerk and a short-order cook, each of whom wore a white paper hat. They whipped up vanilla milkshakes and chocolate malt-eds, toasted grilled-cheese sandwiches, constructed BLTs, heated Campbell's soup, and scooped ice cream from round containers before slathering it with hot fudge. "You can get a cup of soup, half a sandwich, and a shake for a dollar ninety-nine!" Frank said. But the drugstore was his private space. *Body & Soul* was set during World War II, so he may have felt a special connection to the place, and we never ate there together. Instead, he took me to diners where he could get a hamburger. I can't remember him ordering anything else. Frank ignored warnings about high cholesterol, got drunk nightly, and couldn't write without a cigarette. Sometimes, he even hastily announced a workshop break so he could sneak into his office and smoke a Marlboro. "Have you noticed," he once said in class, "that characters portrayed as creeps are always cigarette fiends? We're regressing toward Puritanical hysteria. It's insane."

I called Jean and made plans to spend a week in Florida and a week in New York with the Mets. Around that time, I submitted my novel's second chapter for workshop and it escaped the thrashing the first one had received. Some of my classmates actually liked it, and the initial sentence, "I come from nowhere and everywhere" resonated with Charlie, who understood that my subject wasn't baseball, it was America. Other than Frank and Jody, he was the only person I trusted to read my work.

One evening near the end of the semester, Jody and I were washing the dinner dishes when we noticed something odd happening outside the kitchen window. At first, we were puzzled. Then we recognized what the white flakes swirling in the wind were. And, as if we were little kids again, we stood shoulder to shoulder and watched the snow fall.

CHAPTER FIVE

L ike me, Frank didn't compose his first drafts using a typewriter. From what he told me and I later saw, I learned that he wrote in a long, narrow, somewhat dim room on the second floor of his house. He would sit on a twin bed with several pillows pressed against the bed's headboard to support his back, pull up his knees, and rest a legal pad on his thighs. His handwriting fit easily between the lines of a page, and when he revised sentences he blacked out words with a Magic Marker, then substituted new words written in letters so minute as to be indecipherable. Beside his right hip rested an ashtray, a lighter, and a pack of cigarettes. Because of his confidence, he wrote with a ballpoint pen and composed *Body & Soul* slowly, his prose never more than two drafts from perfection. Initially, a paragraph would take shape, but it would often falter after two lines. A second attempt would produce a longer passage, one imbued with direction, a clear meaning, narrative continuity, and dramatic momentum. He would listen to it repeatedly, judging its tone, assessing its tempo, and decide that several weak phrases would be improved by further revision and others would be jettisoned altogether. A third draft built upon the previous drafts' strengths. And then, like a photographer delicately adjusting his lens, Frank would alter a few critical punctuation marks, invert a clause, and remove an ellipsis, until he believed that a striking clarity would resonate in a reader's mind. After three hours, he would set aside his pad and pen, collect his cigarettes and lighter, walk downstairs, past the grand piano in his living room and into the kitchen. There, he'd find his wife, Maggie; their son, Tim; a cold beer; and a shot of whiskey waiting for him. And the novel's world would vanish until the following day.

* * *

When I began Book Two of my novel in December, something odd happened. Rather than being lucid, my thoughts were imprecise. Words stubbornly resisted being linked to one another to form intelligible sentences. Paragraphs seemed endless and muddled, and the work exhausted me. Every day, I left the page with a sense of defeat rather than minor satisfaction. Soon a mild but persistent anxiety spread from my nerves to my abdomen. A circular, golf-ball-sized area burned inside my stomach where my rib cage parted. Antacids relieved the pain, although not entirely, and the persistent irritation added to my lack of focus and my fear that I wouldn't be able to finish the novel. What if I'd created complications of such idiotic magnitude that I couldn't extricate my characters from them? How would I sustain the story's momentum and yet make its plotlines converge seamlessly? Was the book too difficult to write because I was sick? Or was I sick because the book was too difficult to write? I didn't know.

So I made an appointment to see a gastroenterologist at the university hospital. He had black hair and the part on the left side of his head resembled a white candlestick. His glasses made him look slightly adolescent, giving me the impression that he'd gone directly from high school to performing surgeries. As instructed, I removed my sweater, flannel shirt, and thermal undershirt—it was now winter—and lay on his examination table. Then his dry, chubby fingertips pressed my stomach in various locations, so deeply at times that they seemed to touch my spine. He asked me to sit up, told me I was likely fine, but suggested having a peek at my intestines with an endoscope just to be sure. The morning of the procedure, I was not allowed to eat or drink. At the hospital, I wore an open-backed gown and lay sideways on a gurney, facing a television monitor that allowed me to see the progress of the scope. I declined a sedative because I didn't want to be groggy for the rest of the day. The gastroenterologist patted my shoulder with one latex-gloved hand and said, "Try to relax." Then he shoved a scope the length of a fishing rod down my throat. I gagged, and while a nurse held my head in place, I made sounds like air and water being sucked down a drain. An instant later, I saw the scope crawling through my stomach like a worm. Its glass eye illuminated the channels of my intestines and produced a grainy black-and-white image on the monitor. "I'm seeing nothing," he said, "No Barrett's esophagus, no ulcers, no abdominal perforation." He twisted the rod's handle clockwise, hummed a little ditty, turned the rod counterclockwise, and then, with magician-like quickness, retracted the scope. I closed my mouth and stopped choking as I was wheeled into a recovery room. Twenty minutes later, he appeared and said, "You're fine." I found the news disappointing. Since he'd discovered nothing, the pain had to be psychological, existential, or, quite possibly, literary.

Nevertheless, I forced myself to write. But the book's plotlines lost their rigidity and began to overlap. After I'd written twenty new pages I was completely lost. To find the novel's direction, I went back over the pages using three Magic Markers—black, green, and red. I drew boxes around sentences, sometimes as many as ten sequential sentences, sometimes around only one. Once I'd separated each section by color, I retyped and polished it, clarifying motives and events. Then I linked the sections to one another like the boxcars of a train, and the book began to move forward again. I continued to work, feeling ill and isolated. I'd requested a spot in Frank's spring workshop, but I'd been assigned to a workshop taught by a visiting writer. When I appeared in Frank's office bearing my notice, he laughed before I said a word.

"I can't be in your workshop?" I spoke without hesitation, my anxiety about our fondness for each other long since passed.

"I wanted you in another class," he said. "It's a pretty small group. You'll raise the level of discourse."

I collapsed into my armchair, and Frank smiled. He liked knowing that I needed him, but he also displayed an affection that surpassed his hopes for my novel. I'd become more than Frank's student, and more than his friend, although neither of us mentioned what our relationship ultimately might become.

Grudgingly, I attended the new workshop, in which I knew virtually no one and had little confidence in the instructor, although I liked him personally. Our classroom faced north, and by the time class began the sun had nearly set behind the horizon line of bare trees. The buzzing fluorescent lights overhead did nothing to dispel the gloom, which was magnified by the smallness of our group. Rather than the normal fourteen, there were only seven of us, and our fitful discussions lacked verve and acuity. Many stories were weak and I often found myself having nothing constructive to say. I endured the two hours, contributing few comments, concerned only with catching up with Frank at the Mill, or in the parking lot, where he often waited for me, his car idling in the dark, the heat turned up high or the defroster blowing against the icy windshield when I climbed in. One afternoon, a student—I can't remember his name, but he was fair-haired, slight, wore glasses, and was from Canada—put up a story set in a jungle. The story's cardinal sin, in lit-speak, was that it didn't establish a set of rules by which the reader could understand and contextualize the story's meaning. For example, when Kafka announces in the first sentence of *The Metamorphosis* that poor Gregor wakes up to find himself changed into a giant dung beetle, the reader knows that Gregor won't be shopping at Wal-Mart. The less "realistic" a story is, the more precise, concrete, and convincing its details need to be. All fabulists observe this rule: Rushdie, Calvino, García Márquez. Unfortunately, my Canadian classmate did not, even though his story featured philosophizing chimpanzees and a talking piece of luggage. My written comments on a copy of his manuscript were restrained and polite. I wrote, "You lose me here" and "I don't quite follow," and concluded with "Hope these notes help" because I agreed with Kurt Vonnegut, who once compared writing a savage review of a novel to "using a sledgehammer to smash an ice cream sundae." And as I didn't want to hurt my classmate's feelings, I remained quiet. When prompted by the instructor to offer a few words of advice, I kept my response brief. Then he smiled and said, "Come on. I know you have more thoughts than that." Indeed, I did. And had the story not been thirty-eight tedious and confusing pages, I might have expressed them with more sympathy. But having wasted six hours trying to make sense of the manuscript, I'd lost all interest in being kind. For five minutes, I cited grammatical, logical, and structural mistakes. I asked what the suitcase looked like. Was it leather or canvas? Did it have snaps or a zipper? Since the story's set in a jungle, why don't you mention heat? Or macaws squawking. Or smells, like elephant shit, chimp feces, and rotting bananas. And if you insist on interpreting Nietzsche, it would help if you had a clue as to what he actually meant.

Across the room, my classmate had adopted the classic posture of a workshop student who was having his or her work mercilessly criticized. He'd stationed one elbow on the table, pressed one fist against one cheek, and focused his eyes on his manuscript as he chiseled a hole in it with the tip of his pen. Silence followed my comments. Then the instructor said, "Anyone else?" When no one raised a hand, we passed our manuscript copies to the author.

As others shuffled out of the room, a classmate said to me, "Jesus."

"You think he hates me?" I said.

"You were pretty relentless."

"How did that happen? I didn't even want to say anything."

"Yeah, well. I guess you failed."

Several weeks later, I submitted my novel's latest chapter and during a subdued discussion regarding its countless flaws, my classmate didn't say a word. When class ended, we twirled scarves around our necks, slipped into our coats, and tugged on our gloves. Outside, I made my way toward Frank's snow-crusted car, its tail-lights glowing in the dark. I'd promised never to read criticism of my work. I could always return to it later. For the moment, maintaining the novel's momentum was crucial. I couldn't be distracted. Yet curiosity trumped discipline and I peeked. "Congratulations," I read, "you've created the most despicable narrator in American literature!" Although I shouldn't have been stunned, I crept in beside Frank, and with the car's dusty heating vents blowing dry heat in my face I said, "I can't believe it! He hates me!" As Frank's olive green Plymouth swiveled up an icy hill, I read my Canadian classmate's diatribe aloud. The more vicious the rant became, the harder Frank laughed, enjoying my outrage. "Listen to this! 'Your misanthropy is matched only by your arrogance. And your snide narrator isn't a persona, it's you!'"

When Frank stopped smacking the steering wheel with one hand and composed himself, he said, "What did you expect?" (I had told Frank about my outburst in class.) "He got even with you. So what?"

"Is anything he says true?"

"No. You're nothing like your narrator."

"Sometimes it doesn't feel that way."

"It's a mask. You have to wear it to write the book. When you're done, it'll fall off. Just keep working."

"Too much seems to be happening. Half the time I'm confused."

"That's not necessarily bad. It means you're chasing something."

"Can you read the new pages?"

"Sure. Leave them at the office. But hey, it's admission time. Who knows when I'll get to them? So don't hold your breath."

Two nights later, a writer with a huge following came to read at Van Allen Hall, which had several hundred raked seats, a stage, a podium, and a large, sterile, high-ceilinged lobby, much like the one in which I first saw Frank. Charlie had gone into hibernation and rarely came out for social events, so Jody and I went to the reading without him. We were standing amid the crowd when Frank appeared, cloaked in a gray raincoat. He grabbed my forearm. "Come over here," he said.

Frank found an empty, padded bench and pulled me down next to him. "The new pages are terrific," he said with an urgency in his voice, an unmistakable but grave excitement.

"You're sure?" I panicked and felt light-headed.

"Yes, I'm sure."

"Because I haven't felt well for months."

"It doesn't show."

"I thought you wouldn't be able to read the pages for a while."

"I read the first sentence and couldn't stop. The voice is incredibly strong. And the rhythms, my God. I read some of it to Maggie." Then he added, "Listen, you have to finish this book."

"Okay."

"I'm not kidding, it's a big book. You've taken things to a whole new level. You understand that, don't you?"

"I don't know. Maybe. I write sentences and trust my instincts."

"Well, it's working. So keep doing it."

Then Frank joined the famous writer, whose name I can't remember and whose image I can no longer see. Trailing the others, Jody and I walked into the auditorium and found seats. "Good news?" she whispered.

"Sort of. He thinks it's great." The lights around the podium dimmed, and everyone fell silent. Midway through the introduction I said, "But he told me I had to finish it. What if I can't?"

"You can."

"Yeah, but what if?"

"Then he'll understand. He's your teacher, not your father."

CHAPTER SIX

March arrived. In Florida, spring training was under way. My anxiety lifted as the days lengthened, and gradually the mysterious pain in my stomach subsided. Sentences found their shape more easily. I didn't know where the novel would end, but I did know where it was headed. I'd locked into its downward arc, the slope beyond the story's midpoint. Plotlines began to converge. The book regained its momentum. And, in the midst of this, my sister attempted to kill herself.

We rarely spoke on the telephone, yet the Tuesday night before I left for Florida I had an impulse to call her. But it was after 10:00 PM in New York. Her boys would be asleep, and I didn't want to wake them. So I shook off the odd beckoning, although I told Jody that I felt like I needed to call my sister.

"Why?" she said.

"I don't know."

I didn't believe in telepathy, or in the existence of a unique universal vibration that connected my sister's consciousness to mine. If either truly existed, she may have called me. Instead, she waited for her nine- and eleven-year-old sons and her husband to fall asleep. Then she quietly descended the carpeted stairs, walked into the kitchen, opened a cabinet drawer, removed a carving knife, and, gripping its handle tightly, drove it toward her stomach. She must have expected the blade to slice through her fatty tissue and puncture an organ, as if her midsection were no firmer than melting butter. Instead, the blade made a tiny incision, as thin and wide as a stitch, and a speck of blood opened like a rose on her white nightgown. She tried to plunge the knife in again, but she lacked the strength to disembowel herself. She left the kitchen, and her slippers tapped against her bare heels as she padded into the living room. Beside the oak coffee table, she dropped to her knees, pressed the knife's handle against the floor, held the blade upright, and fell on it. But like a thick band of rubber, her stomach formed a small, concave circle around the blade's tip. It stopped the knife from perforating her skin and pushed back her hand. She let the knife fall to the floor, glided into the kitchen like a ghost, unsheathed the serrated blades of an electric carving knife, plugged its cord into a socket, moved the "on" button with her thumb, and when the blades began to grind so quickly that their teeth blurred, she slid them across her left wrist. Blood spattered the floral-print wallpaper. Red drops sprayed the yellow refrigerator door. Blood stained her nightgown, the linoleum tile, the hanging calendar. It rolled down her arm and pooled in the crook of her elbow. The sound woke her husband. When he found her, she dropped the knife, which skittered across the tiles like a top. More blood now smeared her nightgown, clung to her hair, and dappled her face. By the time her boys appeared in the kitchen doorway, she seemed to be wearing a horror mask. The boys began tearing at their hair, trying to rip it from their skulls. My sister's husband wrapped her wrist in a dish towel. As he dialed 911, they ran into the dining room and circled its table, shrieking. In Iowa, I opened a book. While the paramedics hoisted my sister's gurney and slid it into an EMS vehicle, I grew drowsy, turned out the light, and closed my eyes. Twenty years later, I'm still haunted by how different my sister's life might have been if I had picked up the phone and called.

* * *

The following morning, with nearly everyone on spring break, I passed no more than two or three people as I walked to Frank's office, where I found him seated at his desk. White manuscripts surrounded him like piles of fresh snow. They'd been divided according to each applicant's chance for admission to the workshop. Seven hundred had no chance, fifty had some chance, a dozen had already been selected. When I knocked, he peered over the manuscript he was reading and smiled. "Hey, come on in." He tossed the pages onto his desk and swiveled his chair to face me. Then he lowered his voice, feigned concern, and said, "I hope you've bought your sunscreen, Tom." Once again, his expression brightened. "When do you leave?"

Without sitting I said, "I have to go to New York. My sister tried to kill herself."

"Jesus Christ."

I explained what had happened.

"And her boys saw it?"

I nodded.

"How old are they?" Frank's voice echoed the one he'd created to describe his adolescent terror in *Stop-Time*.

"Nine and eleven."

"That's not good. That could be trouble."

I told him I'd try to fly from New York to Florida.

"Sorry," I said.

"What do you have to be sorry about?"

"You arranged the Mets trip. I don't want to embarrass you."

"Your sister tried to kill herself, for God's sake."

I shrugged, acknowledging the fact that one situation paled in comparison to the other. "I know."

"Listen, do what you have to do. If necessary, I'll call Frank Cashen. He'll understand. How could he not? And strictly between us, I've got a crazy sister, too. Nothing this bad, but, you know, telephone calls. 'Look out your window, Frank. The sky's on fire.' That sort of thing."

I zipped up my leather jacket, which I'd begun to wear once the bitterest days of winter had passed. "I'll see you," I said.

"Call me."

"I will."

As I turned to leave, he said, "And remember something." I looked over one shoulder. "This isn't your fault."

* * *

In New York, I stayed with my mother. She still slept in the single bed adjacent to the one left empty after my father died. The house seemed cramped, and I'd forgotten the gloomy atmosphere of my sister's bedroom. Its one window overlooked a virtually sunless alleyway, and on cloudy days dusk seemed to fall by 2:00 PM. A six-by-nine-inch photograph, taken when my sister looked pretty at seventeen, leaned against the dresser mirror. With one fingertip, I slid open the hollow closet door and set my bag beneath a dozen bare wire hangers. I refused to unpack. Emotionally, I wanted to remain detached. I had no interest in my past. In fact, I feared it. Every time I returned home, I had one goal: to feel as little as possible.

Although I'd arrived late, my mother wanted to cook me dinner. Instead, I made her stop on the drive from the airport so I could buy a twelve-pack of beer. Then we sat at the round kitchen table where a cardboard salt-and-pepper set and a ramekin packed with NutraSweet pouches huddled at the center of a white plastic cloth dotted with images of summer fruit. Since my mother was four foot eleven inches, her black, imitation leather lace-up shoes barely touched the indoor-outdoor carpet. A thyroid disorder had caused her to gain weight over the years, so she wore polyester stretch pants and loose-fitting blouses. She worked as a teacher's assistant at a local grammar school. At lunchtime, she monitored kids from the fourth and fifth grades. Once or twice, through the chain link enclosing the schoolyard, I'd seen her ordering them around. It seemed to be the only time she felt anyone in the world respected her. Attached to the yellow refrigerator door by a magnet in the shape of tiny cow was a note scrawled on multicolored construction paper that said, "We love you, Mrs. Grimes!" At home, though, none of us took her seriously, and she had come to believe that she could only command our attention and obedience by acting like a bully.

"How long have I been saying something's not right with your sister?" she said.

"I don't know."

"Since your father died."

Which had been three years earlier.

"Did your brother notice? No."

"He lives in North Carolina."

"Did you notice? No."

"I lived in Key West. Now I live in Iowa." I didn't mention my impulse to call my sister the previous night.

"Her husband. He doesn't notice, either? What state does he live in?"

"He's a licensed mortician in New York. So I guess he lives in New York."

"Don't be a wiseass. Your sister just tried to kill herself. And he should have been paying attention instead of taking her shopping every ten minutes to cheer her up. Do you know people who commit suicide because they don't shop enough? No. Who thinks like he thinks? I'll tell you who. An idiot."

I didn't argue. After years of her plotting with my sister to lure my brother-in-law into an early marriage (my sister was nineteen, he was twenty-one), my mother began to criticize him before the wedding rice hit the church steps, and I no longer found the situation perverse, amusing, or tragic. Years earlier, my family, particularly my father, had decided that I was headed for disaster. At one point, when I was in my twenties, in debt, taking drugs, and drinking too much, they were nearly right. Then things changed. I met Jody, started to write seriously, developed what little talent I had by working twenty hours a week for a decade, and made it to Iowa. But as my life came together, my sister's life unraveled. And all I could do was to watch it happen.

"I'm tired," I told my mother. "I have to go to bed."

"How long are you staying?"

"Not long. I'm supposed to be in Florida."

"You know," she said, "when your sister woke up in the hospital, you were the first one she asked for."

"No, she didn't."

"If you leave now, I have no one to help me take care of her."

"You have her doctors and her husband." I stood, quickly opened a cabinet door, and peered inside. "Do you have a cookie?" I said. "I'm hungry." My mother had decided to make me feel guilty and, as I'd learned over the years, my best defense was to distract her.

"What kind?" she said.

I stared at the array of treats she'd stored, hoping for visits from her grandsons. When I didn't see any chocolate chip cookies, I said, "Chocolate chip," to lay the guilt on her. "Why don't you ever have what I want?"

She came up beside me, her graying hair as high as my chest. "I have Ring Dings."

I saw the box. "Where?" I said.

"Here." She stood on her toes to reach for it. Then I let her take one out and pass it to me in its foil wrapper. "You want two?"

"No. One's good," I said. "Night." I kissed the top of her head. Then, before I could move, her arms circled my waist and she pressed her face against my ribs. She shook for several moments, but I didn't say anything. Finally, I touched her shoulder lightly. I patted it. As I pulled away, she sniffled. "It'll be all right," I said.

"Okay." She wiped her eyes.

"I'll see you in the morning." I started to leave the kitchen.

"You don't want milk?" she said.

"No, I'm fine." I looked at her. Never before had she seemed so small. "Get some sleep," I said. Then I walked through the dark dining and living rooms, climbed the stairs, and closed the bedroom door behind me.

I undressed, pulled back the sheets, and turned out the light. But when I slipped one hand beneath the pillow to cradle my head, I felt something thin and dry. I sat up and turned on the light. In my hand were several desiccated, two-foot-long leaves, each folded in half. My sister hadn't slept in that bed for sixteen years. Nevertheless, my mother had blessed it with leaves she'd collected at church on Palm Sunday.

At 8:00 AM, my brother-in-law picked me up. He was short, sandy-haired, worked sixty hours a week, and earned twenty thousand dollars a year. He wore Brooks Brothers suits and regularly slipped this fact into conversations, and he always tailgated the car in front of him. During high school, walking to my job as a waiter and dishwasher at a luncheonette owned by a callous, penny-pinching old German couple, I would see my future brother-in-law racing along the avenue beneath the elevated train tracks, his bicycle basket filled with fish wrapped in white butcher paper, as he hustled to make deliveries for tips. In college, he studied mass communications and aspired to be a disc jockey. When he decided to marry my sister, he became an undertaker, like his brother, who'd arranged the job. Studying for his mortician's license, he learned how to embalm bodies and apply makeup to a corpse's face. Once hired, he collected the dead from morgues and, often, from the homes where they'd died. (Soon after that, I worked for the same firm as a night watchman and professional pallbearer to put myself through college.) We played hoops together. Years later, when he visited Jody and me in Key West, he asked me why I hadn't lost my mind living on a one-by-one-and-a-half-mile island. I reminded him of the Atlantic Ocean, where I took him snorkeling. I didn't mention the limited scope of his life, from home to funeral parlor and then home again, the trip less than ten minutes by car. I liked him. He was a decent guy and a good father, but completely out-matched by my sister's illness, which he would never comprehend.

"What do you think?" he asked as we sped past buildings and parks vaguely familiar to me, the way the ghost of someone I once knew might be recognizable, yet not quite real.

"I don't know," I said.

"She'll get better, right?"

"I hope so."

My sister had been moved from Queens General Hospital, where she'd been abandoned for hours beside a raving woman handcuffed to a radiator pipe, to the relative calm of Holliswood, a psychiatric clinic surrounded by a leafless arboretum. His health insurance would pay one thousand dollars a day for thirty days. Afterward, my sister would have to be released, or the two of them would lose their life savings in a month.

My sister's wrists had been wrapped in cotton gauze and then taped. She wore a nightgown that repeatedly fell open, exposing one breast, before my brother-in-law refastened it. She stared at me, less animated than a zombie, and her mouth remained frozen, as if she had something to say but couldn't summon the power of speech. She knew me, but I must have seemed like a hallucination to her from the sedatives they'd fed her. If she sensed my impulse but decision not to call her the night she attempted to commit sui-cide, she didn't show it. Still, her gaze seemed to beg me to rescue her from the opaque world she inhabited. When I leaned over to kiss her cheek, her eyes followed me, swinging like a pendulum. While her psychiatrist, a slight man with a brown mustache, hov-ered nearby, observing, my brother-in-law spoke to her. My sister didn't respond. I knew she wouldn't. Ordinary entreaties wouldn't reach her. "How do you feel?" or "Talk to me" were meaningless questions and requests. She didn't need to speak; she needed to be spoken to. And, intuitively, I knew she counted on me to do it. So I said, "Well, you really fucked up."

The others looked at me, as she suppressed a rosebud of a smile, one waiting to bloom.

"You just couldn't wait for someone else in the family to commit suicide," I said. "You had to be first."

My brother-in-law thought my remark would upset my sister. Instead, she tried to keep her smile from widening.

"And you're telling me the best you could do was a knife? You think a knife is original? You couldn't have clubbed yourself to death with a dumbbell?"

She laughed through her nose, which made her sound like a dog sniffing a patch of urine.

"I have to tell you, I'm disappointed. I fly out here and you don't even have the decency to be dead. Next time, get it right. Okay? Otherwise, I might as well stay home."

Her psychiatrist asked to speak to me in the hallway. "Why did she respond to you?" he said.

"Because we have something in common. We both hate ourselves. What drugs are you pumping into her?"

"Lithium and Haldol. Why do you hate yourselves?"

"My father, mother, and twelve years of Catholic school. How long will she be here?"

"Until we get her stable. Do you believe your father molested her?"

"No."

"Why not?"

"Because he never wanted to touch any of us."

CHAPTER SEVEN

I n Florida, the humid air opened my pores and seeped into my skin, replenishing the moisture that had been sucked dry by Iowa's winter. From my motel room, I called Frank. I told him my sister had been taken off suicide watch and was semi-lucid again. "Good," he said. "I'm glad to hear it. Now, you know you can't do any more to help, right?"

"Yeah."

"Okay then. Get your head back into the book and do what you went there to do."

Which was to study professional baseball players; to use, as Flannery O'Connor advised young writers to do, my five senses. What did the stadium and its locker room look, sound, smell, taste, and feel like? For my novel to succeed I had to be able to write, "In the air I could smell the vinegarish aroma of sauerkraut, the musty fragrance of ballpark beer." I needed to transform what I saw into the words "It was a sky-high fly ball. At its peak, I lost sight of the ball as it climbed above the band of light that crowned the stadium, into the envelope of darkness and low-flying smog." I was required to know that every professional team employs a public relations manager. For the Mets, this was Jay, a pudgy, curly-haired forty-year-old who wore wrinkled suits, eyeglasses that slid down his beaked nose, and a perpetually wide-eyed expression, as if he feared someone might push him off a cliff at any moment. After I'd been cleared to enter the players' parking lot by an armed guard to whom I'd shown the invitation from Mr. Cashen, Jay confronted me the instant I stepped out of my rented car.

"Who are you?" He tore the letter out of my hands. "What paper are you with?"

"I'm not with any paper," I said. "I'm writing a novel."

He pushed his glasses up toward his feathery eyebrows. "A *novel?*" He pronounced the word as if he suspected me of trying to steal nuclear launch codes. "What for?"

What for? I didn't have an answer. What *are* novels for? Entertainment? Metaphysical inquiry? Chronicling one's times? Could I tell Jay that the world is chaos and an artful novel satisfies our human desire for order, or that the novel excavates meaning from the rubble of incomprehension? That a novel is a thing to be read upon a beach in July for pleasure, or that I was an Iowa Writers' Workshop student and writing a novel was my homework? Or that I never want to die and when I'm writing a novel I believe I never will? Then it became clear to me. My novel had changed my life. A year earlier, I'd been a waiter. Sixty pages of prose later, I had a letter permitting me to dissect the lives of millionaire athletes.

"For a lot of reasons," I said.

He studied Mr. Cashen's signature, searching for any hint of forgery. Then he said, "Fine. Get a press pass inside. And whatever you do, don't talk to Darryl."

He was referring to the team's superstar, Darryl Strawberry, who shared a common trait with my narrator, Mike Williams, who appears on *Sports Illustrated*'s cover when he's twenty-one. Strawberry had appeared on it when he was nineteen. He stood six foot six inches tall and had a chest as broad as a refrigerator door. When he strode through the locker room wearing only a towel, his abdominal muscles resembled ice cubes. His biceps swelled to the size of grapefruits whenever he curled his arms, he hit home runs the way normal people swat flies, and he had a temperament as brittle as an eggshell. In successive years, he had been a Most Valuable Player finalist, and, in 1986, he'd won a World Series title. But the season before I arrived, his ability to hit the ball vanished, and the fifty sportswriters who covered the team had only one question for him: "Why?" Frustrated and brooding, he stopped granting interviews. Several columnists punished him by penning savage articles that belittled his talent and criticized his sullen behavior. Finally, he checked into an alcoholic rehab facility after threatening his wife with a loaded pistol. Before I could assure Jay that I wouldn't interrogate Mr. Strawberry, he darted off to intercept members of the press who had descended on Bobby Ojeda, a starting pitcher who had slowed to a halt in a red Ferrari, which he left purring as his fashion model girlfriend, a creature minted, it seemed, out of pure platinum, circled the car, kissed him, and then dropped into the driver's seat and sped out of the lot.

I walked to the office Jay had directed me to and collected my press card. In my back pocket, I kept a small, gray memo pad and a blue ballpoint pen, although I'd vowed never to scribble notes in anyone's presence. To the players, I wanted to become familiar to the point of invisibility. Professional athletes live in a fishbowl. Therefore, they tend to be skittish around people who ask them direct questions. So I planned to ask as few as possible. I entered the locker room and drew a few curious stares. Within an instant, I was forgotten. I found a corner chair, sat, listened to reporters conduct interviews, and watched the players dress. First, they pulled long white socks above their knees and secured them with navy blue stirrups. Next, they hoisted jockstraps over their hips, stepped into Spandex shorts, and then reached inside them to snugly place a hard rubber cup over their testicles. They tugged short-sleeved Mets T-shirts over their heads, slipped into immaculate white, blue, and orange pinstriped uniforms, and then knotted the laces of their polished black cleats. Finally, they crossed the cool, low-ceilinged locker room and studied the blackboard bolted to a cinder-block wall to see who was in the starting lineup. The ones who weren't said, "Fuck." The ones who were said nothing, but their bodies swelled when they inhaled, which said everything. Alone and in pairs, they headed for the tunnel that led to the dugout. Civilians were not allowed to follow.

I wandered out to the field. For a moment, the blue sky made me light-headed. I'd become accustomed to Iowa's muted winter landscape, its subtle shades of gray. I scanned the grass, looking for Strawberry. Instead, I saw Mr. Cashen peering through the fence behind home plate. He wore a tan suit, eyeglasses, and his signature bow tie. Despite being nearly seventy, his dull blond hair and short, swift gait made him appear younger. He and tall, lean Al Harazin, the team's senior vice president, studied hitters taking batting practice. From a distance, the two seemed to whisper to one another, but mainly they frowned, as if they had been forced to choose between one piece of rotten fruit and another. As I strolled toward them, noting the texture of the third-base bag, the brightness of the white baseline, the palpable calm radiated by the empty expanse of left field, and the stadium's small scale, I recognized the three sources of my disorientation. Sunshine, a balmy breeze, and the freedom of being outdoors, which Iowa's winter had erased from my memory. Also, I'd escaped the pressure of my novel. The six months I'd spent hunched over my desk in a small, cold room near an ice-glazed storm window had ended. I felt as if I'd ascended from the ocean's frigid, black floor, broken the water's surface, and taken a deep breath. A world did exist apart from the intensity of making sentences and the anxiety of scratching my way toward an ending. The stadium no longer seemed unreal, the players no longer like images in a dream. The shift from one reality to another became complete. And I went to meet Mr. Cashen.

* * *

On the evening news, I appeared in the Mets dugout, standing beside the team's manager, Davey Johnson. I immediately called Frank and said, "I was just on television!"

"Great!" he shouted. A moment later, he dropped his voice an octave and said, "Remember your friends, Tom."

I laughed. Then I said, "Mr. Cashen told me to say hello. He asked about *Body & Soul.*"

Frank said, "Tell him it's going well."

After *GQ* published its first chapter, a dozen countries bought the rights to publish the novel, only half of which was written. The circle of readers who had read the manuscript loved it. Now, all Frank had to do was finish the book. And, like him, I had to finish mine. But if his expectations for my novel were high, public expectations for his were far higher. Frank had written *Stop-Time,* which, over the years, had become a vibrant thread in the tapestry of American literature. Now he had to write one as good, or better. As for me, although I'd been too embarrassed to mention it to him, fearing that he'd consider it simplistic and poorly written, what was to become my first novel would be published in two months, and when I returned from Florida I would have to sit down in Frank's office and tell him about it.

* * *

On a nearly deserted practice field, I stared through the small squares of the fence behind home plate and talked to a retired pitcher who taught me how a knuckleball moves. I listened to him without taking notes, and when I returned to my desk I transformed his descriptions into prose. Then I revised the prose seven times to find my narrator's voice. The pitcher's words had the unpolished yet cohesive quality of speech. "The pitch'll do this," a twist of his hand, "and then that," another twist. Mine formed a single sentence designed to allow a reader to see the movement of a knuckleball and understand that "by virtue of its practically spinless nature—the ball only rotates a quarter of a revolution during its trip from the mound to the plate—the pitch has a tendency, when it's thrown correctly, to assume the flight pattern of a bumblebee, a thing prone to random loops and dodges."

Standing at home plate was Darryl Strawberry. I hadn't spoken to him, but I'd followed him. He wanted to practice hitting a curveball, which he called a "hook." One of the team's stellar pitchers, David Cone, obliged him. After assuming his stance, Strawberry said, "Hook." Cone reared and threw. Then the ball floated toward us lazily, following a C-shaped path, until it met the barrel of Strawberry's bat. The ball flew skyward, then dropped into left field. "Hook." A line drive zipped to right field. "Hook." A ground ball rolled toward second base. After five minutes, he said, "Okay, throw what you want." Cone unleashed a fastball, which made a faint *whoosh* as it hurtled toward us. For a millisecond, the ball seemed to swell. Ten feet in front of home plate, it vanished, then reemerged half an instant later in the catcher's mitt. Instinctively, I jerked my head and ducked. So did the pitching coach. Once we relaxed, he smiled at me.

I said, "It disappeared."

He nodded. "That's what a fastball does."

"Then how do you hit it?"

"If it's a good one, you don't."

That evening, I called my sister, who could talk, although her sentences were strung out, like a junkie trying to speak when she's high. "I'll see you in June," I said, "when I'm in New York. We'll talk then."

For several days, I made myself inconspicuous, but I paid attention. In the locker room, players undressed and dropped their uniforms on the floor. They untied their cleats and kicked them out of their way. A frail old man with walnut-colored skin pushed a huge canvas laundry basket on shopping-cart wheels and stopped to collect their grass-smudged clothing as he moved past them. Later, he scrubbed caked mud from each player's numbered cleats with a wire brush. Then he buffed the leather tops until they shone like new coins. The players showered, slipped on their thousand-dollar jackets, their silk shirts and custom-tailored trousers. And when they disappeared, the room became so hushed that I could hear the barely audible *clink* as the old man hung spotless uniforms in every locker.

Once I'd returned home, I found the uncorrected galleys of my first novel lying on the dining room table. The next morning, I sat down with them in my study. As I sharpened a pencil, I noticed that the angle of the sun had changed. A bright light now fell across my desk. I pressed the lead point to the pages. In my six months in Iowa, I'd learned more than I thought there was to learn. Bearing that in mind, I began to revise what I'd once considered perfect.

CHAPTER EIGHT

Shortly before I applied to Iowa, I'd submitted a manuscript to a small New York publishing house. I'd read about the new venture in a literary magazine I found on the dusty, wooden shelves of a Key West shop that seemed to stay in business by selling absolutely nothing. Each week, I passed a few hours in the deserted place, listening to flies buzz and the ceiling fans overhead tick as I flipped through periodicals, used paperbacks, and comic books. I'd enter through the shop's warped screen door, which drifted shut behind me and barely clapped when it touched its frame. The owner sat on a stool behind a long counter with a glass top. He had a gray beard, which he trimmed perhaps twice a year, and coconut-brown skin. His age lines looked as if he'd slashed his face with a razor. He always wore an unbuttoned Hawaiian shirt, and his sweaty, slightly hairy stomach bulged above the waist of his crinkled shorts. At his elbow, a beer can stuffed into a rubber holder to keep it chilled stood like a sentry. He'd nod at me with a lizardlike slowness whenever I entered the store. Then he'd return to his crossword puzzle.

Often, I'd skim *Esquire*, which in the 1980s annually printed a map of the "literary universe." In order of importance, publishers circled the sun like planets. Against the blackness of deep space, editors were depicted as either comets or black holes. "Hot" agents burned like supernovas. And writers with fading careers sailed toward an abyss beyond the margins of the page. With my few published stories, I didn't even register as a mote of stardust.

The magazine article featured two frustrated young editors. They'd quit their jobs to start Four Walls Eight Windows, a press dedicated to publishing books rejected by their corporate employers. Their idealism and naïveté matched mine. Since they accepted submissions "over the transom," I decided to submit a novel that had once been three hundred pages but had been whittled down to one hundred and fifty. I'd written it in my midtwenties, and, like most first novels, it evolved through a series of failures. I had no sense of form or structure. I imagined skyscrapers when all I could build were tree houses. I wasn't an architect; I was a kid with wooden planks, a hammer, and a box of nails. My sentences were imprecise. As a result, the characters and landscapes I described were difficult for a reader to see, like blurry images observed through an out-of-focus lens. And I didn't understand the difference between action and dramatic action. Action alone has no consequences: a character washes a dish and the dish is clean. Dramatic action has *consequences*: a character flings a dirty dish at another character, splits his upper lip, and cracks his front teeth; the assaulted character then grabs a conveniently placed meat cleaver, flings it at the other character, and splits open his head like a halved cantaloupe. I had another problem, too. I imitated authors. On Monday, I sounded like Vonnegut, who, on Tuesday, became Nabokov, who, on Wednesday, became Toni Morrison, who, on Thursday, became Philip Roth. My voice hadn't developed to the point where it was distinctive. And, repeatedly, I made the same mistake. I thought literature existed outside of me, that it was static rather than dynamic, that I had nothing new to add. If I couldn't write about debtors'

prisons with Dickens's authority, I failed. If I couldn't outwit Jane
Austen, I failed. If I couldn't philosophize like Bellow, I failed. For
a year, my novel remained ten pathetic pages, each successive draft
worse than its predecessor.

Then, not for the first time, I got drunk. My first wife had taken
our car, I didn't know where. We were broke. Our marriage clearly
had been a pitiful mistake made by twenty-one-year-olds who felt
guilty about having an abortion. We'd left New York and moved
to North Truro, a hamlet near the tip of Cape Cod. We lived in a
small cottage. To stave off total poverty I worked at the fishery in
Provincetown's harbor. It was winter; no other jobs were available.
So at 7:00 AM, I made my way, often through fog, along the wooden
pier. Inside, the warehouse smelled of dead fish because most of us
wore the same clothes for days and the stench was absorbed by our
stiffened jeans and thermal jerseys. An oily residue of fish scales
made the slick floor dangerous to walk on in boots with hard rubber soles. My job consisted of two tasks: dropping a metal winch
into the bellies of fishing boats to retrieve metal baskets filled with
the day's catch, and then filling splintery pine crates with twenty
pounds of fish packed in crushed ice. My gloved fingers were always
numb, my beard glazed by sleet, my wool watch cap soaked with
perspiration. The evening my wife was out, our cottage's windows
were ice-covered, and the small bundle of firewood I'd bought had
burned down to orange cinders no larger than glowing cigarette
tips. I'd put on gloves to keep my fingers warm while I held cold beer
cans. I couldn't concentrate enough to read, and we didn't own a
television set. I glanced at our scratched Formica kitchen table. On
it, my blue electric typewriter nested beside a cracked sugar bowl,
as if the machine might hatch a novel if it sat there long enough.
Alongside it was the skimpy stack of pages I'd composed. Revising
them had become brain-racking torture. Yet I wouldn't quit. So I
walked to the table, pulled out one of its padded chairs, dragged the
typewriter toward me, and reread the novel's opening paragraph
for the thousandth time. Whatever life it once may have had, I'd

wrung out of it. If a moment's authenticity had ever sung out from the page, I'd silenced it. I didn't believe the narrator's voice. I'd forced it. I'd sentimentalized my family. I didn't know the happy household on the page. My father's bitterness, my mother's theatrical self-pity, my sister marrying at nineteen, my brother deemed an idiot by all of us: that world I knew. I fetched a blank sheet of paper, fed it into the typewriter, drained my beer can, grabbed another, and waited. Five minutes passed. Then I pecked at the keys. After I read the words I'd tapped out, I obliterated them behind a scrim of xxxxxxxxxxx's. I tried again. And then, rather than gravitating toward sentimentality, I instead described the night my father crashed our car, drunk and doing ninety:

> The car's front end had been pushed in and up, like snow that had been plowed into a pile. It was a heap of metal, twisted and creased. The headlights had been smashed and two pools of glass were scattered on the ground. The windshield was shattered but in place, with a hole the size of an orange directly over the steering wheel. I peered inside the car and saw that the apex of the wheel was cracked and dappled with dried blood. Beer cans, an empty Jack Daniels bottle, cigarette butts, and maps that had fallen out of the glove compartment littered the floor of the car. One of my father's neckties was on the backseat, and beside it, as if he'd been undressed at some point during the night, his undershirt.

I paused, astonished. I'd written something true. And, as I continued to type, and the story grew blacker, I laughed, partially at my family's life, and partially at the unexpected authority of my voice. I wrote until I passed out. In the morning, I woke to find my soon-to-be ex-wife still absent and pages scattered on the kitchen table. I brewed coffee. Then I poured some into a mug, ladled in two teaspoons of sugar, and lifted a page from the table. Habit prepared me to stop listening the moment my words sounded false, clumsy, and sickeningly meaningless. But oddly, I was able to continue reading.

I trusted the voice. I could imagine characters and places from the way the words had been strung together, as if by a stranger. I had a story to tell. Four years later, I had a novel.

Not that I knew exactly what to do with it. At twenty-eight, *Esquire*'s "literary universe" still intimidated me, even though I'd published several stories and lived with Jody in a West Village apartment two miles from the center of that universe. The anonymous sting of rejection letters no longer bothered me, but I lacked the confidence to contact agents. However, Houghton Mifflin, a Boston publisher, ran a First Novel contest. The winner's novel would be published, and its author would receive a seventy-five-hundred-dollar advance. So I mailed in my novel.

I also submitted it to the PEN American Center for its Nelson Algren Award for Best Novel-in-Progress. One evening, a letter from PEN arrived. Out of two thousand applicants, I'd been named one of three finalists. (I didn't win.)

Meanwhile, Houghton Mifflin seemed to have forgotten me, but I was reluctant to send an inquiry, fearing it might be interpreted as impatience. Six months passed before a letter from the company's editor in chief appeared. He admired my novel, he said, but, in his experience, an author's second novel often was stronger than his first. So, whenever I was ready, would I please send him a section of my new novel, which he would read eagerly, and with great pleasure. Once I showed Jody the letter, I put the rejected novel in a blue, wooden storage box and didn't look at it again for six years.

Within a few months, I had one hundred pages of a new novel and I mailed them to him and to PEN. For the second year in a row, I was named a Nelson Algren finalist. (Again, I didn't win.)

Three days later the Houghton Mifflin editor who had recommended my first novel for publication wrote to say I'd "gone off track." Nothing he liked about my first novel existed in my new novel, the rest of which he didn't ask to see. Instead, he advised me to "follow the often-lonely road to literary achievement." Earlier that day, I'd stopped work on page two hundred and seven, midsentence. I read the letter to Jody. Then I opened the blue box, placed the new novel inside it, and didn't touch it again for a decade.

Not long after the morning Frank ignored me in Key West, I received a note from the Four Walls Eight Windows editors. They wanted to publish the *first* novel Houghton Mifflin had rejected. As an advance, they could offer me five hundred dollars. They promised the book would never go out of print. For several days, I carried the letter with me. I would unfold it, read it, refold it, and then place it in my back pocket. I even brought it to work, as I wanted to feel it against my hip while I took orders from customers. I didn't tell Jody about it. Instead, I bought a seven-dollar bottle of champagne and hid it in the cooler we took to the beach with us. In February, the water was too cold for swimming, but we went there on our afternoons off anyway. I'd sit at a picnic table and write, and Jody would either read or walk along the deserted shoreline, scavenging for shells. Before sunset, I'd open a can of beer, Jody would uncork a bottle of wine, and we'd listen to music through our tape player's tinny speakers. The evening I gave her the letter, we shivered in our sweaters, and the wind swept her hair across her face. "Open it," I said, handing her the envelope.

I watched her furrowed brow as she concentrated. Then a smile bloomed on her face and she smacked my forearm with the sheet of paper. "You see?" she said. Meaning, you're not the failure you think you are.

"It's only five hundred dollars," I said.

"Who cares? It's a book!"

I poured champagne into two clear plastic cups.

"Do you have a new title?"

The editors had requested that I change the original, *Domestic Depravities*. "No," I said.

The next day, I accepted their offer. A day later, I donned my waiter's outfit. But I felt as if I'd become two people. One had achieved a measure of success; one hadn't. Otherwise, my life remained unchanged, until Frank called.

* * *

Frank and I had written our first books in our mid- to late twenties. Each concerned an absent father and adolescence. All comparisons end there. *Stop-Time*'s achievement eclipsed my novel by such magnitude that I dreaded telling Frank of its existence. I believed the book's publication might diminish his affection for me, and he'd lose interest in the novel he expected me to write. He might even feel betrayed. Jody said he wouldn't. When I admitted my anxiety to Charlie, he agreed with her.

In my study, Charlie sat in the gray armchair. I leaned forward in my desk chair, hands clasped between my knees. "I sold my first novel," I said to him. "Not the one I'm working on, another one."

"No shit."

"Yeah."

"Great. When does it come out?"

"May. You think Frank will resent it?"

"No."

"Then would you do me a favor? Read the edited version, because the book sucks."

The clumsiness of my prose stunned me. Why would anyone want to publish the novel? I felt ashamed to have it attached to my name. For two weeks, I worked at the dining room table, rewriting the novel sentence by sentence. I red-lined deletions and penciled in additions. The finished pages resembled a Pollock canvas. As I retyped them, I continued to improve the book one word at a time. Exhausted, I let Jody read the new draft, and once she'd approved it, I handed it to Charlie and hoped for his blessing. I trusted his judgment for a reason besides friendship.

During our first workshop, he'd written a story called "The Point." Frank, who rarely doled out praise, suggested it might even be publishable. "Although you use 'and then' a lot," he said. "And you overdo the physical description of Mrs. Gurney." He then read it aloud: "'Her breasts sagged away like sacks of wet sand, slumping off to either side.'" Frank paused. When he continued, his voice rose as he pinpointed a textual flaw. "'There were long whitish scars on them, as if [and I'm italicizing to convey Frank's emphasis] *a wild man or a bear had clawed her.*' They're stretch marks, for Christ's sake! Jesus! She's thirty-seven! From where I'm sitting, that looks pretty good. Lighten up!"

Before class, I'd found Charlie seated on the hallway floor, his back tilted against the brick wall. I squatted next to him. "The story's great," I said. "I don't mean workshop great. I mean, *great* great." I told Charlie to mail it to the *Atlantic Monthly.* Its fiction editor, Michael Curtis, had liked my work, and I wrote him a letter, praising "The Point." He rejected the story. A month later, the *New Yorker* accepted it, and, later, the story appeared in *The Best American Stories 1991.*

Why had Michael Curtis rejected Charlie's story? Why had Frank been enchanted by my novel, which someone else had rated B-? No one knows. The ground a writer stands on is no firmer than water. Still, I needed Charlie's assurance that my book was, at some level, good.

Several days passed, and I interpreted his silence as disappointment. But something else had kept him away. He found the book unspeakably sad. "At one point, I just had to put down the pencil and take a walk," he said.

The revision astonished my editor. "What happened?" he said. I answered, "I went to school."

CHAPTER NINE

The week I submitted my revised novel with its new title, *A Stone of the Heart* (a line taken from a Yeats poem), Frank read in public from *Body & Soul*. I sat in the crowded auditorium's balcony as he shuffled into the spotlight much like he had in Key West. His woolen blazer drooped from his shoulders, its visible pocket misshapen and baggy from being reached into repeatedly for a pack of cigarettes. Perhaps the balcony's angle changed my perspective, but he appeared shorter than six foot two and projected less power from this distance than he did in class, which was the only setting where I'd seen him assert authority—authority that pertained solely to, as he called it, the "text." At times, I believed Frank could run an entire workshop without students and not notice our absence. He and the "text" would argue.

As a boy, he'd lived in New York City in a small, Upper East Side apartment where his bedroom's shelves held eight hundred paperbacks. He wrote in *Stop-Time*:

I read very fast, uncritically, and without retention, seeking only to escape from my own life through the imaginative plunge into another. Safe in my room with milk and cookies I disappeared into inner space. The real world dissolved and I was free to drift in fantasy, living a thousand lives, each more powerful, more accessible, and more real than my own. It was around this time that I first thought of becoming a writer. In a cheap novel the hero was asked his profession at a cocktail party. "I'm a novelist," he said, and I remember putting the book down and thinking, my God what a beautiful thing to be able to say.

In *Body & Soul,* he transferred these feelings, almost without a fictional filter, to his protagonist, Claude, a gifted pianist. Every writer has obsessions. A boy's vulnerability was Frank's. (He once asked our class to appreciate the main character's plight in an otherwise weak story. "But you feel the defenselessness of the boy," he said, "the boy.")

Frank adjusted the podium's brass reading lamp and microphone. Then he began to read about the summer afternoon Claude wandered into an RKO movie theater on Eighty-sixth Street and saw:

Cartoons! Followed by a newsreel, the narrator's voice both urgent and important, sounding over the flash of images. And then the first feature, about a tough sailor who marries a librarian but doesn't take life seriously until they have a baby. The second feature described the adventures of a boy who could talk to horses. Claude watched with total attention, so captivated that it was a shock when the movie ended, as if his soul had been flying around in the dark and had now slammed back into his body. Outside, the unnaturally still street and the implacable heat seemed to claim him, to smother the quicksilver emotions of the films and flatten him in his contemplation of the meaningless, eternal, disinterested reality of the street, of its enduring drabness. To come out of the RKO was to come down, and he rushed home to the safety and company of the piano.

The prose had vigor. Frank's voice didn't. It became apparent that he hadn't prepared for the reading. His voice lacked inflection. He mumbled. At one point, he faltered when he read a passage concerning Claude's abusive, and freakishly large, "six-foot-tall, three-hundred-pound" mother:

Claude sat down on the floor. He was attentive to her mood, to its direction, in case escape was necessary. Sometimes when he ran around the couch or slipped under her arm she would lose interest. He knew that almost always when she hit him, she held back.

Then Frank's voice croaked. He didn't stop reading for long, but he adjusted his glasses before continuing:

There were times, for instance, lying on his cot with the radio off or sitting on the floor motionless, staring into space, when Claude would become sharply aware of his own existence and the fact that he was alone. Either the basement apartment was empty, his mother out to work or her discussion meeting, or she was holed up in her room. The sense of being alone would come over him, causing not so much fear as uneasiness.

Briefly silent, Frank reached into his pocket, removed a handkerchief, turned his head (I could see his profile), and blew his nose. He barely finished the chapter. The following morning, I went to see him in his office.

"I can see the headline," he said, the moment I walked in. "Doddering Professor Bursts into Tears over His Own Work!"

"I don't think anyone noticed," I said.

"No?"

"Only a few hundred of us."

"Bastard." Then he smiled.

"Listen," I said, "I have to tell you something, and this is kind of awkward." I hesitated. "I'm having a novel published—but by a little house. The advance is only five hundred dollars." I wanted to underscore the publication's insignificance.

Unfazed, Frank said, "Well, you'll get a lot more for this one."

"There's no problem?"

"Why would there be a problem?"

"I don't know," I said. "I thought there might be." At the time, I didn't consider my persistent anxiety unusual. "Do you think I should ask people for jacket quotes?"

"No," Frank said, "let's save them for the new novel."

When my slim book review galleys arrived, I gave him a copy. At one hundred thirty-one pages, the book felt measly. Frank must have read it in an hour.

* * *

I received a sample of the dust jacket and, like most writers, I hated it. When I called my publisher I was told the jacket couldn't be changed. Besides, the sales force loved it. (My publisher had no sales force.) In the illustration, my narrator had thick black hair and a face so fat that the boy appeared to be chinless. I'd been overweight as a kid (and lean, almost skinny, ever since), but I may have overdone the physical description of myself and left the illustrator with only this to work from: "I undressed, and while I was naked I caught a glimpse of myself in the mirror which hung above my bureau. I was enormous. There were two thick crescents of fat hanging from my pectorals and my navel was deep and wide enough to hold a walnut. Over my hips were bands of flesh as thick and soft as loaves of packaged bread. Beneath my stomach the wild, unfinished hair growing above my genitals seemed pathetic." I studied the cover up close. Then I set it on a shelf and backed away to see how it would look to a stranger who noticed it in a bookstore. As I did, space became time. With each step, eternity swallowed another second, and the sensation matched the slight melancholy I felt whenever I looked through a car's rear window, watching my life vanish at sixty miles an hour. The past turned the book into an object that belonged to someone else. Even my name, nine red letters at the base of the jacket, seemed unfamiliar, and rather than reinforcing my existence the finished book drained it of meaning. Years of work, frustration, doubt, anger, longing, and, finally, a tentative satisfaction with the novel no longer mattered. Notebooks, dulled pencils, typewriter ribbons, reams of paper, keystrokes, letters daubed with Wite-Out, smoked cigarettes, coffee rings, postage stamps, and letters—"Dear Editor, Thank you for your consideration," "Sorry, it's not right for us"—were erased in an instant, like a superfluous word from a page. I crossed the room, removed the dust jacket from the shelf, and filed it with the complete manuscript. Then I put it out of my mind and resumed work on the new novel, which, now, was where I lived.

* * *

Several weeks passed, and although Frank and I saw each other every week in class, neither of us mentioned the book. But after our final workshop, Frank tilted his head and I followed him into his office. He said, "I've read the book. It's okay." Seated, he laid one hand on his desk to indicate *A Stone of the Heart.* "But how you got from here," he said, "to here," he raised his other hand a foot above his head to indicate the new novel, "is amazing." Then he lowered his arm and leaned back in his chair. "Honestly, I don't know how you did it."

"I wrote twenty hours a week for ten years."

"Well, it shows."

Connie simply said, "I loved it." She didn't discriminate between the two novels. To her, I was one continuous being, rather than one who had developed in stages. But to Frank, my life began the moment he read my application manuscript.

With the semester over, people began to leave town. A few friends and I had agreed to help another friend and his wife move. As we hoisted their washing machine and attempted to maneuver it through a doorway, one of them said, "Nice review of your book in the *Times.*"

"What review?" I said. "When?"

"The one in this coming Sunday's *Times Book Review*."

"But it's Monday."

"Prairie Lights sells copies early."

I continued to hold my share of three hundred pounds. Then, not wanting to seem egotistical, I hauled boxes for another two hours. When the last one had been stuffed inside the truck I said, "I have to go." I walked to the corner, turned, then sprinted to the bookstore. Outside its front door I stopped, winded, less than a yard from Frank.

"The *Times* reviewed my book," I said.

Inside, we each removed a copy from the periodical stand near the register. The review appeared on page seven. Frank said, "It's up front, that's good. It means they like it." We read in silence:

May 20, 1990

A STONE OF THE HEART By Tom Grimes. 131 pp. New York: Four Walls Eight Windows. $15.95.

Creative writing programs have been springing up around the country like weeds and, for the most part, they've been given a bad rap, with critics complaining that they produce only derivative "workshopped" writing. Now here's strong evidence to the contrary. Tom Grimes is a member of the Iowa Writers' Workshop, and his compact and affecting first novel, which records a few days in the life of a disintegrating Irish-American family, is a very professional job. "A Stone of the Heart" is set in Queens in 1961, as Roger Maris is striving to break Babe Ruth's home-run record, a goal that rivets the attention of Michael, the 14-year-old protagonist. "The feat seemed so herculean," he recalls, "compared to the accomplishments and work of my father."

Why had I been linked to Iowa? I hadn't even written the novel at Iowa. I skipped to the final paragraph:

"A Stone of the Heart" renders the afflictions of adolescence in both unique and universal terms, and Tom Grimes is, in workshop terminology, a "natural" writer. He would probably have developed and flourished on his own, but perhaps not so soon or so well.

Frank said, "Not bad," and returned his copy. While I opened my wallet to pay for one (I wanted to buy five, but was too embarrassed to do so), he said, "See you." Then he left, as if nothing out of the ordinary had happened.

Prairie Lights had arranged a reading and Frank, breaking his policy of not attending student events, arrived with Maggie. He lingered behind the last row of chairs. At one point, he wandered off to browse in the bookstore's mystery section. Once I finished reading, he appeared, carrying two novels under his arm. Before I began to sign books, he drifted toward me. "You should read slower," he said. Then he patted my shoulder and added, "Don't waste the summer. See you in August." He strolled toward the doorway, and I didn't see or speak to him again until he returned from Nantucket and fall classes began.

CHAPTER TEN

My mother met me at La Guardia airport. Then we drove to
Holliswood, where my sister's psychiatrist had released her
for the second time. Early summer had descended on New
York and when I stepped out of the car to collect my sister's suitcase
humidity encased me like a glove. Trees surrounding the clinic had
bloomed, sunlight shone through gaps between their leaves, and
the day's brightness dulled my sister's pale complexion, lending her
affectless face a putty-colored pallor. She'd been weakened by her
medication and, as I hugged her, she felt as boneless as a sponge.
After my visit in March she'd been discharged, but within weeks
she saw a sign from God on a seltzer delivery truck, she couldn't
remember how to fold laundry, the purpose of socks eluded her,
and she again tried to commit suicide, this time by swallowing a
quarter, believing it would slice open her stomach and intestines
and allow her to bleed to death.

On the ride home, she remained silent and stared out the window beside her, watching the world pass. Her face was puffy, a pouch

of flesh hung from her chin, and, although she was only thirty-two, white roots lined the part in her hair. She'd been prescribed Haldol, an antipsychotic, which slowed her movements and deadened her emotions. As I drove, my mother leaned forward from the backseat and placed her mouth inches from my sister's left ear.

"Do you want lunch?"

The concept of food seemed beyond my sister and she didn't answer.

"Your brother's here." My mother glanced over my right shoulder. "How long are you here for?"

I'd come to spend a week with the Mets. "Seven days."

"Your brother's here for seven days. You think you have all the time in the world to talk to him? You see him once a year, if you're lucky." My mother's use of "you" actually meant "I."

My sister's head turned as if a puppet master's hand had reached up inside her skull and twisted it toward me. But her lips didn't move.

"And you," my mother said. "You don't have anything to say to your sister? Look at her. She could be dead. Does she look like a healthy person?"

I stared at the rearview mirror and waited for my mother's reflection to appear. When she looked up, I narrowed my eyelids. She understood my warning. I wouldn't join her campaign to undermine my brother-in-law or influence my sister's decision to choose her caretaker and living companion. With my father dead, my mother could devote herself to nursing my sister. I also didn't doubt her ability to infantilize my sister. They'd never lived more than a mile from each other, my mother had a key to my sister's house, and, excluding my sister's two-week honeymoon, I don't believe forty-eight hours passed without them being together. Now, if my sister's dependence on her became complete, the loneliness that trailed my mother through the house the rest of us had left behind would vanish like an exorcised ghost.

I said, "She looks fine."

A moment later, my mother leaned back. To avoid my gaze in the mirror she placed her elbow on an armrest and dropped her jaw into her open palm. "Well," she said, "she doesn't look fine to me."

Without speaking to one another, we rode to my sister's brick row house. Her sons stood behind the storm door's glass pane as we walked their mother, unsteady from her medication, along the grass-bordered concrete path. The older boy's hands stayed in his pockets. The younger one's clutched his brother's wrist. When we entered, they moved out of our way and my sister glided past them. Inside, the living room's palpable stillness seemed eerily funereal.

An hour later, I left for Shea Stadium, yet the stillness clung to me until, near midnight, the roar of fifty thousand cheering fans shook it loose.

*　*　*

On my way to the stadium, I stopped to pick up a newspaper. Unlike the sedate *Times* or the middlebrow *Daily News*, the *New York Post*'s sports section stylistically mirrored the front pages of tabloid scandal rags sold at supermarket checkout counters. I dropped thirty-five cents into the newsstand keeper's palm. Then I turned the paper over and read the afternoon's headline: "BRAWL IN METS' LOCKER ROOM!!! STRAWBERRY SLUGS TEAMMATE!" The reason: an unpopular rookie, considered by some to be arrogant, had replaced a well-liked player. The situation may have been tolerated had the team been winning, but when a team loses more often than it wins its locker room grows unnervingly quiet. Some players blame themselves for the losses, some blame others, and some blame everyone: the owner, the manager, the press, the fans, their friends, and their families. Initially, losing streaks irritate players. But when the streak continues, they become angry. The streak's nature mystifies them. Their losses seem preordained. They feel cursed. Then they begin to play as if they *are* cursed. On the field, their attention wanders; they fumble easy catches; they swing and miss and aren't surprised by their inability to hit the ball. What's happening is clear, but no one knows what to do about it. Hence, the silence, then the search for a scapegoat. So when Darryl Strawberry threw a punch, he struck not only his teammate, he also whaled on the team's superstitions. He pummeled them. He provided the catharsis they'd longed for and ended the locker room's silence. The players now had something, other than losing, to talk about.

When I reached the ballpark, an armed guard admitted me. I drove past the autograph seekers and girls hoping to score a date with a player, then found a parking spot amid the array of BMWs, Mercedes coupes, Ferraris, and, beside me, a single van with a toy-littered interior and an infant's car seat secured to the rear bench. Crossing the asphalt, I glanced up. The stadium dwarfed the team's spring training ballpark. As a kid, I'd come here to see games, and inside the stadium's twenty-story-high walls, the vivid green field, the random, multicolored pattern of shirts, jackets, and caps that spanned the upper and lower decks, and the crowd's restless buzz before game time electrified me. Unfortunately, the directions I'd been told to follow led me beneath the field into a painted cinder-block tunnel illuminated by caged, yellow-tinted light-bulbs. Voices bounced off the walls, creating a harmless but dispiriting bedlam. Players hurried past me, some out of uniform, some carrying travel bags, some towing children toward the ball-park's playroom. Ahead of me, I saw Jay standing with his arms spread and his back pressed against the clubhouse doors, denying reporters locker room access, even if it meant being crucified. I took the executive elevator up to Mr. Cashen's office. In it, a prim, middle-aged woman sat at a large, elegant wooden desk. Championship plaques hung from the room's walnut paneling and a plush carpet muffled my footsteps. Dressed in jeans and a polo shirt, I felt conspicuously poor. I said hello, then showed her my letter. She lifted the telephone receiver and whispered into the mouthpiece. Moments later Mr. Cashen burst through a pair of tall doors, wearing a blue suit, white shirt, and bow tie. "Thomas!" he said, shaking my hand. "Here to steal more secrets?"

"As many as I can," I said. Then I handed him a signed copy of my novel. He studied its cover, flipped the book over, looked at my photograph, and read aloud the quote my publisher had added to the jacket. "'Talented newcomer Grimes writes elegantly about inelegant lives in this debut. . . . Small, polished, and moving. *Kirkus Reviews.*' You're famous!"

"Not quite." I extended a copy of Alice Munro's new story collection, *Friends of My Youth.* "I brought this, too," I said. During spring training Mr. Cashen had mentioned that his favorite author was García Márquez. But García Márquez had published nothing since *Love in the Time of Cholera,* two years earlier, so I chose the Munro book as a gift, hoping their narrative similarities—their fluid use of time and flashback, their complicated characters— might appeal to his imagination. "I thought you'd like it," I said.

He examined the dust jacket, smacked the book against mine, and said, "I'll read it." Then he handed the books to his secretary, who, I later learned, was his wife.

"How are things?" I asked.

"How are things? Things are, one day you're a genius, the next day you're the village idiot." Three years had passed since the Mets championship season, and now, regardless of Mr. C's having lifted the team from last place to the World Series, second-guessing his judgment had become every New York sportswriter's pastime. He said, "Are you free for lunch tomorrow?"

"Sure."

"Twelve o'clock, VIP dining room. Jean, give him a pass. I have to run." Then he slapped my back and returned to his office.

Next I went to find Dr. Lans, the team's psychiatrist. He'd spoken to me during spring training and offered to do so again when I rejoined the team in New York. His clubhouse-level office was dim, windowless, and adjacent to the media room, where the team's public relations staff taught players how to sit, face the camera, enunciate words, and show no emotion whenever they answered press conference questions. Some players were naturally at ease, others jittery and self-conscious. "Those are the ones we worry about," he said.

He sat behind his desk and I sat across from him. Quickly and defensively, he said, "I can't talk about Darryl."

"I don't want to talk about Darryl."

"Great," he said. "What do you want to talk about?"

"The losing streak."

He barely paused before he answered. "The team has no center. That's why it's losing. A team is supposed to cohere, to shape an identity. This team hasn't."

"So how do you help players?"

"*I* may not be able to help them. But, I do know *what would* help them. Winning. One win can restore a team's faith in itself. Now, I can talk to players individually about marital problems, money problems, self-esteem problems, and substance-abuse problems —don't make a note of that—but I can't do one thing. Make the team win. No. *They* have to win." He raised an index finger, as if he wanted me to concentrate on an issue I might find baffling. "By the end of nine innings, they have to score more runs than the other guys. If they do that, then what's complicated becomes simple. But we don't want things too simple. If things are always simple, I don't have a job. Don't write that down, either."

"I won't."

On the field, I watched batting practice for a while. An hour before game time, I found the cafeteria where the reporters ate. I placed a sandwich and a Coke on a plastic tray and looked for a place to sit. The scene reminded me of high school. Certain groups crowded around tables and talked loudly; others whispered and seemed meek. Individual writers focused on their work. Seated alone was a man with a slight build, a ring of gray hair, gold-rimmed glasses, and a pale mustache. I can't remember if I recognized him, or if we introduced ourselves to each other once

he said it was okay for me to join him. But I knew his name and
his work: Roger Angell. He covered baseball for the *New Yorker*. I
would read his articles when they first appeared and then reread
them when they were collected and published in book form several years later. I regarded his work with a minor sense of awe. He
had a detached, nearly Olympian view of the game, and a graceful
prose style untainted by the grubby, workmanlike banality of daily
journalism. But then, his stepfather had been E. B. White, author
of the children's book *Charlotte's Web*, and coeditor of the classic grammatical usage manual Strunk and White's *The Elements of
Style*, a book that explains, for instance, how to enclose parentheti-
cal expressions between commas: "If the interruption to the flow
of the sentence is but slight," the authors write, "the writer may
safely omit the commas. But whether the interruption be slight or
considerable, he must never omit one comma and leave the other.
Such punctuation is indefensible." I never thought I might have
to take up arms to protect the integrity of a sentence, but, as Mr.
White obviously did, I imagined Mr. Angell at age eight, having
nightmares about comma splices. He asked what paper I wrote for.

"I'm not a reporter," I said. "I'm researching a novel."

He stopped eating. "You're a novelist?"

I nodded.

"What's your name?"

I told him.

"Don't know it," he said, dismissively. Then he lifted his fork.

"I published my first novel last month."

He lowered his fork and snapped at me the way a dog snatches a
slice of meat from midair. "Who published it?"

"Four Walls Eight Windows."

"Never heard of them."

At that moment, his publishing pedigree made me feel more
than ever like a literary mutt. So I said, "The *Times* reviewed it, and
then listed it in its Bear in Mind section." Without saying a word,
he lifted his tray and left the table. At game time, when he saw me

enter the press box, he turned away, as if I didn't belong in the chair he, on some other night, may have occupied.

Forty thousand fans filled the seats, darkness embraced the stadium, and, above it, a halo of light dimmed to a milky blackness that obscured the stars. On the manicured field, players in white uniforms moved, whenever the ball was struck, with startling precision. For eight innings, the Mets played well enough to outscore the other team. But when they surrendered a lead in the top of the ninth, Mr. Cashen left his skybox and strode toward me, crouched like a pit bull ready to tear off a piece of flesh. "Disappointing, Thomas," he said, hurrying by me, "very disappointing." Kevin McReynolds, the Mets' left fielder, had stepped to the plate. Without hesitation I said, "Don't worry. McReynolds is going to hit one out of the park." Mentally, I *saw* the ball sail over the outfield fence, and the act seemed uncannily real. Still, I mentioned it simply to cheer up Mr. Cashen, who was on the elevator when, moments later, McReynolds knocked the ball into the left-field stands. Immediately after the win, tension in the clubhouse vanished. Players spoke freely to the press, smiled, and joked with one another. Reporters surrounded McReynolds, demanding quotes for their columns and articles. I walked past naked players heading for the showers, and a seldom-called-upon relief pitcher who used his bullpen time to study for a degree in accounting. I stopped in front of Ron Darling's locker when I noticed several Zen philosophy books on the shelf above his uniform. I nodded at them and said, "Does reading them help you pitch?" He glanced at the books, then looked at me and said, "Not unless they can tell me how to throw a better slider."

The Mets won eleven straight, and twenty-three out of twenty-four. Secretly, I wanted to take semidivine credit for their winning streak, but the next day at lunch Mr. Cashen told the man seated beside me, Fay Vincent, the commissioner of baseball, that each time he rode an elevator near the end of a game, the Mets won. "So they want me on an elevator, any elevator, whenever we're behind in the ninth inning!" Others at the table laughed. I felt slightly disoriented when a waiter said, "May I take your plate?" Then I understood why. A year ago, I would have been the waiter.

I took notes for several days, then said good-bye to my sister and mother. At the airport, I bought a Sunday *Times*, found a seat, took out the book review section, and opened it. *A Stone of the Heart* had been included in the Editors' Choice Summer Reading List. I called Jody to tell her. Then my flight was announced and I flew to Key West, not to wait tables but to see my first play produced. If someone had asked me who I was, I'm sure I wouldn't have had an answer.

CHAPTER ELEVEN

I'd written the play mostly on guest checks and time cards. Standing around before the hostess—who happened to be Jody—seated customers at my tables, I imagined lines of dialogue, often without intending to. I simply heard voices. This double-edged gift helped me as a writer but later amplified my paranoia. On good nights, particularly during autumn when hypomania kept my brain bubbling with words the way water boils in a mad scientist's test tube, I wrote one or two pages of dialogue while waiting tables. When I got home, I pulled bits of paper from my pockets, dropped them on my desk, and the next morning I typed and revised them.

I had begun writing the play when Jody and I lived in New York. Around this time, I met the lawyer who handled my divorce and then Jody's. His *Village Voice* ad had said, "No-hassle divorces, $105." So I made an appointment to see him. After entering a grungy midtown building, I climbed a dim, narrow stairway. On the landing, I checked the office number listed in the ad. It was correct. The brass plaque nailed to the wooden door said "James

Ingrassia, Attorney-at-Law." Inside, a teenage girl seated at a cluttered desk held a baby in her arms. With her telephone's handset lodged between her left shoulder and ear, she raised her chin to indicate the tattered armchair in which I should sit and wait. I glanced around the room. Old movie posters had been Scotch-taped to its dingy walls. Stacked below them were dull, nickel-colored film canisters. The infant burped, and the girl stroked the back of its head. Then she asked the person at the other end of the line to hold and shouted, "Your five o'clock's here!" A door to my left opened. Beside it stood a man, perhaps five foot six inches tall, built like a wine barrel with arms and legs. He wore a tan corduroy suit, a striped shirt, and a mismatched paisley tie. He looked to be about forty and spoke in a soft, almost conspiratorial voice. "How you doing? Come on in," he said, angling his head. His curly, chocolate-colored hair remained in place. I followed him. On his desk, screenplays bound with gold clasps lay beside court documents. And rather than legal casebooks, filmmaking how-to manuals filled his shelves. He sat, grabbed a notepad and pen, and said, "Okay, so. Why do you want a divorce?"

"I love someone who's not my wife."

He looked at me. "Do you know how often I hear this?"

"No."

"Daily. I traffic in tragedy. I'm in the tragedy business." Then he scanned the room, smiled, and said, "But I'm moving into the film business." He coughed, expelling dusty air from his lungs. "Okay," he said. "So. What's your *legal reason* for a divorce? In New York, you can't file for divorce just because you love someone other than your spouse."

"Well, what are my choices?"

"Adultery, physical abuse, mental anguish." He ticked off several other options.

I didn't want my marital situation to be construed as excessively hostile. My first wife and I had married young. We didn't hate each other, although when I moved out and asked for a towel she gave me one with a hole in it. "I guess I'll go with adultery," I said.

"Has your wife had affairs?"

"Two."

"So do you want to be the plaintiff or the defendant?"

"Defendant," I said.

"Noble."

I shrugged.

As he made notes, he said, "What do you do?"

Instinctively I said, "I'm a writer," even though I'd been paid less than two hundred dollars for my work.

He paused to stare at me. "Really? What do you write, fiction, nonfiction, plays, screenplays?"

"Fiction," I said.

"You're published?"

"Some short stories in journals."

"Can you write a screenplay?"

"I don't know."

"Because I have ideas."

He actually said this. But by the time I'd embellished his words the line in my play became "I have notes. Outlines. Ideas. (Beat—which means a subtle pause.) I want to lay them out for you. I want you to dwell on them. (Beat.) Can I lay the first one out for you?"

While writing the play, I changed our names. I became Mike; he became Al. And Mike said:

Go ahead.

AL
VIRUS.

Pause.

MIKE
Virus?

AL

VIRUS. That's the title. The idea. Can't you
see it? Ten million movie marquees, in black
plastic lettering—VIRUS. (Beat.) You like it?

Short pause.

MIKE

It's simple.

At some point, I actually said this. But, to write the play, I com-
pressed conversations that took place over several years into one scene,
then mixed what we said with what I invented, and the scene continued:

AL

It's familiar. Everyone knows what a virus
is, so there's no lack of audience identifica-
tion. This is what makes it universal. We start
with a common cold. Do a real Spielbergian
domestic Cuisinart blender household number, open up with a lot of real Americana
tracking shots, establish the scene. Now. The
parents leave pretty seventeen-year-old Sally
home for the weekend. You want to get the
parents out of the way immediately. Parents
are death at the box office. Kill the parents.

Mike begins to take notes.

MIKE

Parents dead.

AL

OK. Good. Now. Sally calls her friends the

instant her parents leave in the Saab. They invite
some boys over. This is where we throw in the
sex angle.

MIKE
They all start jumping into bed.

AL
Right. OK. Now, little Joey, Sally's little
brother, suddenly comes down with a fever.
He comes home from school . . . he looks like . . .

MIKE
Casper the Ghost.

AL
Great! Terrific! Write that down.

MIKE
He picked up the virus in school. Like, we'll
see him at the water fountain with some
lower-middle-class kids—

AL
No. School is out. You gotta get a building, fill
it full of kids, the whole thing costs too much
time and money. I want to keep it simple. I
want a virus to appear, wreak havoc, then get
wiped out by some new brand of mega-
antibiotic. The virus can run rampant, but
only on one block. Remember: horror movies
are microcosms of society. So: Think small.
Think microcosm.

Short pause.

AL
Help me. I'm totally lost.

MIKE
Joey.

AL
Right. Joey. Joey comes in, his stomach hurts.
Sally, like a good sister, tucks him in, etc. In
spite of this, his temperature climbs. Sally calls
the doctor, a good-looking intern named . . .
Matt, who Sally has a crush on.

MIKE
And he wants to get into Sally's pants.

AL
No. Sally's the heroine, therefore her pants
never come off. Pants come off secondary girlfriend characters who are slaughtered by this
raging out-of-control virus ten seconds after
they have sex with their boyfriends. Got it?

MIKE
Got it. Secondary characters fuck and die.
Keep lust to a minimum.

AL
Good. Now, Matt leaves, the other kids
come over, they're jumping into bed, etc.
What happens? Little Joey's temperature
SKYROCKETS! He starts changing, getting

more hideous. He's turning into this, this,
this . . .

MIKE
Thing?

AL
Thing! Exactly! You know, the red spots in the
eyes, the vomit spewing across the room.

MIKE
Sounds like *The Exorcist.*

AL
The Exorcist. Nobody's made an *Exorcist* rip-
off for years. It could be viable.

MIKE
Are Sally's parents religious people?

AL
When confronted by grief and death, yes.

MIKE
So this couldn't be a speaking-in-tongues,
gospel-type experience then, could it?

AL
Definitely not. (Beat.) Although, if you could
imply that without stating it, so that we have
this straightforward virus thing, and then tie
in on a subliminal level this cultlike Black
Mass religioso mumbo jumbo–type theme, we
could double our audience.

MIKE

Like, " Was it a virus . . . or was it . . . God?"

Ingrassia settled my divorce within weeks. My wife kept everything we owned (which wasn't much); I became solely responsible
for our five-thousand-dollar credit card bill. But Jody's husband
refused to surrender a penny of their joint property and ignored
motions demanding his appearance in court; her divorce took seven
and a half years. During that time, Ingrassia closed his office and
would vanish for months. When he reappeared, we'd meet him in
odd places. One afternoon, Jody waited outside a Banana Republic
store while he bought a safari jacket. Then he emerged and had her
sign some papers on a metal trash-can lid. One evening, over cock-
tails in the Cornelia Street Café, he said to us, "But forget Jody's
divorce. I can get financing for a biker movie. You want to write it?"
    I said, "Okay."
    Then, on spec (the Hollywood term for writing a script, then
hoping someone buys it), Jody and I wrote Ingrassia a biker script
in three days. As I sat at my battered desk and typed, Jody stood
behind me and read over my shoulder. We began our marathon
sessions by drinking coffee. After sundown, I switched to beer, and
Jody switched to wine. Our task was to craft an interestingly terrible
script, and we exchanged ideas like, Should the car sail off the bridge
here? (Ingrassia planned to rent a car, have a stuntman drive it off a
bridge into a lake, and then report the car as stolen. "Insurance pays
for the loss," he said. "It's win-win for everybody.") Then he saw a
Sylvester Stallone movie and he liked the knife Stallone's character
used. "Give me an unusual knife," he said. "Something menacing." I
gave him a mechanical arm that fired six-inch bullets. "We can actually fake this," he said. "I love it." But his mysterious investors backed
out and we didn't make the biker film. Instead, we made Hot Splash,
a semi-soft-porn surfer flick, which went straight to videotape and
late-night American TV. For the play's next scene, I didn't even need
to invent dialogue. I simply transcribed Ingrassia's words verbatim:

MIKE

So you want me to throw in a little more character.

AL

Character is a wonderful thing. But we don't have the money to buy actors who can act like characters.

MIKE
Well, what do we have?

AL
Basically . . . ? Some girls who'll take off their clothes.

The *Citizen Kane* of Ingrassia's oeuvre, however, was *Snake Island*. By the time he began filming it, Jody and had I moved from New York to Key West. Up the coast, in Cocoa Beach, Ingrassia had bought a modest villa, turned it into a small production studio, and convinced a retired stuntman who'd worked in James Bond movies to loan him his house, which was inland, surrounded by palm trees, near a swamp, and an ideal location for shooting *Snake Island*. The guy said, "Just stay out of my bedroom." Otherwise, Ingrassia had permission to transform the two-story hut into a creepy, decrepit hovel, inhabited by snakes. Crew members leased machines that worked like vacuum cleaners in reverse and sprayed dirt, dust, and mold over the living room, dining room, and kitchen walls. They infested the place with spiders and let them spin webs. They slathered the house's exterior with mud. A makeup person showed Ingrassia a sample of fake blood. "Darker," Ingrassia said. "Use more chocolate." Filming began with two couples—the girls wearing bikinis, the guys wearing swimming trunks—who get lost in the swamp.

When their motorboat's engine sputters and dies, they're forced
to step onto the island. "Stay together," one of them said. (I didn't
write that line.) They soon lost track of one another anyway. The
blonde couple's response is to immediately undress. A few days
later, the rented snake and his trainer arrived. Uncoiled, the snake
was four feet long. While two dozen of us stared at it, Ingrassia
sent for Murray, the twenty-three-year-old actor who played
"Snake Boy." As a child, a snake had poisoned him. Now he could
inject venom with his tongue. We waited. Twenty minutes later,
the casting director returned. Murray was having difficulty "getting into character" and had locked himself in his EconoLodge
motel room. Baking in the hot sun, the snake rested in his cage,
coiled like a bullwhip. Ninety minutes later, Murray showed.
Ingrassia raised his megaphone, ready to shout, "Action!" Then he
signaled the trainer to release the snake. But the snake had fallen
asleep. The trainer dragged him out of his cage, and the snake
uncoiled, but remained limp. We gathered closer and watched it
lie on the ground in a stupor. Ingrassia shouted, "Okay, forget it.
We'll shoot the fight scene on the roof." But the roof's sundeck
had been sturdily built, and as one of the crew's carpenters sawed
partially through a wooden railing so the actor punched in the
jaw during the fight sequence could fly backward through it to his
death, the house's owner bounded down his dirt driveway in his
Jeep, skidded to a stop, stepped out, looked up, and yelled, "That's
it! Everybody get the fuck out!"

Ingrassia finished the movie on another location and released it
with the title *Kiss of the Serpent*. We never made *Virus*, but Ingrassia
read its script. After we talked about it I had:

SCENE FOUR

*Al's office. Lights up. Mike paces, eyeing Al. Al, seated,
reads Mike's script intently. When he turns the last page,
Al flips the binder closed and launches into his speech.*

AL

I have to tell you something. This is a script
I could love. (Beat.) If there could be physi-
cal bonding between a man and a screenplay,
Virus, for me, would be that screenplay.

MIKE
The gasoline . . . ?

AL
On the hair—

MIKE
The beach, the night—

AL
The terror, the bondage—

MIKE
The whole sexual subtext—

AL
The gunpowder in the mouth—

MIKE
The exploding head!

Beat.

AL

I cried. (Beat.) I'm a man, I cried. (Beat.)
Sweet little Sally dead? This was the death of
innocence.

But I had a collection of scenes, not a play. I needed a plot, a
through line, and a time frame within which all action had to take
place. The play was stillborn.

One afternoon at the restaurant, I'd finished polishing wine-
glasses, filling salt and pepper shakers, folding napkins, and
setting electric candles on my tabletops. It was August. We
wouldn't be busy. So I sat on a stool at the short service bar and
opened *Premiere*, a new movie magazine. I read an article about
films currently being made in South Africa. Apartheid was ending
and wealthy, white South Africans wanted their money out of the
country. But transferring funds was illegal. If wealth disappeared,
the regime would collapse. Money had to be invested in projects
developed in South Africa. Except there was a loophole. *Profits*
from investments could be deposited in overseas accounts. This
money became known as "flight capital." One of the best ways
to create it was to make a movie. Investors pooled their money.
Fading Hollywood stars were recruited to play the leads in mediocre action films. South African death squads supplied weapons,
transport vehicles, helicopters, and planes. And military person-
nel were hired as extras. I put my own twist on the story. Browner,
a CIA agent, convinces Ted, an investment banker, to make an
action film, which is a cover for a coup:

> TED
> You want a script.

> BROWNER
> That's right.

> TED
> Of this idea.

Ted indicates the envelope Browner has set beside him.

BROWNER

Right.

Short pause.

TED

What is this idea, Petey? As you see it.

BROWNER

In a nutshell? An exiled leader, a hero of the
people, puts together an army of freedom
fighters. He trains them in a country adjacent
to his homeland that is sympathetic to his
plight. The freedom fighters go in, depose the
brutal, non-Westernized dictatorship, democ-
racy and free trade are restored, and our hero
rides off into the sunset with pledges of U.S.
economic aid and contracts for billions in
military hardware. So get us a script, Ted. And
a crew. A film crew.

In order to tie the story lines together, Ted knows Al, who says:

What type of situation is it, Ted?

Short pause.

TED

A high-concept synopsis? A man has been
exiled from his home by a brutal, let's say, a
fundamentalist dictatorship. And now, the
only way he can reclaim his home is if we
help.

AL
By making an action movie.

TED
Yes.

A year later, I gave the finished play, *Spec*, to a director at Key West's Red Barn Theater, which had a ninety-nine-seat space with a proscenium stage. Its board deliberated for three months. On the afternoon Jody and I were packing the U-Haul truck that would carry us to Iowa, its members agreed to produce the play. A month before it opened, rehearsals started, and every evening from seven to midnight I sat in the theater, watched the actors, conferred with the director, and made revisions. During the day, I worked on the novel. I needed to maintain its momentum and hear the narrator's voice. I didn't want to leave the novel's world entirely and return to it feeling like a stranger had written it.

But I also felt like a stranger when I became a minor Key West celebrity. To my embarrassment, the restaurant's owners had mounted an enlarged copy of the *New York Times* review of *A Stone of the Heart* and placed it on an artist's easel beside the hostess's podium, where Jody had stood for three years, scanning the reservation ledger prior to seating customers. Soon afterward, I appeared on the cover of *Focus*, the weekly entertainment section of the *Key West Citizen*. As directed, I sat at a table, held a pen above a revised page of the play, beside which lay a copy of my novel, and stared at the camera. The following day, while buying groceries, the woman behind me in the checkout line said, "You're much better looking in person." The reporter who wrote the article emphasized my waiter-turned-writer phenomenon, equating it with the evolution of ape to man. "Shortly after he arrived in Key West in 1986, Grimes worked first as a busboy, then as a waiter at Louie's Backyard." She also developed an anthropological interest in my work habits. "Grimes writes in longhand, perhaps one of the few remaining writers to do so." I added, "Frank Conroy and I are the only two (at Iowa) who write in notebooks and transcribe." Then, perhaps mindful of Frank's minimal admiration for *A Stone of the Heart*, I said my new novel would "come in at around 750 to 800 pages" and "be considerably different than" my first, which she called "a small gem." A week later, she described *Spec* as the worst play the Red Barn Theater had ever produced.

Nervously wandering the grounds the evening before *Spec* opened, I noticed someone seated on a bench outside the theater. He had long, brownish-red hair and a ragged mustache. He looked familiar, but I couldn't decide whether he was an actor or a Key West bartender who had served me when I was drunk. Anyone was allowed to attend the final dress rehearsal, and he sat in the last row. When he laughed halfway through act one, I recognized his voice. I'd seen him in a Sam Shepard play; his name was Jim Gammon. Between acts, I stood, turned, and began to introduce myself. Before I could, he said, "Hey, Tommy." He'd seen my photograph near the theater's entrance. He shook my hand and said, "This is a hell of a good play. After you wrap up for the night, I'd like to talk to you about it."

I said, "Sure."

We met in the courtyard. He would be in town for several days, he said, shooting a Goldie Hawn movie, in which he played an aging hippie, hence the long hair. He asked for my number. I gave it to him and expected never to hear from him again. He called the next day, and the following afternoon he took Jody and me, along with his wife, Nancy, to lunch. He told me that he'd run the Met Theatre in Los Angeles for twenty years. Briefly, it had closed. But recently he'd found a new space for it. He, Ed Harris, Holly Hunter, and a dozen other actors planned to lease the space and reopen the theater. "If you wouldn't mind," he said, "I'd like to show them your script." I said okay, gave him a copy, and thought nothing would come of it. In Key West, *Spec* ran for six weeks. Then Jody and I flew home to Iowa. A month later, with a hundred new pages to show Frank, I was back in his workshop.

CHAPTER TWELVE

Frank looked up when he sensed me standing in his office doorway. "Hey, babe. Come on in."

I took my usual seat and said to him, "How was your summer? Did you write?"

"I goofed off. I wrote maybe fifty pages."

"Lazy fuck."

"How's the novel?"

"Long."

"Well, let it be what it wants to be. Don't force it."

"Okay. Catch you in class."

Then I went to see Charlie in one of the windowless offices we'd been given as second-year teaching-writing fellows. He'd read the new pages and had drawn a map, hoping to chart my novel's course. He said, "You must feel completely at sea."

"I'm lost. I know that much. What do you think of the chapter with Mike and his wife?"

"I think the furniture's doing too much."

"Like it's about their house rather than about them."

"Exactly," he said, "exactly."

Earlier that summer, his story "The Point" had appeared in the *New Yorker*. Before it ran, the story's editor had flagged fifty-three corrections and changes. Charlie said to me, "They want to change Kurt's last name." Kurt was the story's teenage narrator. "They don't want it to be Simpson because of *The Simpsons*. If readers picture Bart Simpson, the whole story's skewed."

"That's a stretch."

"I know."

But in the published story, Kurt has no last name.

The editor also objected to a quote from the French philosopher Blaise Pascal. "You have a kid walking a drunk woman home at night, along a beach," Charlie said, reading a margin note in the galleys aloud. "From here, how do you leap to Pascal?"

"I like the Pascal passage," I said.

"Me, too."

"I don't think it's out of place."

"Neither do I. I'll keep it."

Pascal got axed.

But, in the final version, the story was better without it.

"The *New Yorker* has a house policy about commas, though," Charlie said. "It leans toward using a comma for clarity, whereas I believe the English language has more power with fewer commas."

"Commas aren't so bad."

"The style just bugs me," he said.

Frank treated comma splices mercilessly. "Meaning, sense, clarity," he repeated. Then, on room 457's blackboard, he drew the identical diagram he had drawn the preceding year, a diagram he would draw for as long as he taught. "The prose can be dense," he said, "as long as it doesn't confuse the reader. Learn how to use commas and periods. Rarely use colons, semicolons, and exclamation points [even though he used exclamation points frequently in *Stop-Time*, which proves that workshop mantras are always reductive]. And," he added, "compose paragraphs logically, as units of dramatic action and narrative."

Seated at the far end of the table, I said, "But García Márquez doesn't use paragraphs in *The Autumn of the Patriarch*, and some of his sentences are seven pages long."

Frank said, "I don't think it's effective." Then he added, "But listen to me criticizing García Márquez. The idea is grotesque."

Nevertheless, one rule applied to everyone who either typed or held a pencil: if you don't write with the reader in mind, you are not a writer, period.

I continued to work from 8:30 AM until 12:30 PM. Ideally, I would produce five hundred words. But some days, forty-five minutes would pass before I entered the language. I had to find my way in; language wouldn't open the door for me. Once I was inside, time dissolved. When I felt myself back in time, I knew I'd completed the day's work.

On September 30, I leaned back in my chair and stretched my arms. I glanced at the clock. I'd worked fifteen minutes shy of four hours. But I'd reached the end of a scene. I thought, *Maybe I should stop.* I believed I had several hundred pages left to write. The conclusion of the scene, in which Mike leaves everything behind, his wife, his daughter, and his life as a ballplayer, was simply the story catching its breath. Only this didn't happen. Instead, first I saw, as if the words were imprinted on blank white space, the novel's final paragraph. I felt the rhythm of conclusion, a slight elevation in tone, the flow of a single sentence. Five minutes later, the book was done, and the pressure I'd been living under for thirteen months vanished. Like a diver rising too quickly from the ocean's floor to its surface, I felt disoriented. My typewriter, desk, notebooks, and pencils seemed surreal. My hands trembled. I thought I might pass out. Oddly, I felt as if I needed to apologize to someone. Slowly, I stood up, walked into our bedroom, and called Jody. My chest shuddered the way it did when Iowa's air was so cold I couldn't breathe. Her voice seemed to be a universe away. I made incoherent sounds, and when she asked me what was wrong I started to cry. It took me a minute to say, "I'm finished." When I began to breathe again, my shudders diminished. I remained seated on one edge of the bed, waiting for my thoughts to flow, as my seizure subsided.

Jody said, "Are you okay?"

"Yeah."

"Do you want me to come home?" She was at work.

"No."

"You're sure?"

"Yeah."

Downstairs, I took a beer from the refrigerator and emptied it in three gulps. Ten minutes later, the alcohol ran its warm hand over my brain and my muscles unclenched. I put on a jacket and left the house. I wandered through town. Near dusk, I saw Maggie at the food co-op. I can't remember what she said, only that she smiled when I said, "I think I finished my novel."

Once Frank read the final pages, he said, "You're right."

* * *

Frank mailed a clean copy of the five-hundred-sixty-seven-page manuscript to his agent, Candida Donadio, who had represented Frank for twenty years and had sold *Stop-Time*. She also had represented Philip Roth, early in his career. Given Roth's influence on me—at least once a year I reread *The Ghost Writer*—I viewed his publisher, Farrar, Straus and Giroux with awe. For me, the FSG acronym embossed on the spine of Roth's novels was sacrosanct, and I was surprised, and disappointed, when it no longer graced his book jackets. In 1989, Roth signed with the agent Andrew Wylie, known in literary circles as "The Jackal" (he supposedly enjoys the nickname). Wylie had earned his reputation by demanding, and usually extracting from publishers, huge advances against royalties for his clients—with one exception. When he significantly upped the price for Roth's 1990 novel *Deception*, Roger Straus told Wylie he could "go fuck himself," and Roth moved to Simon & Schuster.

Frank expected my advance to be roughly one hundred thousand dollars. If Roger Straus wouldn't pay that much for a Philip Roth novel, how much would he pay for one by me?

Ultimately, Candida did not become my agent. Her partner, Eric Ashworth, a respected agent in his midthirties, did. He would represent the next generation of writers, but I suspect Eric would not have signed me as a client had Frank not recommended me. Eric read my novel, then called to discuss it. His voice had the clarity, but not the aggressiveness, of an anchorman's, and he muted the gay inflection that would become more prominent and relaxed over time. As he didn't know me, and hadn't yet gauged my temperament, he said, quite gently, and not wanting to hurt my feelings, "I'm afraid it needs a lot of editing."

"Uh-huh," I said, unprepared for the remark, but not upset by it, either.

"The only person I can think of sending it to in this state is Cork Smith," he said, the editor to whom Candida had sold Pynchon's V. Mr. Smith, I was told, had a great talent for line editing, which Eric felt my novel needed.

Despite Frank's severe scrutiny of language in workshop, he hadn't line-edited my novel. In fact, our discussions about it tended to be unspecific. Referring to the novel's narrator, Frank once said, "He's very Hamlet-like." Skimming a few pages in his office a month or so later he said, "You use 'that' a lot." Mainly, Frank believed I could write the book, and when he felt he needed to, he reminded me of this.

I said to Eric, "I can edit the book, if you think it needs editing."

"Well," he said, sounding doubtful, "let me try Cork first."

"Why don't I send you my play? You'll see that I can write sparely, when I believe it's necessary."

"Okay," he said.

Eric's coolness toward my novel in its current shape puzzled Frank momentarily. Then he shrugged. "So you'll edit it. Listen, trust Eric, he knows what he's doing."

To my knowledge, Cork Smith never replied. But a week after we'd first spoken, Eric called and said, "I love *Spec*."

By then, I'd hacked away fifty manuscript pages. I said, "I promise, I'll send you an entirely new draft before the end of the month."

I deleted scenes, trimmed sentences, condensed descriptions, and collapsed two characters into one. Three days before Thanksgiving, I mailed Eric a manuscript ninety-eight pages shorter than the original.

Then I waited.

After our final workshop in December, Frank and I leaned against the Mill's bar and ordered. Frank said, "I got it," and pushed away my wallet. "Buy me a drink when your ship comes in." When we were served he lifted a shot glass filled with bourbon and tapped it against my beer mug.

"You think someone will publish the novel?" I said.

"I do." He spoke with absentminded conviction, as if the book not being published could only happen in another universe.

"If I have a choice, I'd want the publisher to be either Farrar, Straus or Sam Lawrence," I said. They were my dream publishing houses; each published the best writers in the world. And whereas, two years earlier, Frank had ignored me when I asked what he thought I should do *if* I were admitted to Iowa, now, he listened.

Frank eyed his watch. He had become a fan of the TV drama *Law & Order*—"Hey, don't laugh. Its writers are really good at intricate plotting!"—and he wanted to make sure he had ample time to drive home to watch it. "Well," he said, "I'll send them letters and tell them to read it." Half an hour later he set his glass on the bar and said, "Let's go."

Across the street from my house, he stopped the car. "Call when you hear from Eric."

"I will," I said. Then I stepped out, and once his red taillights glided past my knees I hustled through the cold to my front door.

On December 2, the *New York Times Book Review* named *A Stone of the Heart* a Notable Book of the Year. As an early Christmas present, my sister, whose mania was temporarily in remission, sent me a T-shirt that read "Almost Famous."

But with the novel in limbo, I felt like a ghost. I'd inhabited my narrator for eleven months; without him, I felt formless. I paced through our house, hoping to hear from Eric. When I sat in my office, I heard my desk clock tick. When I lay on our bed, I heard our bedroom clock tick. When I watched the news, time appeared digitally on the TV screen. And when I went to a bar, the second, minute, and hour arms of a Pabst Blue Ribbon clock swept the present into the past.

Jody and I had planned to drive twenty-three hundred miles to spend Christmas in Key West. We would leave on Monday, December 20, but I couldn't call Eric to give him telephone numbers where I could be reached, or expect him to work over the holidays. Protocol demanded authorial patience. The agent made contact, not the writer. On Friday, December 17, at five o'clock Eastern Standard Time, I surrendered. I wouldn't hear from Eric until after the New Year. Shortly, Jody would be home from work. But first she'd call to ask if we needed anything from the grocery store. So when the phone rang, I expected to hear her voice, not Eric's. Pensively, he said, "Now this I can do something with."

On Monday, January 2, he sent it to five publishers.

Two days later, Frank called at 9:00 AM and said, "I just got off the phone with Roger Straus. He's going to buy your book."

PART TWO

CHAPTER THIRTEEN

I remember only a few dozen sentences spoken over the following two weeks, which is appropriate. Every "true" memoir must be incomplete; what I remember may not be "true"; and people who know me may disagree with what I recollect. Neuroscientists suspect that the difficulty in retrieving long-term memories depends upon how recently the memory was used, how the memory is connected to other memories, and how unique the memory is. Over the years, I've "used" these memories, some more often than others, and my novel's fate connects them. But what makes certain memories "unique" is their relation to causality. I remember that Frank asked me to meet him for lunch. Then I called Jody to give her the news. Then I called Charlie and he, Frank, and I ate in a downtown restaurant with pine-tinted wooden booths. The place may have served pizza, I can't say. But I do recall its aggressive sterility. Faux Tiffany lamps hovered over each table; plastic ferns dangled from hooks in midair; and framed posters of gondoliers and the leaning tower of Pisa clung to the walls. I picture Frank seated beside me, and Charlie across from us, but I can't remember a word we said. Time, and perhaps the room's soullessness, has erased our conversation. The three of us were happy, that's my only memory, to which I've assigned a feeling, instead of recalling an action or a conversation that had consequences.

Earlier that morning, Eric had contacted the four other publishers to whom he'd sent the manuscript and told them he'd have an offer by Friday. Each demanded more time to read the novel; no one had expected a two-day response. But "Roger Straus sat down with the book the moment he read my note," Frank told me. Then he added, "Roger won't edit the book, though. He's giving it to an editor he's grooming for a top spot in the house."

On Friday, I received a call from John Glusman, who seemed tentative and reticent. I recall a shared sense of awkwardness. Finally, I said, "Do you like the book?" and he answered, "I like the second half better than the first." I understood then that had the novel been submitted to John, he wouldn't have wanted to publish it. Instead, Mr. Straus had handed him the book and instructed him to shepherd it into the marketplace. Of course, John couldn't refuse. But how could I ask him to do what he'd been ordered to do, rather than what he wanted to do? And how could I entrust and burden him with my novel? I'd hoped to hear, "I love the book." Instead, I heard the opposite of what I'd heard the afternoon Frank called me. In less than three seconds, John's remark undid the hundreds of hours it had taken me to write the book that Frank said was good. And so, rather than welcoming me into the house I desperately wanted to step inside, John partially closed the door to it. After a decade and a half's work, I was, to my astonishment, speaking to an editor at Farrar, Straus. To see my name beside the names of Nobel Prize winners would validate my work and me. All I had to do was say yes. But I didn't.

Near the end of our conversation, John said, "If you have any questions, feel free to give me a call."

"Okay," I said, "thanks." I knew I wouldn't call. He didn't like the book. There was nothing more we needed to say to each other.

I put down the phone. Then, once again, I found myself waiting. And, as absurd as this may sound, the person who made me wait was Saddam Hussein.

* * *

On August 2, 1990, Iraq invaded Kuwait. The following January, U.S. President George Herbert Walker Bush deployed 550,000 U.S. troops to fight "The Mother of All Battles." With the holidays behind us and the New Year rung in, everyone waited for it to commence. A curious, excited sense of doom wove its way into news broadcasts, magazine articles, conversations, and, possibly, our dreams. Still, workshops were not canceled, publishers continued to buy and sell books, readers continue to read, and yet, despite Roger Straus's offer, editors asked Eric for additional time to read my novel in order "to see how the war plays out."

I said, "This is a joke, right?"

"I'm afraid not. But several editors this week want to talk to you to see if you'll be difficult to work with," Eric said. "No one likes a prima donna."

First I spoke to David Rosenthal, an editor at Random House, who said, kindly but directly, "I think the book needs editing." I assured him that editorial suggestions were welcome. Gerald Howard, an editor at Norton, had told Eric that the only other writer who could have written my novel was Don DeLillo. Eric said, "Let's avoid labels." Gerry may or may not have used the word *love*, but his enthusiasm made it unnecessary, although he had a slight problem with the ending. "I just wish Mike would kick Mr. Percy [Mike's team's owner] in the balls." I said I'd think about it. My first publisher, John Oakes, told me that, like Frank, he couldn't believe the extraordinary growth in my work. He knew he'd be outbid and wished me luck. Pat Mulcahy, a senior editor at Little, Brown, called more than once and mentioned the word *love* on several occasions. Everyone at Little, Brown "loved" the book, too. Pat and I often talked at length, and I liked her. She was persuasive. She even summoned our ethnic kinship and said, "Come on, Grimes, us Irish have to stick together." Finally, rather than speaking to Sam Lawrence, I spoke with his assistant, Camille Hykes. I didn't know what to do about the awkward FSG problem. I still wanted to place my book next to Roth's and stare at our matching logos, but my longing to become one of Sam Lawrence's authors was equally intense. So I hoped Camille's excitement would convince me to let him publish the book. Instead, she was gracious and detached, her voice faint, as if she weren't near the phone as she spoke into it. She named Sam's distinguished authors and emphasized the attention he paid to each of them. I listened, and then, after ten minutes, I said, "Do you like the book?" She hesitated. Then she said, "Mr. Lawrence seeks his authors' input on the jacket design and end-papers. The book's spine is linen, and your signature will be gold embossed on the cover." Believing (mistakenly) that she was an editor, I said, "That's nice, but do you like the book?" When she paused I understood why: she hadn't read the novel. I may have been wrong but had no reason to believe I was. And so, at the two houses that I hoped would define me as a writer, one editor liked half the book, and the other person I spoke to wasn't an editor.

Frank told me not to worry about it. "They're not just buying your book," he said, "they're buying your mind." A few days later he said, "Sam Lawrence called to ask me if anyone had offered six figures yet."

As I spoke to Eric, debating what to do, I paced in my living room, stretching the phone cord like a strand of taffy. At dusk, the street lamps brightened, and the television's images reflected against the windowpanes. I had muted the set's volume, and, while staring at CNN's live footage of a city twelve thousand miles away, I continued to believe in an idyllic literary world where an editor nurtured an author's career. Foolishly, my potential editor's age concerned me. Nonetheless, Eric indulged me.

"Roger is in his seventies," he said. "John's in his thirties. He's extremely smart, but, of course, he has his own taste."

"And Sam?"

"Sam's in his sixties."

"Why did Kurt Vonnegut leave him?" (Frank had told me, "The money got too big. Vonnegut's advances were off the charts.")

But Eric said, "Because over lunch he found out his editor wasn't reading his books."

"And Gerry?"

"Gerry's in his early forties. He can line edit if he has to, and he really throws himself behind a writer. The problem with Gerry is he never has much money to spend. Norton can't afford a big loss on a huge advance."

"And Pat?"

"Pat," Eric said, soberly. "Now Pat's becoming a real presence. She's acquiring literary authors for Little, Brown, and she's very loyal to her writers."

"And she's how old?"

"Late thirties."

"So, possibly, I could be with her for a long time?"

Before Eric had a chance to answer, phosphorous light dappled the TV screen and I said, "The war just started."

Having called me from home, Eric yelled to his partner, "Turn on Brokaw! The war just started!" Then he said, "Why don't we talk tomorrow?"

Once we were disconnected, I raised the television's volume. Iraqi air-raid sirens whined and red tracer bullets arced across the sky while smart bombs pulverized the city.

* * *

One week later, on the Tuesday following Martin Luther King Jr.'s birthday, five houses, as scheduled by Eric, bid on my novel. Stupidly, I didn't ask Jody to stay home from work. I also neglected to ask Charlie to sit through the negotiations with me. I didn't ask Frank, either. Or Connie, who had read my novel and whose opinion I trusted. I was nervous, but also embarrassed, and too meek to insist that the day wouldn't be an ordinary one. I would simply talk over the situation with Eric, and then make a decision, although I had no idea what my options would be, or what I would, or should, do. I wanted the decision to be so obvious that it would require no thought or emotion, just acceptance.

Eric called midmorning. "Well, I've heard from everybody," he said. "Promptly at nine o'clock Gerry called. 'Twenty thousand and that's as high as I can go.'" Gerry had recently acquired a baseball novel and his editorial board didn't want it to become a Norton tradition.

"But I haven't written a baseball novel," I said.

"I know. We'll deal with that later. Roger Straus offered twenty thousand. David Rosenthal offered twenty-five. Pat Mulcahy offered twenty-five. Sam offered twenty."

"Twenty? What happened to six figures?"

"Sam rides in his limousine and forgets the real world. Everyone's worried about the recession."

I earned ten thousand dollars a year as a teaching assistant; Jody earned twelve as a graphic design consultant. The recession's impact hadn't worked its way down to our pay grade. "So what do we do?" I said.

"Wait." An hour later, Eric called. "Roger's at twenty-five, David's at thirty, Pat's at thirty, and Sam's at thirty. I told them each we had higher offers. We'll see where things stand after lunch."

"Lunch?"

When I reached Frank, he seemed surprised by the low offers, and somewhat disappointed, as if he'd let me down. Incorrectly predicting the outcome slightly deflated his confidence. Then he rebounded. "Hey," he said, "there's a recession, and the thing to keep in mind is, five houses want your book. That's a good sign. Remember, this is only an advance. So don't get too down."

"I won't. But what do I do if nothing changes after lunch?"

"First, wait to see what happens. Then we'll talk."

Frank didn't suggest that I come to his office and have Eric call us there. And it didn't occur to me to ask him if we could do that, which is strange. Our hopes for the novel had begun in his office, yet now that they were close to being realized we remained apart. Instead of waiting separately, Frank should have been sitting behind his desk, and I should have been sitting across from him in my chair, the river outside flowing past, attuning my internal clock to nature, a force that had the power to diminish, and make seem almost petty, the anxiety I felt, and that Frank, in his way, shared. Because no matter what Eric had to say, the sun would set that evening. Then Frank and I would leave EPB together, our breath would visibly cloud the air, and, while walking to his car, we would long only for one thing—to be warm again.

But things didn't happen that way. Perhaps waiting to learn what was to become of my book was too intimate a moment for me to share with Frank. I may have felt so emotionally naked—I'm sure I was—that leaving me alone with my confusion preserved my dignity. That day, my book's fate was the only thing of consequence to me. Every part of me was tethered to it—my identity, my expectations, my future—and the intensity of that feeling, and the place that novel came to assume in my life, haunted me for years afterward. But a third of my lifetime later, it's only a memory. And all questions about what Frank and I should have done have grown so faint from asking them so many times that I now barely hear them at all.

After lunch, Roger came back with thirty, David with thirty-five, Pat with thirty-five, Sam with thirty-five. Once again, Eric said he had better offers. Roger said thirty-five for world rights, and that's it. Pat and Sam went to forty. So did David, who added, "After that, I'm out."

The phone didn't ring for an hour. To distract myself, I watched the war. Yet it didn't put my situation in perspective. Staring out the living room's front window did. As he always did in the early afternoon, most likely after he'd finished writing for the day, a workshop student who lived across the street and with whom I shared an office on campus stepped out of his apartment into the cold and lifted the black lid of his tin mailbox. When he plucked out some envelopes, I sensed his hopefulness. Just like me, he sorted through them quickly, no doubt looking for an envelope from a literary journal or a slick magazine bearing good news—someone would publish his work; he'd feel elated. But most days, this being another of them, he exhaled, and his upper body briefly slumped once he understood that he had received no news about his life as a writer.

When the telephone finally rang and I picked up the receiver, Eric said, "Okay, Pat went to forty-two, North American rights only. Sam went to forty-five for world rights. His financial officer, Joe Kanon, said it's a baseball book, baseball books are hard to sell overseas, and there's a recession. We're done. So," Eric said, "what do you want to do?"

I thought for a moment. "What do you think you can get for foreign rights?"

"Well, let's see. I'd say ten in the UK, ten in Germany, seven in France—it's a baseball book and the French don't get baseball—and Japan ten. So, thirty-five, forty."

This meant a possible advance of seventy-seven to eighty-two thousand if I accepted Little, Brown's offer. If I went with Roger or Sam, they would retain twenty percent of all foreign advances until my U.S. advance paid out.

"What if Roger or Sam sells the foreign rights?" I said.

"What do I think? I think Sam's a lot of hot air. But Roger," Eric paused, ruminating. "He's a real force overseas."

The kitchen clock read 3:45. I had to be in class in three-quarters of an hour, where I had a novel chapter up in Marilynne Robinson's workshop. "Okay, let me think about it," I said, "and call you in the morning."

As if he had to tell a child that his dog has died, Eric's voice took on a plaintive quality. "Tom, I can't ask these people to wait until tomorrow. They're sitting by their phones. They've been at this all day."

"I have to decide now?" I said.

"I can't put them off. They want to know, and it's five o'clock."

I said, "I have to call you back."

I reached Jody and synopsized the day for her, but she had no more sense of what to do than I did. We were confused, anxious, and too timid to insist on having more time to decide. "Have you called Frank?" she said.

"I'll call him now."

I reached Frank in his office and laid out my final options. Eric had told me he thought David Rosenthal was a superb editor, but not the right editor for my book. I had FSG, Sam, and Little, Brown. I didn't want to give up Farrar, Straus, but John and I would be put in terrible positions. And Sam's offer was ten thousand dollars higher, my entire year's salary. Frank said, "Roger's out then," and I felt as if a needle had pierced my heart.

"What about Sam?"

"Sam's a good publisher." For the first time, Frank sounded tentative. Perhaps he didn't want to bias me toward the man who published him. If the novel's publication were a disaster, he would feel responsible for it.

"I idolize the people on his list," I said.

"It's a hot list."

"But he never spoke to me. And how did he get from one hundred thousand to forty-five thousand?"

"Times are tight."

"At the end Little, Brown came up with an extra two grand. Eric thinks he can get an additional thirty-five to forty overseas."

"Take the money," Frank said. Just like that. No hesitation, no equivocation.

It was 5:10 PM in New York. "I have to call Eric," I said. "See you later."

Eric said, "Tell me what you want to do."

I said, "I don't know" several times. I closed my eyes and saw publishers' logos and the face of one of my classmates. He didn't dislike me, although he didn't like me, either. But I interpreted what might have been indifference as disdain. Frank had guided, defended, praised, and, in a way, isolated me from my classmates.

With the exception of Charlie, I existed apart from everyone. I had Frank's approval, friendship, and affection. When it came to most of the other students, he barely knew their names. And I imagined my classmates thinking, *Tom Grimes was published by Frank Conroy's publisher. He didn't write a good book; he received an undeserved gift.* I didn't want to feel ashamed, disgraced, or haunted by second guesses. So, at 4:15 in Iowa City, I said, "Okay, Little, Brown. Go with Little, Brown. I have to run."

Breathless, my earlobes burning from the cold, I walked into class, apologized for being late, and found a seat.

Virtually everyone hated the chapter. At one point Marilynne said, "It should be 'were,' not 'was,' in this sentence. It's the subjunctive, right?"

After workshop, I started uphill alone in the dark. Bill Lashner caught up with me. We trudged along, heads down, our faces shielded from the wind. "Forget workshop," he said, trying to cheer me up. "Just write."

Without any joy I said, "Five houses bid on the novel today. I sold it two hours ago."

Frank had reached the Mill and he glowed as I walked toward him. At his table, I sat across from him. Charlie may have been with us, I can't remember. My tunnel vision includes only Frank, and the blur of space behind him.

"Hey, hey," he said, "the famous author."

He raised his glass, but I said, "I've made a terrible mistake."

"What are you talking about?"

"I went with the wrong house."

He smiled. "No, you didn't."

"I did. I should have gone with Sam."

"Don't be crazy."

A tremor coursed through my body. Then, perhaps having noticed it, Frank leaned forward. As he gripped my arm, his smile disappeared. Softly he said, "Listen, everything's going to be fine."

And I sat there, wishing I could believe him.

CHAPTER FOURTEEN

F ive days after I sold the novel, Jim Gammon called me. The Met Theatre, he said, would reopen in May, which was only four months away. After listening to a staged reading of *Spec*, the board wanted to mount it as the theater's premiere production.

The speed of events seemed surreal. A decade had passed since the night I'd accidentally discovered (or at least began to shape) my literary voice. I'd begun to search for it while enrolled in a freshman composition class at Queensborough Community College. I read *The Sun Also Rises* and wanted to be Hemingway. Naively, I also wanted to be Jake Barnes, a journalist, and the novel's narrator. He rose late, showered leisurely, then drank coffee and read the daily paper at a Paris café. After a long lunch, he'd "go upstairs and get off some cables." In the office, he "worked hard for two hours." Once he'd typed his articles, he "sorted out the carbons, stamped on a by-line, put the stuff in a couple of big manila envelopes and rang for a boy to take them to the Gare St. Lazare." Then he went "to the Café Napolitain to have an *aperitif* and watch the evening crowd on the Boulevard." The only problem was, I'd romanticized Jake's life so completely that, until my professor pointed out this fact in class, I didn't realize Jake was impotent. Still, I wanted to be a writer, and Hemingway's memoir, *A Moveable Feast*, validated my fantasy about how I could become one. I would move to Paris, live in a charming attic, and each morning I would carry a notebook to the Place Saint-Michel, where I would find "a pleasant café, warm and clean and friendly" and order a café au lait. Once the waiter brought it, I would lift my pencil and press its sharp tip against one of my notebook's empty pages. At first, I struggled with the prose. But soon I found that "the story was writing itself and I was having a hard time keeping up with it." So I skipped lunch and ordered a rum St. James. Then "I went back to writing and I entered far into the story and was lost in it. I was writing it now and it was not writing itself and I did not look up nor know anything about the time" until "the story was finished and I was very tired." After lifting my head, "I closed up the story in the notebook and put it in my inside pocket and asked the waiter for a dozen *portuagaises* and a half carafe of the dry white wine they had there." At dusk, as the streetlights came on, "I was sure this was a very good story although I would not know truly how good until I read it over the next day."

Only I didn't go to Paris. I stayed in Queens and worked as a funeral parlor's janitor to put myself through college. By my sophomore year I began to call myself a writer. At first, I wrote poorly in a plain, direct style; then I wrote poorly in a self-indulgent, complicated style. But, slowly, I improved. Using cheap paper and purplish-black ribbon that stained my fingers whenever I changed the spools, I pecked out manuscripts, each as tall as a layer cake. I hid embarrassing sentences behind a hedgerow of xxxxxx's, or else I smeared them with Wite-Out until they disappeared beneath a crust of hardened goo. When I moved to Manhattan and found a day job, I woke at 4:00 AM to write for three hours, often dozing despite drinking several cups of tea. For years, no one published my work. I received unsigned rejection letters in envelopes I'd addressed to myself. My stories seemed to operate according to the laws of a boomerang. I'd fling one into space, and a few months later it would return. Now, within days, people told me they wanted my work. I seemed to be leading someone else's life. Frank called it "the impostor syndrome."

"You can't believe good things are happening to you and you're worried someone will find out you're a fake," he said. "Don't worry, it'll pass."

So I said okay to Jim Gammon. Several weeks later, in February, a squib appeared in *Variety*: "A group of stars are reviving Hollywood's Met Theatre, which has been dark for five years. The board includes Ed Harris, Amy Madigan, Beth Henley, Arliss Howard, and Holly Hunter. The first planned play is *Spec*, a comedy about a frustrated scripter penned by Tom Grimes, who is turning into a hot property as well. His novel, *Sweet Illusions of the Game*, will be published by Little, Brown."

I felt more confused than elated. "This is weird," I said to Frank. He answered, "Hey, enjoy the ride while it lasts."

After Eric had told me I couldn't change publishers, I resigned myself to remaining with Little, Brown. I scanned my bookshelves and looked for its logo. The company had published Mailer, Salinger, and Pynchon, who, twelve months earlier, had released his first novel in seventeen years. Not bad. Plus, Pat Mulcahy's presence comforted me. As the novel's in-house advocate, she maintained everyone's enthusiasm for the book—the editorial board, the sales force, the marketing division, and the PR people. Even before she'd edited the book, she'd convinced them to print three dozen "Cape Cods," which are expensive advance reader copies sent to famous authors for jacket quotes. Chain-store sales executives and respected independent booksellers received them, too, as a sign that the publisher planned to promote the book aggressively. A year before the finished product would be snugly placed on a shelf—ideally showing the front cover, not simply the book's spine—or, if Little, Brown paid for the premium space, on the table every customer saw the instant he stepped into the bookstore, the buzz started.

But my novel didn't have a title. Amend that: my novel did not have a good title. Initially, Little, Brown used the manuscript's final six words and entitled the novel *The Sweet Illusions of the Game*. To me, it sounded syrupy. "Titles are hard," Frank said. "They have to imply everything and reveal nothing." So we sat in his office and stared at the frozen river, aware that Fitzgerald's original title for *The Great Gatsby* was "Trimalchio of West Egg." That Hemingway's *The Sun Also Rises* left his typewriter entitled "Fiesta." And that Pynchon's *Gravity's Rainbow* emerged from its literary chrysalis entitled "Mindless Pleasures." We began in earnest, but came up with nothing. So we pondered our titular abyss for perhaps a week before we began to leave notes in each other's workshop mailboxes. The spontaneous and unspoken rule of the game was to suggest the worst title imaginable. I'm no longer sure who dreamt up *The Great Batsby*, but Frank contributed *Across the Infield and Into the Showers*, I hold the copyright on *The Fastball Also Rises*, he gets credit for *The Mound and the Fury*, and I take the blame for *The Satanic Bases*. One cold night I went to a Paul Simon concert and a song lyric attached itself to my brain the way a barnacle adheres to the hull of a ship. The next day, by pure coincidence, Frank and I approached each other on a deserted, downtown street. With our woolen scarves wrapped around our faces and the two of us nearly deafened by the wind, we paused beneath the illuminated bank sign that displayed the time and the temperature. Briefly, I lowered my scarf and yelled, *"Forever Blessed!"* Frank shouted back, "Great!" Then he pointed at the numerals overhead. It was fourteen degrees below zero. Without saying another word we scurried in opposite directions. At home the tiny icicles that clung to my beard melted. With my tongue, I snatched drops of water from my mustache the way a lizard snares flying insects. As I wiped my face with a dish towel the telephone rang. When I answered Frank said, "It sounds like a bodice ripper." I pictured a swooning duchess having her white blouse torn open by a duke wearing platform shoes and a powdered wig. A week later, I heard two words: *Season's End*.

They signaled the end of youth and innocence. And, as my narrator believed liberalism died the day we elected Ronald Reagan president of the United States, the new title's resonance captured my protagonist's nostalgia and disillusionment. In sequence I called Frank, Jody, Charlie, and Connie. In response I heard, great, exactly, perfect, and terrific. The book had its title.

Eric said to me, "We'll do everything we can to make this book a best seller."

"And he means it," Frank assured me.

As Pat edited the novel, February and March passed. In early April, her comments arrived. I read them and showed them to Jody and to Charlie. Then I carried the seven, single-spaced typed pages to Frank's house, where we sat shoulder to shoulder at his dining room table and went over them. Despite Frank's intense enthusiasm for *Season's End*, this was the first time we had scrutinized the text word by word. During the two workshops I'd taken with him, his input had been minimal. Once, beside a simile, he'd written in faint gray script, "Superb." But he had never questioned the narrator's voice, or quibbled with my prose. Instead, his impressions were macroscopic. One day, he said, "The relationship between Mr. Percy and Mike has a Faustian quality. Mike's soul is at stake, even if he doesn't entirely understand this. But the reader will." He studied Pat's comments. Then he said, "These are good. She's smart." We debated which suggestions to accept, which to ponder, and which to reject. "Mike never seems to have much fun," Pat had written. "Loosen him up." (Later, I tried to, but the effort felt forced, and the addition interrupted the flow of the book. "Delete it," Frank said. "Ignore the suggestion." I did.) Pat continued, "And this paragraph at the end of chapter seven: it's very Joycean and beautiful, but it kind of makes me gag. Cut it?" "Should I?" Frank shrugged. "Hey, it's your book." I kept the paragraph. That's what Frank did: he allowed me, for better or worse, to write the novel I was able, and needed, to write. At the end of April, I mailed the manuscript's final draft to Pat. For my last workshop as a student at Iowa, I submitted her favorite chapter and my classmates spent twenty minutes discussing how two characters were positioned on a bed. The conversation was silly. Yet the voices I'd once fought to silence would soon be forever silenced, and I would miss them.

After class I told Marilynne that I wouldn't be back.

"Oh?" she said, softly, like a pigeon cooing.

"I have to be in LA," I said. "My play opens in May and rehearsals have started."

Marilynne seemed surprised. I suppose she expected a more conventional excuse. Or perhaps my mysterious success puzzled her. I know she didn't like my novel. But I'll never know if she spoke about it with Frank, or with Roger Straus, who had published her novel *Housekeeping*. So I said good-bye, and then—just like Frank leaving school in *Stop-Time*—"I turned from the window, walked down the hall and went out the door. It was as simple as that. I disregarded the pounding of my heart."

* * *

Rehearsals ran from three in the afternoon until midnight. Afterward, most of the cast and crew sat backstage, drinking and talking. I never got to bed before 2:00 AM, and when I slid out of it the next morning and parted the thick green drapes to let in the sunshine the first thing I saw was Al Pacino as "The Godfather" staring at me from a thirty-foot-high billboard. He wore a brown three-piece suit and a light gray fedora, and he appeared ready to tell me I'd disappointed him. Nearby, on the scrubby hillside, stood white, twenty-foot-tall letters that read HOLLYWOOD. Seeing the word every day demystified it, and changed its meaning. Rather than being grandiose, the sign seemed timid and apprehensive, as if the place it represented was so unreal it needed to remind itself, and convince others, that it existed. Soon, I began to meet film agents who believed I could earn millions penning screenplays based on the fact that they'd *heard* I could write. They were desperate to sign me because I'd accomplished nothing. They'd discovered me in a cocoon and imagined me as a butterfly, and they would love the illusion of me until I produced my first failure. After that, they would never want to speak to me again.

A week before *Spec* opened, Eric called and said, "You're not going to want to hear this, but Pat's leaving Little, Brown next month." Before I could speak, he added, "Don't panic. She wants to take four authors with her and you're one of them."

Pat had been offered the founding literary editor's position at Hyperion, a new publishing house started by Disney. As I held the receiver, I pictured FSG's logo on my book's faux-linen spine and understood that it had become a fantasy.

I said, "Eric, how did I go from Roger Straus to Mickey Mouse?"

"Don't get upset," he said. "Disney has a lot of money. Pat can give you a two-book contract. Fifty thousand for the novel you've written, eighty thousand for the next one you write. All she needs is a one-page outline to show Bob Miller," Hyperion's president. Momentarily, Eric and I were silent. Then he said, "Pat's afraid to call you. She knows you had other offers and went with Little, Brown because of her. Now, I don't want you to worry, I think we can fix this, but there's one other problem." Eric paused. "Little, Brown won't let you out of your contract."

"Why not?"

"I don't know."

"And the other three writers?"

"They don't care about them." The first, a mystery writer, was not under contract. The second had accepted a one-hundred-thousand-dollar advance on a partial manuscript years earlier and hadn't delivered a word since then. Now, Little, Brown wanted its money back. The third writer remained anonymous. Even when Pat called, she wouldn't tell me who he was.

"I promised I wouldn't. Do you hate me?"

"No, I don't hate you. It's a good offer. You have to take it." I recall not wanting to make her feel guilty. After all, she'd been afraid to talk to me, so I assumed she felt remorseful. I'd be fine, I said. I don't recall much else.

After I hung up I called Frank, who said, "Have Eric call Sam. He'll still take the book."

But Eric said, "I can't go to Sam. It's too late. They've started to copyedit the book. Besides, Bill Phillips," Little, Brown's editor in chief, "insists they still love the novel and will do everything within their power to promote it. He's assigning it to another editor."

"What about Pynchon's editor?"

"Pynchon's Pynchon. He doesn't have an editor."

"So who am I getting?"

"Colleen Mohyde," who was sweet, sincere, and worked in Little, Brown's Boston office, which would close by the end of the year, four months before my novel was due to be published in April. I begged Eric to find me another editor. "I like her, she's nice, but she lives in Boston. There's no way she's transferring to New York. Her husband's a Boston police detective. He has fifteen years on the force. Now, does anyone honestly believe he'll quit his job five years before he can retire at half pay? I don't. January will come and Colleen will be gone."

"Bill says that won't happen."

"It will."

Eric said, "Well, I'll call and tell him you're concerned." Eric called. Then he called me back. "Bill says if Colleen doesn't move, he'll be your editor." In the strictest sense of the word, I no longer needed an editor. I needed someone to keep the book from being "orphaned." Little, Brown published ten books a month. Without a "parent" watching out for my novel, everyone would likely forget it within days of publication. Bill promised Eric this wouldn't happen and Little, Brown refused to cancel my contract, in part, it seemed at this point, to spite Pat.

In the meantime, I'd become ambivalent about following her to Hyperion. Six weeks had passed since she and I had spoken. By late June, when I returned from LA, where *Spec* was a success, I'd begun to consider the implications of having a book marketed as a baseball novel published by Disney. I imagined serious reviewers tossing it into a bin reserved for young adult novels, all of which ended with a World Series–winning home run that completed the fairy tale season of a team of plucky underdogs. I'd written a novel about capitalism, pop culture, celebrity, and race, but if Hyperion published it I'd have to go on tour dressed as a Mouseketeer.

By this time, Frank had retreated to Nantucket for the summer. All he'd said before he left town was, "Not to worry."

Frank tested the nature-versus-nurture argument regarding one's temperament. Either Frank was congenitally "cool," as in jazzy, Miles Davis "cool," or as a result of having survived his volatile and terrifying childhood he no longer worried about anything. To me, a fusion of these dual psychological imprints conjured up Frank's character and personality. But I sensed a third, unaccounted-for mystery at work. After all, how had he become the workshop's director if not by magic? Besides, he loved my book and others had offered to buy it, which confirmed his judgment. So why on earth—a phrase Frank often used—should I worry?

The paramount reason was my stupidity. First, I sold my book after considering my options for less than fifteen fraught minutes. Then, rather than traveling to New York to meet the people at Little, Brown face to face and perhaps secure my novel's potential future, I said to Eric, "What if I talk to Bill?" who agreed to take my call. It was now July, the windows of our house were open, and, as the telephone cord stretched into the sunlight-filled dining room, I sat at its table while we spoke. Bill promised me that my novel would be well taken care of, but he resisted my desire to have someone other than Colleen oversee its progress from manuscript form to its final resting place among the thousands of other bound and dust-jacketed tombstones squeezed indifferently onto one shelf in a book chain's superstore located in a mall the size of an airport. I said I appreciated his offer to act as the novel's guardian should Colleen not transfer to New York. "But," I added, "your eye's on the company's three-million-dollar books," like its tie-in with a PBS miniseries about the Wild West. "So, as grateful as I am for your guarantees, I'm still afraid the book will get lost."

"It won't."

"Well, maybe not. But if I continue to believe the novel is better off with Pat, what do I have to do to resolve this?"

Without an instant's hesitation he said, "Sue us."

Eric said, "He actually told you that?"

"Yes." And despite the fact that people always tell me to speak louder, they can't hear me, at this point I raised my voice. "How the hell did we get from five houses bidding on my book to having to sue the house we sold it to in order to get it published?"

Unsurprisingly, Eric didn't have an answer.

* * *

Nor did my book have a dust jacket. I begged Colleen to "please make sure the illustration has nothing to do with baseball." That autumn, when I slid the prototype out of its FedEx envelope, a player on a baseball card appeared beneath my name. And to make sure I got the point, the card had been torn in half.

Frank didn't mind the cover. "Hey!" he said when I showed it to him. "It'll look good with quotes on the back." Frank had asked several famous writers he knew to provide them. But as autumn ended, we hadn't received a quote from anyone he'd contacted. Then, at a Christmas party thrown by him and Maggie, Frank tugged me aside, and as we sat on their living room couch he opened an envelope and pulled out a letter from Norman Mailer. During Mailer's Iowa visit (which, it seemed, no one but Frank, Charlie, Jody, and I appreciated), Frank told Mailer I was "into some heavy existential stuff." Mailer also was an idol of mine. At night, during college, after I'd finished scrubbing the funeral parlor's toilets and scooping the crumpled and often lipstick-smeared cigarette butts out of sand-filled standing ashtrays, I would stay up, often until sunlight pooled on the spaces of the parking lot outside the building before the hearses arrived, to study his work. Within a month, I'd read every word he'd written. At the time, I was nineteen, and I never dreamed I'd meet him, so the morning I ate breakfast with him and Frank at the Cedar Rapids airport seemed hallucinatory, a sensation intensified by the fact that each of us was hungover from the previous evening's party. On the drive from Iowa City, I sat in the station wagon's cold backseat and studied, in profile, Mailer's gray eyebrow. Wizened hair sprouted from it like an insect's tentacles. He stared at the fallow cornfields alongside the highway. Then he said to Frank, "Are they taking good care of the land?" The remark was ludicrous, and yet Tolstoyan and touching. Here was a Jewish boy from Brooklyn surveying an expanse of fertile Iowa earth that had been sprayed with pesticides by an agricultural conglomerate expressing his patriarchal concern for crops he envisioned being scythed and harvested by serfs. Knowing absolutely nothing about farming, Frank—not wanting to disappoint *his* idol, friend, and guest—answered, "Yeah, I believe so."

In the airport's cafeteria, Mailer ordered eggs, then looked at me and said, "You have to eat eggs on the road," as if defending a masculine code of honor. I dishonored the code, perhaps disappointing him, and ordered an English muffin. Frank had tea. After breakfast, Frank and I watched Mailer board the plane. Returning to Iowa City, Frank said, "Well, I think that went off okay."

I hadn't sensed Frank's anxiety over Mailer's visit and was surprised to hear him admit he was relieved. Not wanting to disappoint *my* idol, I said, "It did."

Still, Mailer didn't have time to read my novel and offer a jacket quote. "Every other day there's a new genius on the block," he wrote. "It's too hard to keep up." Frank folded Mailer's letter, slipped it inside its envelope, and said, "There you have it. He tried."

Since no one else had, one morning in his office Frank called E. L. Doctorow, who had been sent a galley of the book. When Frank reached for the telephone, he looked at me and said, "I love doing this." Yet after the two of them spoke for thirty seconds, it became clear that

Doctorow wouldn't be providing a quote. "I understand," Frank said. Briefly, they talked about a trip they'd made together to Russia, years earlier. "I can't believe we saw Chekhov's telephone," Frank said. Before he hung up, he added, "It's good to hear your voice." Then he stared at a point in space behind me, the way a stage actor *looks toward but not at* an audience. He shrugged. "Well, he can't do it."

I said, "That's fine," knowing Frank had begun to feel powerless with regard to generating praise for the book. It was out of his hands and out of mine. The book now belonged to the world, and neither of us knew what the world would do with it.

* * *

We didn't have to wait long to find out. January came. Colleen left. And one bleak winter afternoon Eric called and read me my novel's first review.

From *Publishers Weekly*:

This schizophrenic second novel from Grimes (*A Stone of the Heart*) veers from sluggish philosophizing and ponderous verbosity to snappy repartee and crisp narrative. Mike Williams, a left fielder and singles hitter for an unnamed major league baseball team, chronicles the intermittently compelling stories of his marriage to his high school sweetheart and battles with his agent, manager and team owner in the seasons between 1975 and the players' strike of 1981. Proposing baseball as an anchor of sanity in the craziness of the business world around it, Grimes contrasts the sharp realities of life with "the sweet illusions of the game." The first part of the novel, charting Williams's rise to stardom and its burdens, is smugly pretentious and nearly chokes the sly, sardonic humor that is its principal redeeming feature, although the rest of the book is better focused. Williams observes, "We are ballplayers. We accept the ineffable and get on with the game." Grimes should have followed suit from early on.

At that moment, I died in some small but irreversible way. Years later Charlie said, "The book *may* have had the same life in the world, you can't know. What's gnawed at you, though, what you can't let go of, is that you betrayed your own ideals by not signing with FSG. That's what you can't live with."

Having already disowned me, Little, Brown remained silent.

When a copy of the review turned up in my mailbox, I showed it to Frank. Normally, he read with uncanny quickness, but this time his eyes lingered on the page. He scanned the words twice to be certain he understood them correctly. "It's one review," he said, returning the sheet of paper to me. "It's no big deal." Yet disappointment—not in each other; our bond had deepened and I was more Frank's son than his friend—clouded the book's once illusory promise. All Frank had hoped for had not come to pass.

Selling the novel had been deceptively simple and effortless. But the novel no longer existed as a potential success. It was real and, by increments, it was becoming a failure. Not even *Kirkus Reviews'* assessment of it as "passionate, entertaining, and refreshingly confident" seemed capable of reversing its freefall, or restoring *my* confidence in it. Over time it became clear to me that my confidence had all along been Frank's confidence. So deeply had I sought his approval that I never questioned his judgment. I hadn't been able to separate my need for Frank's affection from my need to look at my novel as objectively as possible. Which is why it's taken me twenty years to understand that our unexpected friendship, rather than my novel, was the real work of art.

It's also taken me twenty years to figure out that no matter what decision I'd made regarding the novel, I would not have made the *right* decision because, for me, there is never a *right* decision. I didn't choose the *wrong* house. Whatever house I chose would have been the *wrong* house. In fact, I may have made the *best* decision. But my counternarrative for selling *Season's End* would have been this: immediately after I'd committed to FSG I would have thought, John didn't like the novel, but Pat loved it. I knew this.

So why didn't I go with her? Instead, I took less money and gave away the novel's world rights. Pat had been hired by Little, Brown to find, entice, and sign extraordinarily talented fiction writers, to create a list equal to or better than FSG's and, had I signed with her, I would have been the first to represent it. *Season's End* may have even become a success. But I didn't, it wasn't, and by choosing to define myself exclusively as a literary writer I've chosen a profession and a life that promise to humble me. Every day I face a blank page, knowing that the majority of the words I commit to the page will be wrong, and after I reread my prose, I know a dozen necessary revisions will begin the moment I complete the first draft. But for me writing is a necessity. I exist in sentences. I forget my sense of failure. I forget time. I forget that I'm aging. I forget that one day I'll die. Revising sentences is an act of hope, and connecting with a reader is the only leap of faith I'll ever take. As a boy, I read stories that transported me, just as stories transported Frank, into a world that, paradoxically, was real *because* it was imaginary. Now I write stories because I continue to need imaginary worlds, and limiting myself to *Season's End*'s fate was deeply foolish. The book did change my life, not by telling me who I am, but by not telling me. Its failure left me unfinished. Maybe success intimidates me. Maybe I'm afraid of completion. Maybe I know that if I don't believe I can write a book better than the books I've already written, I'm a ghost.

CHAPTER FIFTEEN

D espite the book's early reception, Frank's faith in my work didn't waver. He'd already awarded me one of the workshop's six annual ten-thousand-dollar James Michener Fellowships. For the first time since I was twelve, I didn't have either a full-time job or a part-time job while I was in school. As a kid, I mowed lawns and shoveled snow. I delivered newspapers. I jerked soda and washed dishes. In college, I hoisted coffins as a professional pallbearer. Later, I iced dead fish for a packing plant on Cape Cod. I managed a stationery company, a Soho housewares store, and, in Key West, I waited tables. Now, all I had to do was write. And, as a favor to Frank, I read fifty of the workshop's eight hundred application manuscripts. "The borderline ones," he said. Afterward, he selected the final twenty-five. I'd gone from being among the eight hundred to judging fifty of the eight hundred, a reversal of fortune I found incredible. Then he added, "I'm also nominating you for a Whiting."

"What's a Whiting?"

"An award for young writers, first books, et cetera. You'll get thirty thousand. Just give me a finished copy of the novel." At some point I learned that Whiting nominations are supposed to be confidential. But Frank had expected me to receive a larger advance, and annoyed, surprised, and slightly embarrassed by the fact that I didn't, he not only wanted to help me, he also wanted to prove he still had the clout to bestow upon me a major literary honor solely on the strength of his name.

During the autumn of my Michener year, I'd begun my third novel. I wanted to have a new book under way before *Season's End* was published, but Jody wanted to leave Iowa City. If you're not in the workshop, it's a gruesome town to live in. Hot, humid summers; glacial winters. No ocean, no museums, no theater. Lousy food, juvenile movies, and four hours from the nearest interesting city: Chicago. Also, Charlie had left, and from the time I finished my day's writing until Jody returned from work near dusk, the house felt hollow. Yet I had difficulty imagining life without Frank's constant, fatherly approval. I'd written a million words hoping to fill my emptiness and erase the perpetual sense of failure I'd lived with since childhood. But they hadn't; Frank's affection had. In his eyes, I didn't feel like a flaw in the scheme of things. Jody had touched and healed one part of me, Frank another, and Charlie completed the family I'd longed for. I wasn't prepared to lose it.

Nevertheless, Jody deserved the chance to leave Iowa City. So, in December, I dutifully entered the job market. Since I had no interest in finding a job, I was so relaxed during interviews that I was immediately offered three. Even the university I advised *not* to hire me wanted to hire me. The school was located in Texas and, in an effort to distinguish its new MFA creative writing program from the country's other hundred and fifty, its administrators had decided to focus their program on "literature of the Southwest." So, while attending the Modern Languages Association's conference in San Francisco two days after Christmas, I sat in one of their hotel suite's cushioned armchairs and explained to three English department faculty members employed by Southwest Texas State

University that I had absolutely no connection to the region. "I was born in New York, I grew up in New York, and my literary imagination sees the world through the lens of New York. If you're looking for someone who writes about the Southwest, please," I said, "look for someone else. It'll be better for your program." I hoped to end the interview with that remark because I wanted to see a documentary about making *Apocalypse Now* and needed to catch a bus. Instead, I was asked if I read literary theory. "No. It has nothing to do with literature." Did I believe creative writing could be taught? "It's not a valid question. Do people ask if painting, dancing, and playing music can be taught?" Once I was free, I dashed out of the hotel, sprinted to nab the crosstown bus and, certain I'd impressed no one during my interviews, I enjoyed the movie guiltlessly. I'd tried to find a job but I'd failed. Selfishly, and no doubt childishly, I was content. I could return home to subzero temperatures and my new novel. But that evening, by telephone, I was invited to Texas for a campus visit. Grudgingly, I accepted. Near the end of January, three months before *Season's End*'s publication, I flew to Austin and then, in the dark, was driven thirty miles south to San Marcos. The following morning, sunshine and an immense, cloudless blue sky mocked my dreary mood. As if to spite me, the temperature was seventy-two degrees. Everyone I met was nice. All were eager to have me join the faculty. But the next day it rained while I was given a tour of the area. Sights I had no desire to see were pointed to; places I had no interest in were explained in historical detail. On the return trip to the airport, the program's director said, "If we offer you the job, do you think you'll come?" I stared at the muddy field bordering the interstate and, instinctively, said, "Nothing about the place speaks to me." I hated the houses, the landscape, the horizon, and the ground. Only after the plane climbed above a thick layer of gray clouds did my fear of exile slowly fade. And only when I stepped off the plane did I, despite Iowa's ear-scorching cold, feel my spirit bloom and my muscles unclench. In the Cedar Rapids airport terminal, Jody hugged me and I gave her a kiss. As for what I thought of Texas, my expression

made it known that she had no reason to ask. Within twenty-four
hours, I had a tenure-track job offer.

"Take it!" Frank said.

"Frank, it's Texas."

"So what?" he said. "Go! Ride out the recession. You don't have
to stay forever."

As I slumped in my chair and sulked, Frank laughed. Then he
said, "You're always worrying. Stop it. This is good news." He lit a
cigarette and flipped the matchbook onto his cluttered desk. After
he'd blown an eddy of smoke toward the dingy ceiling he added,
"Professor Grimes. I like the way it sounds. Hey, I've been thinking. Don't buy a guitar with your book money." Frank's career as
a jazz musician had influenced his conversational style because he
changed subjects as unexpectedly as he changed chord progres-
sions. "Buy a piano," he said. I had played both instruments as a
kid. "You can get those electronic keyboards now. The quality's not
bad, and they cost less than two hundred bucks. How's the new
book going?"

I shrugged. "Yours?"

Leaning back, he swept one hand over the manuscripts piled
behind, beside, and in front of him, as smoke trailed his curled
fingers. "Speaking of which …"

By the time I reached his office door, he was reading again.

* * *

Often, I took long walks in the woods, fifteen miles west of town,
to look for fossilized arrowheads and Indian burial mounds. One
afternoon, I walked deep into the forest and paused when the sun
dipped below a ridge of high, leafless branches. The workshop had
changed me, not simply as a writer, but emotionally, as well. I had
Frank's affection, and I couldn't let go of Iowa.

But Jody liked the prospect of Texas. Before we met, she'd traveled extensively in Mexico, and living within five hours of its border

appealed to her. Plus we needed a steady paycheck. Only, I'd been so determined to turn down the job that I'd forgotten the salary. "You don't know how much you'll be paid?" Jody asked, stunned. Forced to remember, I did. In a dismal, windowless office, the English department's chair, a petite, stylishly dressed middle-aged woman who spoke with a pronounced Texas twang, had leaned toward me and said, "After you leave, we have to vote before we can offer you the job. But, unofficially, the salary's twenty-seven thousand. Since we really want you to come, we've raised it to twenty-nine." As a workshop teaching-writing fellow, I taught two classes and was paid ten thousand dollars. Now, Southwest Texas State wanted to pay me *barely* three times that amount to teach three times as many classes—six altogether, four of them freshman composition. If I took the job, I'd earn *less* per class than I'd earned as a teaching assistant. But Jody didn't want me to wait tables while I waited for my literary career to take off. On the other hand, I wanted time to finish my new novel, which, in my mind, would secure a large enough advance for us to live on while I wrote my next one. Plus, Frank had given me a summer teaching position. In a thrilling yet disorienting way, I would occupy his office while he retreated for two months to Nantucket. So why would I leave Iowa for Texas?

Several reasons: my timidity, Jody's wisdom, and a compromise. We'd spent three years in Iowa; now it was time to move on. The problem was, I'd received an offer from a Virginia university but declined after meeting its embittered faculty, and another university's offer disappeared when its position's funding did. Texas was my only remaining choice.

Returning to my car, I traipsed over dead leaves and intermittent patches of snow. Other than the sounds I made, the world was silent. Occasionally, I'd pause to listen. Then I'd move when wind bent the tree limbs until they creaked.

In town, I went to a restaurant called the Sanctuary and sat at the bar. The other stools and booths were empty. No one had dropped a coin into the jukebox. And as I drank, an emotional twilight softened my resistance. Defeated, I called Jody and told her to meet me.

When she arrived I smiled and said, "Okay, we'll go." Without removing her coat, she put her arms around my neck, kissed me, sat down, and said, "Now buy me a drink."

The next day I told Frank about my decision. He said, "You're doing the right thing. And I can promise you, you'll be back."

CHAPTER SIXTEEN

I called SWT—at the time, this was the university's acronym—and told the department chair I would arrive in August. Jody and I put our house on the market. And, surprisingly, *People* magazine planned to run a long, flattering review of *Season's End*. Its editors dispatched a photographer to take my picture. In my office, I leaned, as requested, against my floor-to-ceiling bookshelves. I sat at my desk, held a pencil, and concentrated on a spiral-bound notebook. I looked down, as if staring into a grave; up, as if contemplating infinity. Then the photographer asked me to don a baseball cap. "I don't own one," I said. A baseball jersey? "No." How about a bat, do you have a bat? "No," I lied. I had a blond, thirty-two-inch Rawlings behind the office door. And I'd hidden a graphite-smudged baseball. Whenever my writing stalled, I'd lift it from the dictionary beside my typewriter, toss it overhead, and catch it until I'd emptied my mind so new sentences could fill it. I also owned an outfielder's mitt, which, at times, I wore on my left hand as I scribbled with my right. But these were private talismans, so the photographer left Iowa City without a snapshot of me wearing a base-ball costume, leaving me my dignity. But what might be forthcoming, according to Eric, was a hundred-thousand-dollar option for the nov-el's film rights. And a foreign book scout's synopsis hyped *Season's End* as a "masterpiece of American fiction," which, she believed, would "travel because it is fundamentally about universal themes and it is truely [*sic*] great writing." I might have trusted her judgment had she'd spelled *truly* correctly. Yet, maybe Frank's prophecy had been true: everything would be fine. I'd been a fool to worry.

Or maybe I hadn't. Little, Brown arranged a brief, odd book "tour." I would read in Dayton, Columbus, and Toledo, Ohio. Cedar Rapids, Iowa. Iowa City, Iowa. And Madison, Wisconsin. Also, the novel's publication date coincided with major league baseball's opening day, meaning it would be released with fifty other "base-ball" books. Little, Brown's marketing strategy seemed to involve keeping the book a secret in large cities, and confusing reviewers by having it arrive for reviews along with *Timmy of the Little League*. My hope withered, my anxiety bloomed, and, not wanting to be caught in public looking for copies of my novel, I avoided Prairie Lights. Instead, I checked the university co-op's bookstore, where no one knew me. In the center of the store, a round table no larger than a beach umbrella displayed important new books. As the table was impossible to ignore, nine out of every ten customers stopped, selected a book, studied its jacket, opened the back cover, glanced at the author's photograph, flipped to the first page, read it, skimmed a few random pages, and, nine times out of ten, returned the book to its spot. I knew. I kept count as I loitered in the fiction section and imagined copies of *Season's End* standing on the table, dar-ing customers not to buy one. But the book failed to materialize. Copies had to be in storage, no? I considered inquiring, anony-mously, about the novel's availability, but repeatedly lost my nerve and bought, as a cowardly diversionary tactic, a dozen paperbacks I didn't need. Finally, publication day arrived. Confident that I'd find the novel prominently displayed, I descended the stairs, turned into the center aisle, and saw a hardcover pyramid, twenty copies high, of—*Jazz* by Toni Morrison. Her first novel since she won the Pulitzer for *Beloved*, arguably the greatest American novel of the late twentieth century, and my novel had identical release dates. I now had to contend with Timmy *and* Toni. I imagined the table's legs buckling under the weight of two hundred books, then I left the store without checking to see if *Season's End* had been shelved, in alphabetical order, between novels by Martha Grimes and John Grisham.

That was Tuesday. On Thursday, *People* magazine appeared. As if I were buying pornography and didn't want to be caught and embarrassed, I walked to an out-of-the-way 7-Eleven and opened that week's issue. The lead review and its large author photo: Toni. A week later, the second review and no photo: Tom. But, as a compliment, the reviewer said *Season's End* read like a "baseball" novel written by Kafka. The *Seattle Post-Intelligencer* disagreed: it read like a "baseball" novel written by Pynchon. The *Boston Globe* didn't say anything; although the *Patriot Ledger* in Quincy, Massachusetts did, positively. Maggie, who'd lived in Boston for years, said, "Oh, all the smart people read the *Ledger*." Which was good, except the *Ledger* had five hundred thousand fewer readers than the *Globe*. A stunning review from the *Flint Journal* streaked across the literary firmament, and readers would have stampeded local bookstores if one thing hadn't held them back: Flint, Michigan, had the highest unemployment rate in the country. As for the *Times*: silence. Frank said, "Don't worry, it's early. And I've sent off the Whiting thing."

I landed in Dayton several hours before my evening reading. At the hotel's registration desk, I gave my name. The clerk checked her computer. She said, "Mr. Grimes, one night." Then she looked at me. "I'll just need your credit card."

"My publisher's paying for the room."

She rechecked her monitor. "Sorry, I'm not seeing that."

"You mean I'm getting billed?"

"I'm afraid you are, if you want the room."

I opened my wallet, removed my MasterCard, and handed it to her. She returned it with the room key, the hotel's floor plan, and a *Sights to See in Dayton* brochure. "Have a good night," she said.

At 7:00 PM, a young man about to graduate from college picked me up and drove me to the bookstore. It was one of three owned by a small, independent chain. I'd been scheduled to read at another location, but, before I flew out of Iowa City, my PR person called to say the venue had been changed. When I asked why she said, as calmly as if she had the statistic to prove it, "More baseball fans live close to this store." Inside, fifty folding chairs had been lined up in tight rows. Beside a podium stood a table supporting fifty copies of *Season's End*. And on a table adjacent to the audience a second table was topped with a coffee urn and several platters of cookies, which would eventually be carried home by the staff because there was no audience. The young man and I waited, expecting at least one customer to take a seat, if for no other reason than to rest. Occasionally, someone would swipe a cookie, then scurry away as if I might begin reading to him. Soon the manager, a trim woman in her forties, ventured out of her office to apologize. "We usually have a good turnout," she said.

"Don't worry."

"Well, wait a while, it's only," she eyed her wristwatch, "ten to eight." She told me to autograph copies of the book before I left. I promised I would.

Bored, the kid and I chatted about his major, literature. Then he asked me if he should apply to MFA programs. I waved at the empty chairs. "My audience," I said, "is chocolate chip cookies." Feeling slighted, he stared at his shoes. "Look," I said, "if you have to write, you'll write. You don't choose the writer's life; the writer's life chooses you." He raised his head and looked at me. "Take a year off," I said. "Stay out of school. Get a job, travel. Whatever. After that, if you still want to sit alone in a room three to five hours a day, every day, call, and I'll answer any questions you like." I lifted the pen from the book-signing

table and jotted my number on a napkin. Then I said, "Are there read-
ings at your other two stores tonight?" He nodded. "Who?"

"The Galloping Gourmet and Gail Sheehy," whose book about
women's sexuality had sold five million copies.

I autographed every copy of my book, then said, "Take me back
to the hotel." On the way out, he grabbed a cookie.

In Toledo, my audience of six kept saying they couldn't hear me
over the espresso machine's hissing.

But the Columbus store owners had designed and mounted on
foam core a baseball-shaped advertisement for my reading. It weighed
a few ounces, but was thirty-six inches in diameter. On it they'd
printed baseball stitches, Ann Beattie's blurb for *Season's End*, and
a snippet from the *New York Times*' review of *A Stone of the Heart*.
After the reading, they told me to take it with me. Thinking it was
sweet of them to make the effort, I did, but as I was about to board the
flight home a stewardess said, "I'm sorry, that's too large to store in the
cabin." We decided it would be crushed in the luggage compartment,
so I said, "I'll just toss it." She said, "Wait a second." She disappeared,
reappeared, and said, "The captain will stow it in the cockpit." I said,
"Thanks, that's really generous." At thirty-four thousand feet, the
captain announced over the intercom that we'd reached our cruising
altitude. "The weather between here and Iowa is clear," he added. "So
sit back and enjoy a smooth flight." My face was tucked between two
pages of the *Times* when I heard, "And we have a celebrated author
with us today. His new novel is *Season's End*." I pulled the paper closer,
like a turtle retracting its head into its shell. "'Persuasively touching
and comical,' the *New York Times* called his first novel." Around me,
people seemed to worry about who was flying the plane. In Cedar
Rapids, the stewardess handed me the huge, round poster. The captain
shook my hand and said, "A pleasure." I smiled, then marched up the
ramp, mortified, and disappointingly famous to nearby passengers.

While I was away, Little, Brown mailed Eric twenty-four review
clippings: each positive, each approximately twenty-four words
long, and each from a newspaper's sports section. With a trace of

exasperation and complaint in his voice Eric said, "Tom, I can't do anything with these," meaning, the reviews were worthless. He couldn't use them to promote the book, particularly to foreign publishers, all of whom, despite the literary scout's enthusiasm, ultimately declined to publish it. I don't believe Eric intended to make me feel responsible for the length and nature of the reviews, he was too kind and supportive; nevertheless, he did.

If I could ask him today, no doubt his recollection would differ from mine. Our conversation has been replayed, reshaped, and re-remembered so many times that the divide between memory and imagination no longer exists. I am trying to remember not only events and conversations but also emotions related to who I was, what occurred, and how I felt about what occurred a third of my lifetime ago. And as I write, I revise these sentences. I will revise them again and again, hearing them differently, satisfied with them one moment, frustrated the next, even though I'm sure they're the best sentences I can make. But one day, I'll reread them and want to change them again. They'll no longer be the sentences I trusted.

Now, I'm fifty-four, and it's 6:28 PM. It's summer and the sunlight is brighter than my room's lamplight would be in autumn, when I would call the same hour "evening." Yet despite how I feel about my memory of Eric, I still want to relive those few moments when I had to decide who would publish the book and he waited for my answer. I want to see and feel the alternate life I would have lived had I answered differently. And if I were not seated at this desk in a warm, sunlit room, if I were cold, and typing by lamplight, my memory of that conversation would not be the memory I've conjured up at this moment. Our voices, Eric's and mine, are fainter now than when I began to describe them. But these words are the only accurate record of what I thought and felt in a warm, sunlit room, at this time in my life, which, at 7:06 PM, has already become my past.

* * *

Several days later, Eric told me the *Times* wouldn't review *Season's End*. That evening, I found Frank, standing at the Foxhead's crowded bar, a drink before him, a cigarette in one hand. He wore the rumpled tweed sports coat that made him look like a disheveled prep-school boy. I glanced at the blackboard near the pool table. Through the smoky haze, I saw his name. The one above his had been erased, meaning Frank would play next. As usual, the space beside him was empty. Students didn't approach Frank, he approached them, usually to bum a cigarette. When he saw me he said, "Hey!" As always, his voice rose an octave. It was this sound of happy surprise I would miss more than anything once I left Iowa. I delivered the news bluntly. The reviewer had nothing kind to say about the novel so, as an act of kindness, the *Times* decided to say nothing at all. Frank didn't react, other than to look away, without moving his head. He had distanced himself, not from me, or his estimation of the book's quality, but from the book's fate. To protect himself, intellectually and emotionally, he'd moved beyond anger and bewilderment. The book's critical and commercial failure implied his failure to predict its success correctly, and being wrong puzzled him. As we stood at the bar and Frank waited for his next game of pool, he pondered the news about the *Times* with profound equanimity. Then he adjusted his glasses and said, "Well, maybe the *New York Review of Books* will get what it's about. But who knows what those Columbia dons think?" (He was referring to Columbia University intellectuals associated with the review.) I ordered bourbon with a beer chaser, but I didn't answer. "A dark night of the soul," Frank said. For the first time since I'd given him the news, he looked at me. "Listen, don't let it stop you. Write another book." Someone called his name. He said, "I'm up." He patted my shoulder and said, "It'll pass." Then he walked to the table, holding his cue.

And I returned to the novel I had recently begun. I'd written roughly fifty pages. The first paragraph took eight hours to draft over the course of two days. The novel's music—its rhythms, its key signatures, its varying tempos—would be determined by those words. I learned this while reading García Márquez describe, in an interview, the importance of composing *One Hundred Years of Solitude*'s opening paragraph. The novel's symphonic structure needed to be established immediately, he said; otherwise, he risked becoming hopelessly lost. Also, concentrating on sentences makes time dissolve. Your mind searches for the perfect word. You locate it. You type it. You look at it. You hear it. Maybe say it aloud. Then you decide it's the wrong word. You change it. Look at it. Hear it. Say it aloud. Decide it's the wrong word. You try a third word, repeat the above, decide it's also the wrong word, and restore the original. Then you count the word's syllables. You listen to its tone. Is it sharp, flat, or out of key? By chance, you notice the clock. Sixty minutes of your life have been swallowed by eternity and you still haven't found the right word. Famously, Flaubert declined to take a weekend excursion with friends so he could remain home and work. When they returned they said, "Did you get a lot done?" He answered, "Yes. I've decided to keep the semicolon." Writing with ludicrous intensity isolated me from *Season's End*'s disastrous reception. And, naturally, Frank helped. He'd hoped my success would match his success with *Stop-Time*. Knowing it wouldn't happen—the book was dead; Little, Brown couldn't even sell its paperback rights—his allegiance to the novel diminished. But he understood that part of me had died and his concern now was to make it a minor, fleeting death. "Ultimately, writing's a test of character," he told me, although he likely mentioned this later on, so it wouldn't seem didactic. I don't remember. But good storytellers understand that what may sound corny one moment may sound wise the next, and Frank was a good storyteller. He kept the action simple and direct.

"You want to teach here this summer?" he asked me.

"Sure."

"You've sold your house, right?"

"We move out June 1."

"Well, you can live in the new house June through August." He and Maggie had bought it with *Body & Soul*'s latest advances.

"You're sure?" I said.

"Of course. We'll call it seven hundred a month for three months." With that, Frank reclaimed one-quarter of my salary and had his utility bills and a portion of his mortgage paid every thirty days. But, in the process, he rescued me.

My fortunes plummeted while Frank's soared. He'd submitted the first half of *Body & Soul* to Sam and Candida, who mailed copies to foreign publishers and U.S. film companies. Within days, offers from overseas arrived by fax, and producers phoned in bids. Dustin Hoffman wanted to play Claude's childhood piano teacher and substitute father, the angelic Mr. Weisfeld. "The problem is," Frank complained, "Dustin Hoffman ties up the rights and never makes the movie." Spring Creek Productions, known for making high-quality films, topped Hoffman's bid. Several countries bought the novel's translation rights. Soon, and unexpectedly, Frank had multiple six-figure advances in hand.

Joking over drinks one night, he said to Jody, "My son tells me I'm a very rich man and I should buy myself a new car." He did, along with the new house that sat atop a hill west of the river.

Trees lined the neighborhood's grassy curbsides. Sidewalks were tidy and wide, and laid, seemingly, for no one. As I drove, I didn't see a single pedestrian. Polished cars stood in driveways, rather than being parked on the street. And green hedgerows hid some front yards, while yellow daises, white roses, pink carnations, and purplish-blue irises bordered others. I believe the neighborhood was called, quite simply, "The Heights." Understated, tasteful. Compared to "Chula Vista," which meant, but didn't offer, a "beautiful view."

As a boy, Frank had lived there, on a marshy island, "well hidden in the woods," near Fort Lauderdale, Florida. In *Stop-Time*, he writes, "The view in all directions was exactly the same. Flat, sandy land, underbrush, and stunted pine trees. Dismal, to say the least." His mother and stepfather "bought two lots." But to build their house, they had to clear the land. "The young pines fell easily under a sharp ax or machete," Frank continues, describing the work, "but the palmettos were more difficult. Showing only a knee-high fringe of palm above ground, these plants were in fact immense subterranean growths of appalling toughness. Their fat, hairy roots joined together in deep sand, so that when you'd worked your way down to the bottom of one plant you sometimes had to work your way back up along another." The floor of the house was "a twenty-five-by-twenty-five-foot platform set on concrete blocks in the sand. After the floor came the framework of the walls and roof, then the lathing, roofing, windows, and finally two coats of paint outside. The interior was never finished.

"The house was actually one large room. The kitchen was hidden by a curtain and Alison [his sister] and I slept in a double-decker bed behind a partition. There was a pump in the yard and a privy in back."

Frank and Maggie's house, the second one from the corner, sat on the north side of the property. Its massive, two-story-high, dark-hued brick exterior looked fortresslike. To the south, a green meadow, rimmed by hedges, sloped away from a thick-trunked maple tree whose branches extended twenty feet and shaded the front yard. Bolted to the brow of the garage, a basketball hoop lent a touch of classic Americana. Inside, there was a semifinished basement, equipped with a washer-dryer. Up four steps from the back door was a large kitchen, with an adjacent breakfast nook. An archway separated the kitchen from a dining room with a mahogany table that sat twelve. To the left, a spacious TV room overlooked the yard. Directly ahead was a large sunroom. To the right was the living room, in which a long couch flanked by two Colonial wing chairs stood before the fireplace; behind them was Frank's glossy black Yamaha grand, its lid open like the mouth of a crocodile. Across from it, a glass-paned bookshelf held a first edition of *Stop-Time*. Two sets of French doors opened onto an enclosed porch with a desk. Yet Frank wrote in the dim, second-floor room facing the street and the driveway. In it were more bookshelves, and another desk. Off the corridor were Frank's five-year-old son Tim's bedroom, a guest room, and a bathroom. Behind a white door was a dressing room and, finally, perched above the yard, the master bedroom and bath—all of it a long way from Florida.

Still, Frank had to finish the novel, and his work pace accelerated. Writing its first two hundred pages took him three years; writing the second two hundred would take less than one.

Writing *Season's End* had taken thirteen months. Maybe the number cursed the novel. I'll never know.

To forget the cumulative disaster its publication had become, Jody suggested that we drive to Wyoming and hike the Teton Range. We stayed at a Jackson Hole hotel. I'd given Eric the number. One afternoon, he left a message. Frank had called him. The Whiting Foundation wanted to read a new play I'd written.

Since *Spec* had won a Los Angeles Drama-Logue Award for Best Script, I assumed he'd sent it to the foundation's judges.

Eric said, "Frank told me they want *New World*."

Idiotically, I'd listed the play's title on *Season's End*'s flap copy. "But it's a draft," I said. "It hasn't been through rehearsals. I haven't even *heard it read* yet."

I asked if we could exchange scripts. Eric said it would be too embarrassing. When I returned to Iowa and was seated in his office, Frank said, "It's good if they ask for more stuff. It means they're interested."

But the judges read an unfinished play. I didn't receive a Whiting. And you can be nominated only once.

Yet, what would have been worse: to know Frank had nominated me and I'd been turned down, due, in part, to my stupidity? Or to wonder, for the rest of my life, why he'd never nominated me at all?

"We'll go for a Guggenheim in a few years," he said, tossing the foundation's letter onto his desk. "Just write the new book."

* * *

By late April, I had seventy pages to show Eric. Before leaving the house to mail them, out of habit I clicked the television's remote and tuned to CNN. On screen, fires blazed inside roofless buildings. Smoke drifted over East Los Angeles. People smashed storefront windows using rocks and bottles. They carted away half gallons of milk, cigarette cartons, loaves of bread, shoe boxes, bed pillows encased in plastic bags. A bludgeoned truck driver lay on the street. A single police car sped away, backward, from a charging mob.

The riot had been triggered by the acquittal of four white police officers who had beaten a black man named Rodney King. They caught him after a car chase, and once he stepped onto a patch of nighttime roadway illuminated by a squad car's headlights, two cops shot him using taser guns. The electrical shocks forced King to his knees. As eight or ten cops watched, four drew their nightsticks and clubbed King's head, ribs, thighs, and back. They aimed for his throat. When he rolled onto one side, they lifted their nightsticks, then hit him as if they were chopping a log with axes. Someone filmed the incident using a home movie camera. They beat him for one minute and sixteen seconds.

I dialed Eric's office and said, "My book's on television." He asked what I meant and I explained that I'd written about a cop killing and riots.

He said, "You'd better FedEx the pages to me, overnight."

By the next afternoon he'd read them. He said they'd astounded him and he planned to submit them, at once, to every editor who had bid on *Season's End*. Responses were swift and identical: no. Bill Phillips from Little, Brown wrote, "We believe Tom's an enormously talented writer but, based on these pages, we feel he has started down the wrong path." John Glusman (rather than Roger Straus) replied, "We'd love to publish Tom's books, but I'm afraid this isn't the one to start with, if for no other reason than I've just spent a year working on an 'apocalyptic' novel [*Going Native* by Stephen Wright] and don't have the strength to take on another." Gerry Howard said, "This is the kind of book that makes me very nervous," meaning the novel could be a masterpiece or a total disaster. "But I don't think Tom can sustain the energy to write the entire book." He passed.

That evening at a party, a classmate who knew none of this said (I don't remember the context), "You're Tom Grimes. They'll publish every word you write."

I laughed. But, in retrospect, I see my narrative's perfect symmetry. I arrived as a potential success. I departed a proven failure. Only, that isn't the meaningful story. The meaningful story is: I arrived fatherless; I departed a son.

* * *

At 9:00 AM, on June 1, Jody and I walked out of our home, leaving everything in its place. At 5:00 PM, when the movers finished packing our belongings, we returned to an empty house. We wandered through it as if to confirm our absence and affirm that the past was now truly the past.

Maggie and Tim flew to Boston where, after driving cross-country, bearing their summer clothes, Frank would meet them. The evening before he left he appeared in the TV room, where Jody and I were watching a basketball game. "I'm going to Cedar Rapids to pick up some hookers," he said. I laughed. Then he waved good-night.

The next morning, I walked along the neighborhood's immaculate streets. Birds chirped. The leaves were green. And when I reached the bridge, the river flowed.

Inside EPB, Connie handed me Frank's office key. I opened the door, aware of the room's stillness. The Oxford dictionary lay open, perched on its stand, but the heaps of manuscripts had vanished. I brushed my fingertips along the edge of his desk. Then I sat in Frank's chair, swiveled toward the one I used to sit in, and saw nothing, not even a ghost.

PART THREE

CHAPTER SEVENTEEN

Once Jody and I had moved to Texas, I returned to writing the novel no one wanted to publish. On weekdays at 10:00 AM, I'd carry a cup of coffee and a slice of low-calorie toast topped with jam into the small room I used as an office. I'd work until 1:15. Then I'd close my notebook, undress, step into the molded plastic shower, bump my head on its five-foot-high nozzle, curse, dress, grab my freshman composition textbook, and walk out the door. Rated the Best Party School in the Country by *Playboy* magazine, the university was a one-mile hike across town past abandoned houses, a strand of ramshackle apartment buildings, and several dingy mansions occupied by fraternities that decorated their lawns with stained couches, beer cans, crumpled pizza boxes, and the occasional Frisbee. Whenever I was late, I ran. When I saw the twin pit bulls, I stopped, turned, and sprinted a block out of my way in the ninety-degree heat. T-shirt drenched, I arrived in class, breathless. I taught, and held office hours, Monday through Thursday from 2:00 to 5:00 PM, and every other week, I

graded fifty-four freshman composition papers. Twice a month, I
spent Friday afternoons in meetings. Weekends, I wrote until mid-
day. Returning to the novel's beginning, revising its seventy pages,
and then continuing provided the personal affirmation I required.
Every writer is alone, and every good book is difficult to write. I
had forgotten this. I wouldn't forget it a second time.

* * *

On the drive from Iowa City to Texas, I daydreamed as we sped
through the flat midwestern landscape. Then, without expecting
to, I imagined a boy leaping off a rooftop, at night, high above a
city's lights. I didn't make a note of it. If the image needed to be in
the novel, I'd remember it. If it didn't need to be, I'd forget it. This
image resonated. If it continued to resonate, it would end my novel.

"Don't lose it," Eric told me during a telephone call, two months
before he retired at age thirty-seven. After he was diagnosed as
being HIV positive, all that mattered to him were his lover and his
yellow Labrador retriever, who, by the end, would drag Eric along
Manhattan's streets by the leash connecting them. "And don't quit,"
he added. "Write the novel."

I continued to write, but by late autumn my ability to construct
sentences, and shape scenes, began to deteriorate. My muscles
ached. My head felt like a metal claw had buried itself at the base
of my skull. Often, an hour ticked by before I could summon the
word I needed. As winter began, my fatigue intensified. I thought
the cause might be allergies. By four every afternoon, pressure
from clogged sinuses made me feel like my eyeballs would pop out
of their sockets. I'd return from school, take two Tylenol, lie on
the floor, stare at the stucco ceiling, and listen to the water heater's
lime-choked pipes whistle as steam blew through them. Taking
antihistamine tablets didn't help. Every morning, my brain felt
as dense as a cinder block. Working twenty hours a week, I wrote
thirty pages in three months. Maybe Gerry Howard had been right:

I wouldn't be able to finish the novel. I lacked the necessary talent and energy.

A year after *Season's End*'s publication, its paperback edition was nonexistent. Twenty-two hundred hardcover copies had sold. Thirteen thousand were remaindered. And Little, Brown had recouped only forty-four hundred dollars of my forty-two-thousand dollar advance. But the image of a boy leaping off a rooftop persisted, and I understood, irrationally perhaps, that if I abandoned this new novel my life as a writer would end. If I quit once, I could quit again. "Go on failing," as Beckett said. "Only next time, try to fail better."

In May, Connie called. "How would you like to teach here this summer?" Denis Johnson had taught the spring semester, but didn't want to stay. (Years later, he said to me, "They expect you to work up there.")

Once again, we would rent Frank and Maggie's house. Frank told me my salary would increase. "But your rent stays the same," he said, before he added, "Although, I have thought about charging your cats room and board." Then he laughed. Why wouldn't he? *Body & Soul* would be released in four months. The novel, it seemed, would make him more famous than *Stop-Time* had. The only unanswered questions were how long it would remain on the *New York Times* best-seller list and what prizes it would win. Frank had been a finalist for the National Book Award once. This time, maybe they'd give it to him.

* * *

Two years earlier, one evening after workshop, I'd given Frank a bottle of wine. We had left EPB after dark and walked across the parking lot. Sitting in Frank's car, we shivered as its engine warmed. Our breath fogged the windshield, masking the thin, filigreed sheet of ice that would soon melt and be swept aside by the wipers. Once heat streamed out the air vents, our muscles unclenched, and Frank turned on the headlights. With a gloved hand I removed from the crook of my arm the wine bottle I'd wrapped in a brown paper bag. As I passed it to him I said, "Just a little something to say thanks." I'd ordered a bottle of 1934 Château Lafite Rothschild Bordeaux from Morrell and Company in Manhattan when my advance for *Season's End* arrived. Hoping I was a local socialite who regularly dropped $150 for a liter of Bordeaux, the telephone salesman said, "Should I send over a case?" Just a bottle, I told him. While I recited my Iowa City address, I thought he might decide not to sell a legendary vintage to a midwestern rube. But he shipped it, I toted it to class, and then, beneath the parking lot's lamplight, Frank checked the bottle's label. About to utter a polite thank you, he said, "Hey!" Immediately slipping it back into the bag he added, "I'll drink it when I finish *Body & Soul.*"

Those two years passed and, one Sunday in late November, shortly after dusk, our telephone rang. Frank's voice, soft and conspiratorial, said, "I'm opening a bottle of wine."

"You finished *Body & Soul.*"

"Two hours ago."

"You're happy with it?"

"Very."

Then Frank tasted the wine and said, "It's terrific."

Had Jody and I been in Iowa, we would have been standing in the kitchen with him and Maggie, clinking glasses. Maggie would have said, "All right!" Frank would have said something innocuous, like, "Cheers!" He wouldn't play the piano. "Let's go sit by the fire," he would have said, and, in my imagination, he does say it—to phantoms. Jody and I were seventeen hundred miles away. The scene isn't a memory, it's a fantasy. And, over time, its continual recurrence with subtle variations—who stood where, how hot the fire was—hasn't diminished my sense of absence but enlarged it, and reinforced the loss's permanence.

Moments later, Frank said, "Wish you were here. Love to you both." Then he hung up.

The conversation lasted two minutes. Seventeen years later, I still hear it.

* * *

Publishers Weekly reviewed *Body & Soul* in June, while Frank was on Nantucket. The review wasn't "boxed," to distinguish it from other reviews, nor was it "starred," or signed. Its anonymous, but far from objective, reviewer had decided that

> When the author of *Stop-Time* and *Midair* produces a new work, it is an event to celebrate. And although Conroy's bildungsroman of a boy finding his identity in his musical genius has some flaws, it is by and large an engrossing novel, written in a supple and elegant prose and displaying remarkable insight into the mind of a prodigy. Conroy's protagonist is Claude Rawlings, who grows up in the 1940s in the shadow of New York's Third Avenue El . . . neglected by his emotionally unstable, alcoholic, cab-driver mother, he shines shoes, lifts coins from sewers and learns to steal. He is introduced to another world when Aaron Weisfeld, a music store owner and WWII refugee, recognizes his musical gifts and transports him to the Park Avenue apartment of a maestro whose Bechstein piano Claude uses and eventually inherits. Even more in the Dickensian mode, Claude falls in love with a cold, arrogant young woman from a patrician New York family, a character who is eerily similar to Estella in *Great Expectations*. Conroy's depiction of a young boy's discovery of music, the awakening of his sensibility and the flowering of his genius are brilliant. Lucid explanations of musical theory ranging from basic harmonics to the 12-tone scale, from Bach to Charlie Parker to Schoenberg, provide a continuum of insights and discoveries for Claude and for the reader. The first half of the book sweeps Claude along a path strewn with almost miraculous lucky breaks: he has inspired teachers and generous and appreciative patrons; his concerts are unalloyed triumphs—

and only the cynical will wish for a disaster to increase the tension. (Readers of *Stop-Time* will also recognize in Claude's childhood an alternative version of Conroy's miserable youth.) The second half is less successful. Claude's immersion in music, an obsession that makes him fascinating as a youth, renders him hollow as a man, and while Conroy obviously intends to demonstrate that Claude's emotional life is sterile in several ways, as a protagonist for a time he becomes a muted and shadowy figure. Claude's unquestioning relationship with the kindly Weisfeld, his first and abiding teacher, is less credible once he matures. The revelation of Claude's patrimony is poignantly rendered, however, and provides another look at the nature of creativity. And the book as a whole is harmoniously orchestrated and beautifully observed. 125,000 first printing; film rights to Spring Creek Productions; major ad/promo; author tour.

A mixed review that, nonetheless, provided advertising quotes: "[A]n engrossing novel, written in a supple and elegant prose. . . . Conroy's depiction of a young boy's discovery of music, the awakening of his sensibility and the flowering of his genius are brilliant."

Kirkus Reviews' assessment was similar: "From rags to riches— by way of musical genius—in this alluringly atmospheric first novel by Conroy of *Stop-Time* (1967) fame. . . . Claude's awakening to music is splendidly, rivetingly, described, and the Horatio Alger-esque clichés and coincidences are readily forgiven. . . . [But] once Claude is grown and launched, Conroy fills out his novel with more and more soap-opera turns. . . . Still, especially for the first two-thirds: a masterful coming-of-ager set in a now-vanished New York. 75,000 first printing (not 125,000); film rights to Spring Creek Productions."

Again mixed, but quotable: "[A] masterful coming-of-ager set in a now-vanished New York."

Not great reviews, but not damaging, although, unintentionally, the reviews exposed every publisher's exaggeration regarding the size of a book's first printing—more copies, more faith in the book; the totals differed by fifty thousand copies. In either case, Sam Lawrence anticipated a major success.

Before he left for Nantucket, Frank gave me an advance reader's copy. On its front cover, the novel's title and Frank's name appear in one-inch-high dusky gold letters. An elegant red cleft note separates the words *Body* and *Soul*. A slim line of type reads: A Novel by the Author of *Stop-Time*. On the back, above his bio, Frank is seated on a black bench, one arm resting against a black grand piano. He wears charcoal gray slacks and a black pullover turtleneck sweater, which fuse with the photograph's grayish-black background. His hair is silvery white, his skin flawless and light gray. He looks neither happy nor dour, but elegant, and eerily handsome. Without glasses, his eyes are impenetrably black. And he stares at me—I know this is impossible—as if he's certain I will study this photograph many years later. And, he's right, I do. But while I imagine our perpetual, metaphysical bond, his expression seems to say, "*Your* memoir, Tom, is about *me*. Don't fuck it up." Then he laughs. I know he isn't serious. But here I am having a conversation with a seventeen-year-old photograph taken prior to Frank's need for insulin injections to control his diabetes and, later, his use of a cane. Yet the photograph perfectly encapsulates my relationship to Frank. For years, he has existed more as a psychological rather than as a physical presence for me. And this memoir, I now see, binds *and* separates us for a simple reason: it's told in my voice, not his.

Still, I often embodied Frank's absence. I worked in his office. I taught in his classroom. I lived in his house. I slept in his bed. I played his piano. And I wrote in his study, although I deliberately avoided sitting on the mattress where he'd written *Body & Soul*. Instead, I used the small desk near the window that overlooked the driveway. As summer blossomed, the speed and clarity of my writing not only returned, it also increased. I produced a page to a page and a half a day, the prose (to me) virtually flawless. At times, it seemed words appeared on the page before I'd even thought of them. However, a muse didn't enthrall me; neurons zipping from projectors to receptors did. Images flashed across the hemispheres of my brain, and Jody began to ask why I was talking so fast. Every evening, after two tumblers of bourbon, my speech slowed. But every afternoon my thoughts accelerated, racing from swift to scattered, and my actions became impulsive. Once I'd finished reading a galley copy of *Body & Soul*, I knew the novel's latter half could be improved, and, as someone who idolized Frank, I felt compelled to tell him. He would expect no less of me. So I composed a letter, and quoted passages to support my argument.

For instance, I wrote, *take this paragraph with Claude and Catherine and consider its lack of specificity*:

> Passion was a force to be fed, eagerly and gratefully fed like some hungry angel with them in the room possessed of the power to lift them out of themselves. Out of the body, out of the world to some deep blue otherness where their souls would join, in and with the blue. Sailing along together in the blue, the blue insupportable to a soul alone.

You use the word blue four times, and I count nine prepositional phrases. Also, are the words otherness and insupportable precise? And the adverbs: eagerly, gratefully. Do you rely on them too much? Think about it.

Convinced I'd done the right thing, I ignored the obvious. Who would shout, "Wait, Tom says don't print 75 to 125,000 copies?!" Before I dropped the letter into a mailbox, I showed it Jody. As she read it, her expression changed from attentive to astonished. "You can't send this," she said.

"Why not? I'm trying to help."

"This won't help, believe me."

We debated the letter's merits. (It had none.) But for every rational point Jody made, I made an irrational one.

"I can't talk to you when you're like this," she said.

"Like what?"

"Like when you try to force me to agree with you until you drive me out of my mind." Knowing I wouldn't listen to her, she said, "Go talk to Connie. Ask *her* if she thinks you should send it."

Skimming the letter, Connie said, "Oh God, no. Please, please, *please* don't mail this." She may have said, "Are you okay? You seem a little frantic." I can't remember. But I believe she did say, "Listen, Frank knows you want only what's best for him. Okay? And this isn't what's best for him right now. He needs you to be happy for him. Okay?"

She repeated the word *okay* the way a mother assures her child that everything is all right. My energy spent, I nodded. Whether I left the letter with Connie or destroyed it myself, I can't say. Most likely, once my confidence turned to guilt with the ease of a coin turning from heads to tails, I obliterated the letter, tearing it into postage-stamp-sized pieces and then scattering them, a few scraps at a time, into Iowa City's downtown sewers.

* * *

One evening, a week later, the phone rang. Sam Lawrence was looking for Frank. As I said, "Hi," I pictured myself serving him dinner in Key West. His voice sounded gruffer than I remembered.

"He's on Nantucket," I said, calm and terrified. "But I know the number." Once he'd made sure he had written it down correctly I said, "My name's Tom Grimes. I used to live in Key West. A couple of years ago, you wanted to buy my novel."

He paused. Then he yelled, "The waiter! You wrote the baseball book. Whatever happened to that thing?"

"It was a disaster."

"Who published it?"

"Little, Brown."

"Why the hell did you go with them? Why didn't you come with me?"

I said, "I made a mistake. I had only fifteen minutes to make up my mind."

"Who told you that?"

"My agent."

"Listen," he said, "the next time someone tells you that you have fifteen minutes to decide what to do with a book you spent two years writing, you tell him to go fuck himself. You hear me?"

"Yes."

"What are you working on?"

"A novel."

"Well, you send it to me when it's done."

"Okay," I said. "I will."

Several days later, I wrote a tactful letter. This one I did mail.

Dear Mr. Lawrence,

It was nice speaking with you last week—about Season's End, about Key West, and other things. And I do appreciate your generous offer to take a look at my new novel when it's complete at the end of the year. I will have the manuscript sent your way at that time. I hope to have a good book for you, and this time I won't get, as you say, 'distracted.'

Thanks for the advice, and all the good writing you've published over the years. I will be in touch.

Sincerely yours,

Tom Grimes

On July 16, 1993, he replied:

Dear Tom,

Many thanks for your friendly letter of June 22. We look forward to reading your new novel with great pleasure.

Best wishes in your work ahead.

Cordially as ever,

Sam

* * *

Frank's *People* magazine photograph shows him dressed in black and stretched across the closed lid of his Yamaha grand piano, comically reaching for the keyboard as he smiles at the camera. The full-page *New York Times Book Review*'s ad simply reprinted his book-jacket image. But *Time* magazine's snapshot of Frank, seated, dressed in a striped shirt, one palm pressed against his forehead, captures his irritated expression, as if Frank suspects the tenor of the forthcoming review. And he's correct. The reviewer's tone, which is typical for him—he's an obscure, mediocre novelist who likes to ridicule famous writers—is snide and envious. Titled "Great Expectations, No Satisfaction," the review begins, *"Body & Soul* isn't a minor letdown but a major disappointment. No one could help rooting for this 57-year-old first novelist (even if he is the head of the Iowa Writers' Workshop), whose 1967 memoir *Stop-Time* remains much admired." But "Conroy's characters are well-worn stencils, like the sexy, snooty rich girl (Estella meets Daisy Buchanan) and the gluttonous Italian violin virtuoso (Paganini meets Zorba meets the cartoon chef on the pizza box." Something other than the review, however, must have bothered Frank while the photographer snapped his picture—the heat, perhaps, requests for another pose—because he later said to me, "I was laughing so hard by the time I reached the 'pizza man' line I had to stop reading. I mean, the guy's an idiot!"

As Frank's book tour began, other reviews followed, and the array of conflicting opinions echoed workshop discussions.

Vanity Fair: "Beautifully written, and hypnotically readable, the best story I know of in a long, long time."

The *Boston Globe*: "The novel is a gesture back to those great, wonderful, fat books with character and plot. It also heralds the return of a gritty writer who has kept a low profile for 25 years."

The *Dallas Morning News*: "A big, old-fashioned book as satisfying as a fine evening at the symphony."

The Chicago Tribune: "A literary event, a grand saga. *Body & Soul* was written under the spell of Dickens, not to mention Stendhal, Tolstoy and the other 19th-century titans. Conroy bedazzles readers!"

Elle: "A riveting, neo-Dickensian saga."

Entertainment Weekly even "graded" *Body & Soul*: "This isn't Dr. Faustus or any sort of great novel about music, but the first half is full of enchantment. B+"

Most importantly, the *New York Times Book Review* treated the novel with admiration and respect: "Utterly sincere, unironically devoted to re-creating an America that I would have thought by now had ceased to be an inspiration. . . . A legitimate and moving piece of Americana. Full of rich characters and tricky twists."

I called Maggie to ask how the book was selling, and she sounded cautiously upbeat. "Well, they printed 57,000 copies, but they say any returned books fill new orders." Foreign sales alone had repaid Frank's advance. The $3.75 he earned for each American hardcover sold easily doubled it. Yet, despite being eagerly hoped for—and, to a certain extent, even expected—*Body & Soul* never appeared on the *New York Times* best-seller list. And, given the novel's uneven critical reception, literary prizes seemed unlikely. This disappointed Frank, but—unless I'm mistaken—it didn't drive him into a cave of self-pity. He lacked the gene for dejection. I didn't. Knowing this, he had written to me from Nantucket the previous summer.

Dear Tom,

    I trust you are cheering up? Cheered up? I've seen Season's End at both of the island's bookstores. In one of them (the more highbrow establishment), it is moving well. I don't know about the other place. So your baby goes off and makes its unpredictable way through the world, sans daddy. Look at Patrick O'Brian (and you should). I'd never heard of him, and since June 1 I've read fifteen of his historical novels. (Capt. Aubrey/ Dr. Maturin sea stories, same period as Hornblower but much, much better) and am complètement desolé that there are no more. Let the word carry the word.

But Frank's serenity eluded me. And, compared to his joy, my gloominess puzzled him. As he wrote in the same letter:

I never know what to make of you when you excoriate yourself for alleged bad behavior at a social function. This exists in your mind, my friend. Maybe it's because you get squiffy so easily, but not squiffy enough to forget what you've said. You want bad behavior? Frank at a stuffy dinner being offered salad by a lovely matron, a total stranger. "May I hold it for you?" she says, presenting the bowl. "Don't talk dirty," sez me, never to be invited back again.

One night, driving home from the Foxhead, the two of us shivering, I said, "Do you think you'll ever write another memoir?"

Without taking his eyes off the road—which was good, because he was drunk—Frank answered, "No, I want to do novels now. I want to do the longer work." Then he raised one hand from the steering wheel and, gesturing toward the darkness beyond the streetlights ahead, he added, "Novels. That's where the juice is."

Writers always look toward the future. In a sense, we have no past, only whatever time we have remaining to write the perfect book to mask our emptiness—or my emptiness, anyway—the book that won't defeat us, the book we'd like to be remembered by, if we're remembered at all. And Frank will be remembered; *Stop-Time* is a singular achievement. A sui generis insanity governs its style and the very act of its creation. "I'd write a chapter and then take four months off and fuck around," Frank told me, recalling how he wrote his memoir—after he'd accepted the failure of his first novel, a novel about a priest. I haven't read it, and I won't; Frank considered the work so weak that a sense of shame, perhaps, attached itself to the manuscript. Yet, he didn't destroy it. Boxed and marked, it remains in his archive. I can't ask Frank now why the pages still exist, but I'm a writer and I know why: he *wants* it to be read so that his life's work is understood completely. He's even mentioned its failure. In an essay, he called the novel "dead on arrival." A corpse. This stain of failure never entirely vanished, but *Stop-Time* overcame it. In fact, *Stop-Time*'s anger and bitterness is, I'm sure, grounded in Frank's buried novel. He wrote about a priest, and nothing is interesting, dramatically, about a priest who's celibate and virtuous. My guess is that Frank, like me, wasn't able, in his early twenties, to confront the shame he felt about his family, how broken, sad, confused, hysterical, and nearly tragic his childhood was. But, once again like me, when he was angry enough to see beyond the bullshit façade of "literature," he found *Stop-Time*'s narrative voice. In the first sentence of the prologue, he announces what every writer wants to be able to say: "I worked well." He then describes a harrowing, drunken, high-speed drive to his "small countryside house about twenty miles outside of London." The game is: how fast can Frank drive without killing himself? He leaves the question unanswered, for the moment, then leaps into chapter one, the first sentence of which is, "My father stopped living with us when I was three or four." It's Frank's anger over this wound that smashed his Jaguar's gas pedal to the floor. Then there's the first chapter's title: "Savages," which recounts the merciless beating of Frank's classmate by fellow classmates at an "experimental boarding school in Pennsylvania called Freemont." Reluctantly, Frank participated. Years later, he still considers the boy's beating part of his life. He worries about the incident and his behavior for a long time. But in the end he learns nothing other than that brutality happens easily. Then come *Stop-Time*'s other mad chapter titles: "Space and a Dead Mule"; "Hate, and a Kind of Music"; "Shit"; "A Yo-Yo Going Down, a Mad Squirrel Coming Up"; "The Coldness of Public Places"; "Death by Itself." The book ends when Frank, after escaping his childhood by entering Haverford College, survives, by accident, his manic dash through London's suburbs. And yet he's disappointed when he doesn't die. Swerving toward a concrete fountain, he relaxes. "Let it come," he thinks. And then, gleefully, "Here it comes!" Only, he fails. He stumbles out of the car. All he's accomplished is waking an old man, who yells at him from a window. "My throat burning with bile," Frank writes, "I started to laugh." What killed his first book, I believe, was sincerity, or a striving for atonement. What electrifies *Stop-Time* is its demonic anger. But, ultimately, it's funny: he can't even kill himself. Perfect freedom! Only by reaching the point where he accepts his desire to obliterate himself—and I'm talking about me here, too—does he feel cleansed. Of course, I'm speculating. Frank may not have felt this way at all. But he didn't burn his dead book, and that failure shaped him. He knew it and he remembered it. Failure burned away every slippage of language, intellect, or sentimental feeling in *Stop-Time*. The book's beauty is its darkness; its bitterness is its grace. "The bad work leads to good work," Frank used to tell us in workshop. "You rarely get one without the other." So, he wrote the book he'll be remembered by.

But I'm remembering Frank here and, of course, he's laughing, although bile no longer burns his throat. In me he found his biographer. Yes, he rescued me. I applied to Iowa with an incomplete novel's opening pages. In retrospect, submitting that material was a bold, idiotic move. On the one hand, I risked rejection, and I would have had the justification for it had I been rejected. I didn't submit my best, published work: that was my out. On the other hand, I wanted to court failure, and I did. My all-consuming ambition urged me to write something so far beyond my skill that I could only fail. I insisted that *Season's End* wasn't a baseball book; it was about America. Its scope stretches from America's defeat in Vietnam to Reagan's election as president. The working title for *Season's End* was "Love and Death in the American Novel." Only someone stupid enough to risk failure on a grand scale would brandish that title (which is why the novel was sold untitled). I purposely stole the title from a work of literary criticism by Leslie Fiedler. And it's clear to me now: I'm a failure as a writer because I've overreached; my ambition was larger than my talent. Yet I willingly accepted that risk, believing I could overcome it. Every great novel, it's been said, is a "long story with a flaw in it." Well, I've mastered the flaws and have diligently produced long stories to contain them. But something all along was missing—me. And this book redresses that absence. For twenty years, I believed Frank filled that absence. But he didn't; my idolization of him did; moreover, my fictionalizing of him did. Frank is the protagonist of my best novel, and my best novel is this memoir. In the end, my memoir about Frank is a memoir about me. By writing about Frank, I could no longer turn away from myself, which is what I've done all of my life. Now, I'm gazing at myself.

But, by the time we had become friends, Frank's gaze had turned toward the future he'd imagined for himself. In it, he would write more novels. *Body & Soul* simply materialized first. And if its immediate fate fell short of fulfilling his wishes, he saw no reason to despair. Who could predict any book's future? "For twenty-five years *Stop-Time*'s been in print," he once told me. "I'm constantly amazed."

So, he enjoyed his tour. And he wrote inside our copy of *Body & Soul*:

> *Dear Tom & Jody,*
>   *Your cats left some fleas [which, unfortunately, was true], but I got to talking to them and they have a compelling story*
>
> ———————
>
>   *Much love to you both,*
>   *Frank*

Then he signed a copy for the wealthy New York dowager who would hold a celebratory dinner for him in her posh, Upper East Side apartment, *Let's eat. I'm starving!*

His happiest moment, though, came one evening when his hotel telephone rang and the operator said she had a call from a Mr. Shaw. "I thought, okay, he's the local auto mechanic," Frank told me. "But it was Artie Shaw! One of the greatest jazz clarinet players who ever lived! Once I realized who it was, I was like, 'Maestro!'" Artie Shaw had tracked down Frank to tell him no one had ever written so beautifully about how it *felt* to play music.

Frank never bragged about his writing, but he routinely told me about the amazing jazz quintet he played with each summer on Nantucket. "You have to hear this!" he said one night, after we'd closed the Foxhead. He drove me back to his house. Maggie was seated on a living room armchair when we arrived and she closed the book she'd been reading as Frank inserted into his VHS player a live performance he'd taped of his band. "Listen, the blues number is amazing." It was past 3:00 AM, and, as I sat on the couch, I faded in and out of consciousness. Several feet away, Frank watched with an expression that approached unadulterated bliss. I felt as if the tape had been playing for hours. Desperately wanting to crawl between my bed's warm sheets, I said, "Are they ever going to play the blues piece?" Frank stared at me in disbelief. "They're playing it now!" he shouted. Maggie said, "Frank, let Tom go home. He's sitting on the couch with one eye open." I don't remember walking home, but I'd learned that music, as much as literature, had shaped Frank's identity. During his childhood, he'd taught himself how to play the piano, but it hadn't been easy. "I could not just learn a tune, however slowly," he once wrote in an essay, "and go on to another one. I had to play it over and over, so many times that it became engraved in the neurons of my brain, the muscles of my arms and hands, the nerves of my fingers." Yet he assembled a repertoire. And, in his late twenties, while he still lived in New York, he played nightly gigs at a bar. One evening, between sets, his bass player vanished. Having no choice, Frank nervously took the stage.

"I sat down and began to play midrange chords with my left hand and an improvised line with my right," Frank wrote. "The tune was 'Autumn Leaves.' Sometime in the third chorus a large black man got up from his dinner table and moved forward. . . . As he approached, I recognized Charles Mingus—the foremost jazz bassist in the world—and was afraid. Mingus, a manic-depressive, was famous for sudden onsets of rage."

But he simply grabbed Frank's AWOL partner's bass and began to play, as Frank continued. It was "The most important night of my musical life, because I no longer had to think of myself as an impostor. If Charles Mingus got up to play with me, I must have been doing something right. I was no genius, but I was a musician."

After receiving Mr. Shaw's call, every doubt Frank may have had about *Body & Soul*—could it have been better, should he have taken more care with its latter half?—slipped into silence, the way a hammered piano string ceases to vibrate, and the note it produced can no longer be sustained or heard.

CHAPTER EIGHTEEN

The one hundred and ten pages I wrote in Frank's study generated enough momentum to carry me into the late fall. By early December, the boy I'd pictured leaping off a rooftop began his metamorphosis from image to sound, from sound to sentence, and—if I was lucky—from sentence to music. I'd borrowed the conventions of a crime novel; the book began with a cop killing. But I didn't want the novel to *sound* formulaic. A novel's music *is* its meaning. So I made the details specific, yet slightly strange. When the boy, Ray, comes abreast of a patrol car parked on a deserted street, surrounded by condemned buildings:

> His gloved hands unsheathe the truncated rifle barrel strapped to his chest when the cop nearest him looks out, his eyes meeting Ray's. They don't pick up the gun at first. It's just a simple turn of the head, a reaction to something stirring near the blurry edge of peripheral vision.
>
> The first C-4-tipped shell hits the window and rocks the car, its passenger-side tires lifting off the ground. The plastic explosive in

the cartridge bursts on impact, dappling the windows and doors with small bright stars and kicking back a shower of sparks. Holes open in the passenger window and Ray can hear shouting—panicked, angry, terrified—inside the vehicle. The second round rips through the interior of the car and blows out its far windows, glass leaping from the doorframes and fanning out over the street. This time no voices are heard under the clacking of metal as Ray reloads, just a deep, hoarse whining. He fires again, this blast taking off the steering wheel top. Then he realizes that the whining sound is the cop nearest him trying to breathe. As the gun's report echoes down the street, it becomes quiet enough for Ray to realize that the guy is still trying, though just barely. The spooky thing is that the sound seems to be coming not from his mouth, but from his chest.

Ray peers into the car and sees that the man's head has fallen back against the security grating behind him. His jaws are open, part of his throat torn away. What's left is a thin, bloody, faintly pulsing stalk. His shirt ripped open, a fractured bone juts out from the skinless stump of shoulder, his flesh from sternum to ribs peeled away like a skinned onion. The man's insides gleam, slick and reddish-black in the streetlight. For an instant, Ray thinks he sees the man's heart dangling by a partially severed artery, beating arhythmically outside his ribs. His own heart clutches.

The multiple metaphors disliked by my classmates were gone, as well as *Season's End*'s first-person point of view. And although Frank's subject matter and mine differed, I had studied his use of third person, learning how, in *Body & Soul*, his narrator illuminates Claude's thoughts, yet remains detached, the voice sympathetic, yet impartial.

Over dinner in a Chinese restaurant, before I began my third novel, I'd said to Frank, "Since I may be about to waste two years of my life, do you have any advice?"

"Go in with plenty of energy," he said.

"What do you mean?"

"Bob Stone"—whose novel *Dog Soldiers* I worshipped and used

as a model for the book I'd begun to call "City of God"—"says novels end once they've worn us out. Norman equates writing a novel
with a prizefight. You have to train like a boxer trains. You have to
be in shape. If you aren't, entropy wins, you lose."

These recommendations spoke to Gerry Howard's concern that I
wouldn't have the requisite energy and concentration to complete the
novel. And, given my previous winter's experience when language no
longer streamed through my mind but became as stagnant as a swamp,
they also made sense. Another semester of teaching freshman composition had smudged and worn down my imagination the way corrections
on a handwritten page blacken and diminish a rubber eraser. And I can't
say I followed Mailer's advice (although I doubt he followed his advice,
either). Upon learning from an allergist that my immune system reacted
most to mold, I immediately said, "Beer contains mold, right?" Yes. "But
distilled alcohol doesn't." Correct. So I toted home a sack filled with
antihistamine tablets, nasal steroids, lung inhalants, and a gallon of Jim
Beam. Subsequently, like Frank, I began my evenings with a "bump,"
and ended them nine or ten "bumps" later. The result was less sinus con-
gestion, a crisper hangover, and a resilient buffer between "City of God"
and my anxiety about finishing it. I knew I was close to the end, but I
didn't want to force or rush its final pages.

The previous summer, Frank had responded to a *rational* letter
from me regarding *Body & Soul. I know what you mean*, he wrote,
about the urge to close down too quickly. (I'd suggested that he resist
it; he didn't.) *But not to worry, Part II is done [about a hundred and
ten or twenty pages] and all the anxiety I had about it is now transferred to Part III, which I am about to begin, and which should run
about two hundred pages at least. I doubt I can finish this calendar
year, but for all that, I'll try.*

The letter was dated July. By January, the book was done. In six
months, he'd written two hundred pages. The preceding two hundred had taken him three years. But pressure, rather than haste, was
the issue. Frank often spoke of "the restless, searching soul behind
the prose," and he frequently said that "when the soul is truly on

the page," literature has been created. A reader, he added, must feel the continual, but unobtrusive, pressure of the writer's soul behind every sentence. For five years, I couldn't articulate the anxiety I felt as I wrote my novel's concluding pages. But, in 1999, Frank sent me a note concerning an anthology of essays about the craft of writing he would edit, entitled *The Eleventh Draft*:

> *Dear Tom,*
>   *Want to make a quick buck and be in with some big names?*
>   *But seriously, I hope you'll do this. I'd like to have you in the book.*
>   *Love to you both,*
>   *Frank*

I answered, sure. Then, addressing my anxieties, I wrote in my essay that "pressure builds as you approach the end of a novel. Unlike short stories, the chances are not that you will make a sudden wrong move and wreck everything. With novels, the likelihood is more that you won't get everything in, won't catch every possible echo and reverberation. . . . So as I hurtle toward closure, I need to slow down at the same time. I desperately want the book to end; I never want the book to end. I'm terrified and ecstatic. When I wrote the end of that closing chapter [referring to *City of God*] I literally dropped my pencil, sat up straight, and raised my fists in the air."

But had my two years of work produced a good, publishable novel? "Good" in whose eyes, "publishable" according to what editorial board's opinion? Also, would Frank approve of and perhaps even admire it? I had no idea. Once my fleeting elation passed, I had pages of prose that needed editing.

* * *

I borrowed a Mac classic computer from a student (I still owned a typewriter). Then Jody and I drove to Key West. We'd rented a house with a dreary living room, but a large bedroom, a bright kitchen, and a deck outside of its French doors. Every morning, we walked to the Cuban café, ordered to-go cups filled with *café con leche*, returned to the house, and then worked, uninterrupted, for eight hours. Jody perched at the kitchen counter with the computer and keyboard, while I sat on the deck, pencil-edited the manuscript, and handed her corrected pages through the open doors. Then she entered the changes, I gave her additional changes, and, at dusk, we strolled to the marina's bar, ordered drinks, and watched the sunset. In two weeks, we cut five hundred and sixty-seven pages to five hundred and ten pages. Shortly before Christmas, we took a day off, then returned to our stations and began to revise the next draft.

One evening, a woman we knew invited us to a cocktail party. In the dim light, I recognized Rust Hills, *Esquire* magazine's former but still influential literary editor, and his wife, the writer Joy Williams, whom I'd seen several years earlier on Sam Lawrence's deck. Now, holding my drink, I passed them, unnoticed, which I expected. What I didn't expect was an invitation to the cocktail party they held the following week. The ground floor of their house was one long, rectangular room. Toward its far end, people gathered near the wooden kitchen table. On it stood an array of liquor bottles, plastic cups, and a bowl filled with sliced lemons and limes. Across from it, a shelf displayed perfectly aligned cans, jars, and boxes of Campbell's soup, Skippy peanut butter, and Rice Krispies. I couldn't decide whether Rust and Joy ate the food or if they'd assembled an ironic collection of Americana. When Rust saw me, he interrupted his conversation, extended one arm, and said, "Tom, come on in!" He curled his arm around my shoulders and pulled me toward him. Conversations paused as other guests studied me, wondering why I merited attention. Speaking softly, Rust said, "Frank called and told me you were in town," which explained the invitation. Then he poured bourbon and soda into a glass, placed the glass in my hand, and escorted me to the back deck. Torch lamps cast a dim, gold light as he drew me into a quiet, poolside shadow.

His grayish hair resembled Frank's—parted, yet slightly unkempt—as did his nonchalant, aging prep-school boy's manner, typical of a Wesleyan graduate, which he was, but not of someone schooled at Merchant Marine Academy, his high school alma mater. I could tell that he'd been handsome once, but he seemed to have aged comfortably—and perhaps intentionally—into the role of a slightly dissipated old man.

"What are you working on?" he said.

"A novel."

"Well, when it's done send it to me. I can probably find an excerpt to publish."

Surprised by how swiftly I'd been transformed from a nonentity into a privileged insider, I said, "I will, thanks."

"Now you teach, right?"

I nodded.

"So, you teach my book"—*Writing in General and the Short Story in Particular*—"and I read your stuff. Okay? That's how it works. Make sense?"

"Yes."

"Good."

No doubt he'd made the same, mutually self-serving arrangement with other young writers, but he broached the matter so directly that the exchange seemed innocent.

As new guests arrived, Rust turned to greet them, and when I stepped inside to refill my glass, the bookstore owner who had belittled me for years but seemed to have forgotten the past approached me, smiled, shook my hand, and asked if I would come to his store to do a book signing. I said, "Sure," gave him a fictitious telephone number to call, and then, after speaking with Joy for a while, Jody and I said thanks, good night, and left.

Working on the novel's cleaner, sleeker draft, we trimmed five hundred and ten pages to four hundred and fifty-four. I hated the book. But I printed the manuscript, mailed it to Frank, and waited.

Shortly after New Year's eve, we attended another cocktail party where a woman I didn't know and remember now not as a physical presence but simply as a voice said to me, as if I were an idiot, "The next time you get an offer from Farrar, Straus, take it." She was somehow related to the publishing business. Then she asked what I was working on.

"A novel," I said. "Sam Lawrence told me to send it to him when I've finished it."

About to walk away, she patted my chest and said, "Honey, read the paper. Sam Lawrence died this morning."

The next day, the *Times* published his obituary:

January 7, 1994

Seymour Lawrence, 67, Publisher for a Variety of Eminent Authors

Seymour Lawrence, an independent book publisher in New York City and Boston for almost 30 years who brought the first works of many important writers to the public, died on Tuesday at the Englewood Community Hospital in Englewood, Fla. . . .

Among the dozens of distinguished authors published by Mr. Lawrence, who was known as Sam, were Richard Brautigan, Jim Harrison, Katherine Anne Porter, Kurt Vonnegut and Frank Conroy.

Mr. Lawrence published Mr. Vonnegut's novel *Slaughterhouse-Five* in 1969, after the manuscript had been rejected by the publishing firm with which the author had a contract.

Mr. Lawrence's authors described him as a publisher who was passionately committed to writers and writing, but who was not always tolerant of "misguided reviewers" or the publishing bureaucracy.

Joseph Kanon, an executive at Houghton Mifflin, said: "The first time I met Sam Lawrence, he was making an argument on behalf of one of his authors. The last time I spoke with him, this morning, he was doing the same thing. On both occasions, as usual, he got what he wanted."

* * *

Frank didn't call before Jody and I left Key West, even though he must have had the manuscript for five days. Intellectually, I understood that despite snow, ice, and subzero temperatures, Frank hadn't planted himself on his front stoop to await its delivery. But emotionally, I pictured him standing on the sidewalk, wearing his bathrobe, hoping to spot the mail truck. And what I felt always trumped what I knew.

During our twenty-hour drive to Texas, Jody often slept, or pretended to sleep, in order to protect herself from my obsession with why Frank hadn't called. Crossing Alabama, I debated—compulsively, yet silently—where, in Frank's life, my manuscript resided. Leaning against the front door in its unopened envelope? Lying on his bedside table? Glued to his hands because he was too engrossed to put it down? Or hidden on a shelf, largely unread? Jody knew I'd begin my interrogation regarding Frank's opinion the instant she opened one eye; I knew that, at some point, she had to wake up; and the moment she did, I said, "Why do you think Frank hasn't called about the book?"

Barely conscious, she said, "He probably hasn't read it yet."

"But he *will* read it?"

"Yes, he'll read it, when he has the time."

"Why wouldn't he have the time?" (I'd blocked out the workshop's eight hundred application manuscripts.)

"Because he's busy."

I paused (on purpose). Then I said, "Should I call him?"

"No."

"I mean when we get home?" (She knew I meant from the next gas station.)

"No."

"But you're sure he'll read it?"

"Yes."

"You think he'll like it?"

"I don't know."

She slept through Mississippi and woke in Louisiana.

"What if he doesn't like it?"

"He'll tell you he doesn't like it."

"Why wouldn't he like it?"

She napped again and regained consciousness in East Texas.

"Let's just say . . ."

"He'll love it, okay? He'll love it. Satisfied?"

Once we reached our house—it remains impossible for me to call Texas "home"—I checked our answering machine. I heard several voices, but not the one voice I wanted to hear.

* * *

My anxiety was not unique, however. By uncanny coincidence, while I awaited Frank's approval of my novel, he wrote an essay entitled "My Teacher," prompted by his experience at the man's memorial service. In 1954—the year I was born—Frank was eighteen and a freshman at Haverford College. Like me at his age, he "wanted desperately to be a writer." In an English composition class, he met his only writing teacher, a man he called, in the essay, Professor Cipher. Frank first encountered him "at an informal student-faculty mixer under a striped tent behind the library a few days before the start of classes." Instantly, the man became Frank's idol and, perhaps unconsciously, a model for Frank's behavior, in the same manner that Frank later became my object of adulation. Frank marveled at "the speed and agility of his [teacher's] mind, his intensity and an air of mild cynicism, which," as Frank wrote, "for some reason I thought was terrific." More importantly, "Professor Cipher *had published a novel*." To impress him, Frank submitted, along with his weekly critical paper, a "dramatization" of their meeting, which earned him an audience in the man's office.

Describing it, Frank wrote:

Books covered all four walls and most of the floor. There were no shelves, simply stacks of books four or five feet high leaning precariously against the walls, mounds of books in corners, books strewn across the floor, occasional open volumes whose pages would flip at a breeze through the open window. I handled my own books with reverence, and stored them neatly; Professor Cipher seemed to use a shovel. But," for Frank, "the shock left almost instantly, and suddenly the disorder seemed thrilling—some kind of rejection of materialism, perhaps, or simply the urge to literally swim in books, or a vaguely aristocratic disdain for order. Whatever it was, I thought, it was probably very Harvard, very Oxford and Cambridge, and therefore magically wonderful.

To a lesser degree—thanks to Connie's regular neatening of it—Frank's office maintained the tradition of absentminded disorder—the casual clutter and overflowing ashtray. I had bought, framed, and given Frank a special photograph, which I'd spotted in a magazine. I'd tracked down the photographer and paid him for a negative, as well as permission to reproduce the image. In the picture, rain falls as a pool table stands on a muddy, countryside road. Around it, three Chinese men wear drab, mandarin-collared shirts and baggy trousers. Two smoke cigarettes. And as the three observe him, a fourth man holds a pool cue, leans over the table, and lines up a shot. When I handed him the photograph, Frank studied it. Then he smiled and said, "It'll lend the office just the right touch of insanity. I'll have Connie hang it up." But he didn't. He set it on a shelf and, when I returned to teach the following summer, I found it lying face up, the frame's glass pane cracked, and the photograph puzzlingly crumpled. Scanning the plaster wall, looking for a bent or loose nail, I found nothing, not even an indentation. The negligence was quintessential Frank. So, rather than repair the picture, I laid it on his open dictionary and imagined his momentary bewilderment the next time he wanted a word's definition.

But despite the condition of their offices, on the page Frank and Professor Cipher demanded clarity. Ready to discuss his prose, Frank stood in Professor Cipher's office doorway until his teacher recognized him. "'Ah, yes. Mr. Conroy,' he said, shuffling through the papers on his desk." Once he located Frank's four-page "drama-tization," he added, "'Come around and sit here where you can see.'" After taking his seat, Frank "saw with alarm that the first page was covered with red markings. 'Pay attention,' [Professor Cipher] said. 'I'll walk you through this time, but in the future it'll be up to you to figure out what I mean.' He gave a slightly evil chuckle," Frank wrote. "Then, tapping the pages every now and then to indicate one of his red marks, he began talking very rapidly. 'Awk' is 'awkward,' usually a question of rhythm, usage, grammar, or overwriting. 'Cli' is 'cliché.' 'Rep' is 'repetition,' something you've already said, a device you've already used or a stylistic tic. 'Unc' is 'unclear,' which means either I don't understand what you're saying or you're saying something that can be understood in more than one way. I mean the literal meaning. You understand?'"

This discussion could have been Frank talking to me on any num-ber of occasions, for at the heart of the conversation lies a boy's longing to learn his mentor's secrets, the way his knowledge controlled the world and therefore made him seemingly perfect and absolute.

Frank wrote, "'I think so,' I said, attempting to conceal my excitement. I had always written by instinct, and the idea that he was taking my writing seriously enough to do line-by-line editing made me tremble."

Likewise, in Texas, I trembled. My novel wouldn't exist until Frank acknowledged it, and it wouldn't be good unless he said so.

At first, Professor Cipher's approach to Frank's work was imper-sonal, just as, to Frank, I once was no more than the sum of what I wrote. But our relationships with our teachers—Frank's with his, and mine with Frank—evolved into crippling dependencies.

"I relished every moment I spent with the man," Frank wrote, "especially tutorial. I worked hard to be worthy of his faith and rapidly gained control of my language. ("You are a racehorse," he once said to me, "among elephants." I glowed for weeks.) He was no doubt 'projecting,' (as the psychoanalysts used to say) onto me. His youthful artistic ambitions, perhaps. Much more, I was 'projecting' onto him, seeing him as something close to a god on earth."

The day Frank graduated Professor Cipher said to him, "'You're going to be a writer. . . . Better find yourself a rich wife.' And then— a breathtakingly daring and uncharacteristic thing for him to do—he gave me a fast little hug."

With me, Frank was equally reticent. For years, we shook hands, nothing more. But one cold, drizzly afternoon, after lunch, I put my arms around him, as he was about to open his car door. Startled, he didn't pull away, but his embrace was tentative, as if he didn't quite know how to hug me.

At the end of his essay, Frank wrote:

> It was good that as an adult I had carefully examined the dynamics of my own youthful projections onto Cipher, because that allowed me to deal better with the phenomenon when, now and then, a student would temporarily project onto me. For some young writers, it is no more than a necessary stage and should be handled with respect, tact, as much measured generosity as can be managed and, of course, common sense. There is no need to back off quite as much as Cipher had backed off from me.

Yet Frank and I never "backed off" from each other, emotionally. Instead, we echo each other. He wrote about his late teacher; unexpectedly, I now am writing about mine.

* * *

At the beginning of February I called Frank, prepared to hear his disappointment regarding my novel. I was also afraid that he'd think I'd lost my talent, my promise, and my mind. Three years had passed since we'd sold *Season's End*. In light of its failure, had Frank decided to distance himself from the book and, therefore, distance himself from me? True, he'd spoken highly of me to Rust

Hills and, once again, had invited me to teach at Iowa. But what if the new novel changed his feelings? I wanted to believe that his love was unconditional, rather than contingent upon my literary success, but I wasn't certain. So I called not only to ask about my novel but also, indirectly, to ask about our future.

When he heard my voice, he said, "Professor Grimes!"—not "Hey, babe," or "Tom!" Unintentionally, he'd demoted me from author to instructor.

"The novel's that bad," I said.

Surprised, he paused, then said, "To the contrary, my friend."

"It's good?"

"It's better than good."

Not everyone agreed, but after speaking to Frank and having my questions about the novel and his affection for me answered, I could no longer be wounded. Disheartened, maybe; unpublished, certainly; but not artistically devastated. I'd written a far from conventional novel, in part because I felt constricted by literary realism. But I also wanted to write a novel that none of my peers was attempting to write. In the way that Frank's failed first novel had provided him with the rage necessary to create *Stop-Time*, I used *Season's End*'s failure to write a more, rather than a less, ambitious novel. And while I wanted Frank to tell me the book was good, despite the fact that his enthusiasm for *Season's End* may have blinded him to that novel's flaws, my anxiety subsided because— good novel or bad—he'd committed to taking the trip with me; the *artistic* trip, not the *publishing* trip, which didn't begin well. Neil, Eric's former assistant, had taken on Eric's clients, and his letter to me about the novel began, *Dear Tom, You'll probably want to stick a pencil through my eye.* Neil didn't think the novel accomplished what I'd hoped it would accomplish. Knowing I'd spent two years writing it, he regretted having to tell me so. Separately, Candida wrote, *Tom, your prose is nothing short of amazing. If I wore a hat, I'd take my hat off to you. But I can think of only five or six editors I could send this to.* The book's ironic voice, they felt, didn't serve the book's dark sensibility. Form and content hadn't fused flawlessly to produce a work of art. With Eric no longer working for the agency, I felt more like a burden than a client to Neil and Candida. This delusion, Frank assured me, was all in my head. But in my head is where I live. So I thanked them for their generosity and their effort on my work's behalf, and I started over.

Henry Dunow, an agent who had contacted me in Iowa, agreed to read the novel. Then, with enthusiasm, confidence, and the appropriate touch of intimacy an agent and a writer need to share, he offered to represent me. "Although, the book could use some cutting," he said. Within days, Jody and I trimmed four hundred and sixty-seven pages to four hundred and seventeen pages. Then Henry submitted the book to several editors. This time, no one answered within forty-eight hours. There were no pleas for more time, no clamoring for our attention. Instead, Henry and I waited for forty-one days, April 17 to May 24, 1994. Each morning, I woke hoping to hear the telephone ring. At 5:00 PM, I resigned myself to the fact that I wouldn't. I dreaded Friday afternoons. Once they ended, silence reigned for two days. Yet, rather than diminishing my anxiety, the weekend's silence intensified it, giving my imagination sixty hours to concoct disastrous scenarios. The results were always the same: no one would publish my novel. But my novel *had to be published*, not to satisfy my vanity, not for fame, not even for money, since I knew I hadn't written the type of novel that would yield a life-changing advance. No, my novel had to be published for one specific reason—so I could escape Texas and the university where I taught.

Also, I was determined to have my choice of an editor (if I was to have an editor). Of those who had read the novel's early pages, only Gerry Howard had seen the book's potential. And so, despite his wariness concerning my ability to finish the book, I decided to work with him should I have the chance. I believed he would be the best editor for the book. I'd betrayed my intentions once. I wouldn't do it a second time.

Late one Friday afternoon, Henry called. Gerry had offered to buy the book. The advance: $17,500. Even though it was $25,000 less than the advance for *Season's End*, I didn't hesitate. "Say yes."

"Maybe we should wait," Henry said.

"No. Sell the book."

Amused, Henry said, "Okay." Five minutes later, he called back and said, "Well, you're a Norton author."

As soon as I heard those words, three years of anxiety whistled through the infinitesimal hole in my heart and vanished.

Henry added, "When I accepted, Gerry laughed. He said that was his opening bid. He would have gone to twenty-thousand."

To me, this didn't matter.

"Gerry was running out the door to get to Los Angeles for the book fair," Henry said. "He'll call you next week."

"Okay," I said. Then I added, "Thanks. I mean it. Thank you."

After I returned the receiver to its cradle, I stepped into the living room and dropped to my knees. With my forehead pressed against the carpet, I closed my eyes and remained there until my breathing slowed and I was at peace.

Eight weeks later, I was clinically insane.

CHAPTER NINETEEN

It was 1994 and Frank had invited me back to the workshop for another summer. The day we left for Iowa, Jody and I packed the car, then placed our cats on the backseat in their carrying cases. Since they hated to travel, we'd given them tranquilizers. Stoned, they stared at us from behind their cages' silver bars and meowed weakly, protesting their confinement. By the time we reached the interstate, they were asleep.

In Kansas, we stopped at a motel. I'd packed a bathing suit and when I dove into the pool I was alone. I swam laps, then rolled onto my back and, beneath a cloudless blue sky, wondered how, at thirty-nine, I'd sold my third novel and was returning to Iowa to teach. I'd worked hard for twenty years, but my effort didn't seem connected to who I'd become. I felt like an eggshell that had been dyed with vivid colors, then pinpricked and drained. It may appear solid, but beneath its decorative surface it's hollow and nearly weightless.

At Frank and Maggie's house, we set our bags in the guest room, then walked down to the kitchen, where Frank handed me a cold imported beer.

"I hear we have something to celebrate," he said. Then we tapped glass bottles.

"The advance is only seventeen five," I said.

"Hey," he told me, "it's a book!"

The day Frank left for Nantucket, I stood in the driveway as he crammed the final items into his station wagon. Pausing to show me the interior of a small leather bag, he said, "This is what it comes to." The bag contained insulin vials and syringes. At fifty, Frank had developed diabetes. For several years pills controlled the disease. Now, at fifty-eight, he'd been switched to needles. His health's long, episodic decline had begun, and he knew it.

By contrast, over the next two months, my health seemed to improve. During the day, I taught, read, and played basketball. In the evening, I drank bourbon. Then, after sleeping for three hours, I'd wake at 2:00 AM, walk from the bedroom into its adjacent sitting room, turn on a lamp, settle into the armchair beside it, open a novel, and read until dawn. Not being able to sleep once the alcohol's effects had worn off didn't strike me as unusual. Neither did returning to bed at sunrise, or pouring my first cup of coffee at noon. If what I felt constituted the state others defined as happiness, I was happy. I played scales on Frank's piano. And, after dusk, I sat in the yard and watched glowing fireflies form constellations.

But one night, I woke at 3:00 AM when my body sprung upright on Frank's side of the bed. My heart beat so loudly that the sound filled my ears. For a moment, I thought I'd gone deaf and from then on I would hear only the internal thumps, gurgles, and growls my body made. Sweat had soaked my T-shirt, slickened my forehead, and dampened my beard. I'd leapt out of a dream in which I stood beside my brother near the tenement apartment building where I'd lived, fourteen years earlier. There, on the sidewalk, he handed me a sealed envelope that contained a warrant for my arrest.

Years earlier, I'd fled Provincetown when I had a chance to return to New York. On Cape Cod I had moved into one half of a small, wood-shingled cottage, divided in two by a thin plasterboard wall.

The day I'd signed the lease, I didn't know if I wanted the place, even though all I could afford was its $140 a month rent. Still, I hesitated. But as the afternoon's light faded and shadows swallowed the weedy front yard, the prospect of being homeless frightened me.

The landlord was an overweight guy in his thirties with a pasty face and black hair. He carried a tall, cardboard Big Gulp container filled with Coke and spiked by a clear plastic straw. Between sips, he chewed a hamburger he'd pulled out of a greasy paper bag. "Listen," he said, "it's Saturday. It's five o'clock. You have to be out of your place on Monday and you can't possibly find another apartment by then. This is a good deal. Take it." He removed the lease agreement from his coat pocket and placed it on top of the living room's cheesy, plywood-paneled wet bar. "Sign," he said. Then he tilted a ballpoint pen toward me and his hand remained motionless until, five seconds later, I took it. Once I'd written my name he said, "Someone broke a lease on me recently and I can promise you, I will hound that person to the end of the earth." Then he looked at me and raised his black eyebrows. As I drove away, I knew I'd made a mistake. The following day I called and told him I'd changed my mind.

"Too late, you wrote a check."

I said, "It's Sunday. I know you haven't cashed it. So please, do me a favor. Tear it up."

"No," he said. "And if you stop payment, I'll sue you."

I moved into the cottage and within twenty-four hours I had my radio, my leather jacket, and my ten-speed bike stolen, presumably by the drug dealers who lived in the adjacent cottage. At the police station, the officer to whom I reported the burglary said, "You look like a decent guy. Why are you living there? That's the worst street on Cape Cod. Half your neighbors pedal dope; the other half live on food stamps, welfare, and whatever they can steal."

Two driveways filled with fallen, desiccated pine needles separated our cottages. In mine stood a VW beetle; in theirs, a black Camaro with skull and bones decals pasted to its tinted windows.

Every time I ventured into my backyard to drop a garbage bag into the dented aluminum trash can, the dealers' German shepherds sprinted toward me, snapping their teeth, their nails scratching the rusty aluminum door an instant after I slammed it shut. Eyeing me through the dingy pane of glass above the doorknob, they growled, implying that, next time, they'd chew off my leg.

So when a Manhattan apartment with a monthly rent of $225 became available, I set the cottage's thermostat to sixty-five degrees to keep the water pipes from bursting if the temperature fell below freezing, mailed the landlord a letter that said I would no longer be paying rent, and didn't tell him where he could find me.

Shortly after I vanished, two men tracked me to the restaurant where I'd last worked. They asked the waiters, fry cooks, and dishwashers where I'd gone. A waitress said, "To California," although she knew I'd moved to Manhattan. The pair then traced me to the Queens house I used to occupy and quizzed the new tenants, who told them I'd been gone for two years. Someone called my parents' house and my mother said I'd disappeared. In Connecticut, my brother went to his power company's office to have his electricity turned on. The clerk checked the debtor list, noticed that my brother's surname matched mine, and summoned a manager. When the man asked my brother where I was, my brother told him we weren't even related.

After I'd lived for a year in Manhattan without being found, my fear subsided. But when it returned in the dream that woke me in Frank's bed, it left me drenched and trembling. The following day, rain fell. And, despite it being early August, Iowa City's temperature dropped into the upper fifties. Wearing an old, camouflage army jacket, my hands stuffed inside its pockets, my face angled downward as if a boulder had been dropped onto the base of my neck and forced me to stare at the floor, I trudged through the house. Pressure around my temples threatened to crush my forehead. My jaw ached. My teeth ground against one another. And, that evening, when I drank several shots of bourbon, my mood sunk, rather than lifted. Hours later, I staggered to bed.

Then the voices started. Internally, I heard mostly gibberish. Conversations overlapped conversations until they became incomprehensible. My brain seemed to be hosting a noisy, endless cocktail party. But a vivid and relentless paranoia I'd never experienced before focused my guilt, and provided its narrative. I'd been found; and now, for breaking a lease, I'd be imprisoned. Intellectually, I understood this was idiotic; emotionally, the prospect terrified me.

By late August, when Jody and I left Iowa and returned to Texas, my depression had escalated into a state of manic anxiety I could barely control. Whenever I taught, I expected FBI agents to burst into the classroom and lead me away in handcuffs. As always, I faced my students; but, with one eye, I monitored the door, waiting for it to fly open. My mind split, like the brain's twin hemispheres: one half interacted with people; the other half battled my delusions.

Each evening, I drank until I passed out. Otherwise, I couldn't sleep. Once the alcohol wore off several hours later, I'd wake, wander through the house and, in the dark, I'd lean against the wall beside a window so I couldn't be seen through its partially open blinds and watch for approaching headlights. When two appeared, I was sure the vehicle had come for me, and I would quake until it passed.

Then I did something unfathomable. I told Frank I couldn't meet him for dinner. He had flown to Austin to visit James Michener, the wealthy, eighty-eight-year-old writer whose endowment provided fellowships for workshop graduates. Mr. Michener lay in bed, attached to the dialysis machine that kept him alive, but he had agreed to meet Frank. A week before his arrival, Frank called and we planned to have dinner. But as I believed Frank would think less of me if I acknowledged my paranoia, I remained silent about it, rather than requesting his help. I didn't know he'd experienced a similar "breakdown" until we discussed it several years later. So I seemingly had no reason for canceling dinner when I called his hotel room two hours beforehand. True, a fine drizzle had slickened the oil-stained streets, and the thought of driving in the dark frightened me. Yet how could I say I was afraid to leave the house without offering an explanation? Also, I wanted to see him, and I knew I'd feel like I'd been impolite and ungrateful if I didn't. But when my hand tremors convinced me that I couldn't make the twenty-five-mile drive, I said, quite simply, "I don't feel well."

"Hey!" he said. "Don't worry about it. Stay home. It's crummy out." Then he lowered his voice to convey the grotesque nature of his trip. "And let's not kid ourselves, I'm not here for fun. This is me on my knees at the old man's bedside, holding his hand." He laughed softly, and with remorse, the way you'd laugh at a joke made about someone who'd just died. "I'll tell you," he said, "I don't look forward to requesting money." But, as the workshop's director, Frank's duties included begging ill tycoons and dying heiresses to leave behind millions for student scholarships. "The depths to which one sinks for literature," he said. Then he added, "Listen, take care of yourself. You sound a little rattled." We didn't speak again until spring.

* * *

Jody had to live with my illness, and Charlie knew about it. His youngest brother had committed suicide, another was schizophrenic, and Charlie took an antidepressant. So we spoke a common language, and he understood my insanity. In fact, he was surprised I hadn't cracked sooner. "I thought you would have been on meds years ago," he said, at one point. Otherwise, no one suspected my "inner turmoil," as Frank later described it, referring to himself. My colleagues had no reason to believe anything was wrong with me. I never missed a class, and I never missed a basketball game.

I'd begun to play three days a week in the university's gym. On weekends, I played outdoors with kids twenty years younger than me. I'd become addicted to the game's constant movement, which left me no time to be paranoid. While my thoughts followed the ball, nothing else mattered. But the instant I had to stand on the sidelines, my prison fantasies returned. I imagined that, in order to earn the respect of hard-core cons, I'd play hoops with them. One day, they'd discover I was a writer and I would organize a fiction workshop. Fondly, they'd call me "Teach." Other inmates would ask me to help them write their appeals. Finally, over a dinner of cornbread and lukewarm beans, someone would say, "Hey, Teach. What are you doing time for?" And I'd answer, "Breaking a lease." Then they would stare at me in slack-jawed silence.

But if I could mask my emotional wreckage, I couldn't hide my slow, physical decay. First, I developed a scalp rash. Then I lost hair. Purplish bruises shaped like quarter moons hung beneath each eye from sleeplessness. And, every few minutes, a rib-crunching cough forced me to spit out a gob of green or yellow phlegm.

Each week, I injected myself with a serum that contained a distillate of every allergen that made me sneeze, held an ice pack to my throbbing brow, or slept half the day. One afternoon, toward the end of the semester, I stopped by Dr. Cobb's office to collect a new vial containing a stronger dose of the serum. When he noticed me he pointed to an examination room and said, "Tom, get in here." Illuminating each orifice with his penlight, he gazed into my ears, nose, and mouth. Then he pressed a stethoscope to my chest and said, "Inhale." When he removed the scope's earpiece he said, "Do you know you have pneumonia?" I shook my head. He slipped a thermometer beneath my tongue. Then he held my wrist and tracked the passing seconds on his digital watch. When he released my hand, he checked the thermometer before he looked at me. "Your skin's pale. You have a 101-degree fever. And your heartbeat's elevated. What the hell's going on with you?"

"I haven't been sleeping much."

"Why not?"

Dr. Cobb was gray-bearded, gruff, and built like a college wrestler. But I needed to confess my crime to someone and I knew he'd listen. "I'm wanted by the FBI," I said. "In 1979 I broke a lease and—"

He raised one hand and said, "Stop."

"Do you think I'll go to jail?"

He placed one hand on my arm to stop it from quivering. Then he said, "First of all, they don't put guys who write books in jail. Second, you need to see a psychiatrist. Forget the FBI. The FBI has no interest in you whatsoever. Are we clear on this?"

I nodded.

"I'm going to write you a prescription for antibiotics, and you're going to make an appointment to see a psychiatrist. Are we on the same page?"

I nodded again.

"Good. Now get outta here. And when I see you again, you'd better be healthy."

But I didn't make an appointment with a psychiatrist. I made one with my regular physician and described my symptoms, although I pretended to be unaware of their cause. After listening to me for sixty seconds, he said, "Let's start you on Prozac."

"No."

I barked the word instinctively, worried that—in addition to my mental and physical deterioration—Prozac would transform me into a zombie the way various medications had reduced my sister to a catatonic. After her second suicide attempt, my sister left her husband. And fearing that she might unintentionally hurt her two sons, she left them, too. She moved in with our mother. Several years later, they left New York and bought a small condominium in Florida. Whenever I visited them my sister would stare at me without blinking, her eyes as motionless as the eyes of a corpse. I didn't want to risk descending to the depths of her inanimate madness. I would be fine, I believed, if I could sleep. I simply needed a drug to turn off my nerves the way one turns off an electric razor. I also needed the buzzing that radiated from my skull to my fingertips to cease because my paranoia had enlarged its narrative. I'd no longer only broken a lease. I'd left the heat on, the furnace had exploded, and the resulting fire had incinerated the cottage. Worse, the two women who lived on the other side of the thin, Sheetrock wall had died of smoke inhalation in their beds, before their bodies melted like candle wax.

"All I need is a tranquilizer," I said.

Momentarily, my physician resisted. Then he wrote a script for Xanax.

"Ten pills? That's it?"

He emphasized the drug's addictive power. He also didn't want me swallowing thirty tablets at once, and his suspicions weren't baseless. When I realized I could avoid imprisonment by committing suicide, I felt liberated. As long as I didn't mind dying, I had absolute freedom.

But I didn't want to die, and I didn't want to take Prozac, so I spent several afternoons per week in the university's library, researching arson's statute of limitations. I read legal precedents and weighed the distinction between criminal intent and criminal negligence. In an imaginary, never-ending trial, I defended my actions to a fictitious judge. "Your Honor, I never *intended* to blow up the furnace. I *intended* to keep the water pipes from freezing." The fact that I hadn't been near the cottage for fifteen years, had a valid driver's license, paid my taxes, and maintained a listed telephone number, which meant that any FBI agent who looked me up in the white pages could find me, did not diminish my delusions; it reinforced them.

At one point, I considered flying to Boston, renting a car, driving to the Cape, and turning left onto the dead-end street where I'd once lived. But I couldn't go alone. Jody would have to make the trip with me, rent a car, and book our hotel room using her license and credit card because I couldn't risk using mine. I also had to disguise myself. Of course, I'd aged. But paranoia alters time. To me, fifteen years ago and fifteen seconds ago were indistinguishable. I was being pursued in the present; yet, paradoxically, I was living in the past. I no longer wore an earring; my hair had thinned and been cut short; and my formerly brown beard had faded to gray. Still, I worried about being recognized, and whenever I imagined driving down that street my hands quaked. What if my landlord was waiting for me in the front yard? Or what if the cottages no longer existed? Then, at the local police station, Jody would have to ask the desk sergeant if he had any record of them being burned down while I hid in the car, my face partially obscured by a Red Sox cap. Ultimately, I was too frightened to return. In my imagination, the cottages, driveways, pine needles, the black Camaro, and the dogs remained unchanged and terrifying.

Finally, my madness paralyzed me. I'd promised myself to search for a teaching job if I sold *City of God*. With my experience and a forthcoming novel, my chances for finding a position were good, perhaps as good as they ever would be—because if *City of God* failed critically, my authorial value would dwindle to zero. I would be in my early forties, artistically undistinguished, and close to receiving tenure. Then Texas would own me. So I updated my vita, skimmed the creative writing job list, circled every position I wanted, typed twenty application letters, and slipped each one into a nine-by-twelve-inch envelope. Only, once the letters were prepared, I couldn't risk mailing the envelopes. A postal employee might recognize my name and address, and then tell the FBI where to find me. Like all paranoids, at this stage of my illness, I wasn't simply irrational; I was narcissistic, and phenomenally deluded. I thought the FBI's sole task was to pursue and incarcerate me. At 3:00 AM, I not only believed this was possible; I also believed it was probable. For several days, I considered supplying no name, only my address, but this might make the envelopes seem suspect. If anyone opened one en route to its destination, he or she would discover my name. So the envelopes sat on my desk. Secretly, I wished that while I was out of the house Jody would address and mail them. But after weeks of me explaining, in precise detail, the perils this involved, she didn't.

Dusk now fell earlier; the autumn afternoons ended abruptly; and often, after I left campus, streetlights illuminated my walk home. Soon, it would be Thanksgiving. As the application deadlines approached, I thought it might be safe to mail envelopes to universities located in the Midwest, Southwest, and along the Pacific coast. But mailing any to the Northeast was inconceivable.

After the semester ended, an early December freeze made our lawn glisten like polished silver. And on the date by which all

application envelopes had to be postmarked, I stood over the kitch-
en's wastebasket and tore each envelope in half, and then in half
again, to make its contents difficult to reassemble.

A week later, Jody and I drove to Key West. We'd rented a larger
house with a wooden deck and an unheated, thirty-foot-long lap
pool. Unable to concentrate, I paced beside it for hours. The evenings were chilly and, occasionally, I had to turn on the heat. But I
was afraid to touch the living room's thermostat, which resembled
the cottage's thermostat. So I would walk toward it, close my eyes,
and then place my thumb beneath its small, red lever to raise the
temperature. At midnight, I snapped my tranquilizer in two and
swallowed a tiny, white crumb of Xanax. The drug soothed my
nerves' ragged edges, although I didn't sleep. And I didn't stop asking Jody if I had accidentally committed arson. Once every hour,
she assured me that I hadn't. And I believed her—as long as she continued talking. Because once she stopped, her assurances became
meaningless, and I made her repeat them, which, generously, she
did. Until one peerlessly beautiful morning, while she sat at the
poolside table, reading the newspaper and sipping Cuban coffee.
Seated opposite her, I uttered the phrase, "But what if." Then, without lowering her newspaper, she said, "If you don't shut up, I will
throw you in that pool and drown you. Do you understand me?"

Feeling like a chastised schoolboy, I waited, hoping for a
reprieve. When it became clear that one wasn't imminent, I said,
softly, "Yes."

"Yes, what?"

"Yes, I understand."

"Good. Now go call Bill and leave me alone."

Bill Lashner was a lawyer, a novelist, and a friend I'd made at
Iowa. When he answered his phone and heard my voice he shouted,
"Tommie!" (Bill's one of the few people who calls me that.) We chatted
about the holidays. Then I said, "Can I ask you for some legal advice?"

Perhaps he detected my desperation because he hesitated before
he said, "Okay."

"I think I may be wanted for breaking a lease."

He paused. "When was this?"

"1979."

"You broke a lease fifteen years ago."

"Yeah. I also may have accidentally burned down the cottage."

Patiently, he said, "And you're wanted by?"

"The FBI."

After a moment's silence, Bill said, "Tom, I don't want to play dime-store psychologist. But you don't have a legal problem. You have a psychological problem."

I said I'd broken the lease because I'd been robbed, twice.

"Then you had a legal right to leave," he said. "It's called 'constructive abandonment.' But seriously, Tommie, you need to see a psychiatrist."

And, after being insane for six months, once we returned to Texas, I did.

He was a short, pudgy, cherubic man who wore a gray suit and shiny, black penny loafers. Separated by a coffee table on which he kept a box of Kleenex tissues, I explained what I'd done and why I was wanted. Then I listed my symptoms. When I finished, he smiled and said, "You have major depression with an obsessive feature."

Next, I described a dream. In it, I stood at the front of a classroom. But as I tried to speak, tiny globs of shit, rather than words, spewed out of my mouth and dappled the students' faces like raindrops.

"Feces and depressive guilt are commonly connected," he said. Then he studied me and asked, "Who are you?"

I said I didn't understand his question.

"Who's Tom?"

As I tried to distill an answer, I pictured my brain's dark canals and my mind's eye flying above them as firing neurons brightened the terrain the way a lightning storm illuminates a desert floor. Then I said, "A writer."

He shook his head. "No. I don't mean, What do you do? I mean, Who are *you*?"

The concept still baffled me. Who is anyone? Are our personalities static or fluid? From moment to moment, don't we change? Finally, I said, "I don't know."

"That's the problem," he said. "There's no 'you.' You're a brilliant mimic. But take away the fictional personas you invent and nothing exists. Without a novel to write, you have no idea who you are."

Then he wrote a prescription for Prozac and warned me to stop drinking. "Prozac won't help if you drink every night."

As I took the slip of paper from his hand, I said, "Will Prozac change the way I write?"

He shrugged. "I can't say." Then he escorted me to the door.

So what was I, a void capable of creating masks and imagining voices? If Prozac worked and my obsessions waned, would my desire to worry about characters wane, too? Would the medication scramble my brain in a way that it couldn't be unscrambled?

Once it became apparent that I would not sleep, read, or write well again until chemicals subdued my paranoia, I filled the prescription and brought home ninety green and white capsules. Facing our bathroom mirror, I stared at the hollow shell once known as "me." Then I swallowed a capsule, flicked the light switch, and the room instantly turned black.

PART FOUR

CHAPTER TWENTY

A s it was early summer in Iowa, Frank wore sneakers, khaki pants, and a rumpled long-sleeved shirt with its sleeves rolled halfway up his forearms. When the streetlight changed from red to green, he crossed the narrow, tree-lined, two-lane road outside the Foxhead without looking to see if a car approached from either direction. Jody and I were leaning against the small community theater building. Inside, Maggie was directing *Dogg's Hamlet*, a play in which Tim had a role as one of the schoolboys attempting to mount a production of Shakespeare's tragedy. We hadn't seen Frank for a year. I'd been taking Prozac for six months and had made a modest effort to drink less. Frank hadn't. Smiling like a mischievous teenager, he strolled toward us carrying a clear plastic cup filled with bourbon and ice. He stepped onto the sidewalk, kissed Jody, then shook my hand.

I said, "Shouldn't you be inside?"

Frank jiggled the ice in his cup. "I decided it was time for a refreshment. You know, the play is about Hamlet. That doesn't mean it *is Hamlet*."

Several weeks earlier, in late May, Connie had telephoned to ask

me to teach once again at the workshop. By then, Frank and Maggie
had rented their house to a visiting Israeli professor. For the first time
in three years, Jody and I wouldn't be staying there. We would see
Frank and Maggie that evening only, and the brevity of the time we
would spend together signaled an era's end. Six and a half years had
passed since the Key West morning Frank and I first crossed paths.
The encounter didn't feel like it had occurred yesterday, yet neither of
us noted time's passage. Seemingly, our friendship had no beginning
or end. Instead, we inhabited a continuous now. Frank's presence in
my life and, I imagine, my presence in his, superseded corporeal-
ity. My need to be near him had diminished, but, to me, his voice
had become as essential as air. Silencing it would be like silencing
an octave's note by extracting an ivory key from a piano's keyboard.

As the three of us waited for Maggie and Tim, neither Frank nor
I realized how infrequently we would see each other in the coming
years. But rather than growing distant, like objects observed through
the wrong end of a telescope, our separation created a magnifying
effect and we felt closer to each other. Our telephone conversations
seemed singular and continuous, as if we'd barely paused midsentence. Yes, our appearances changed. Frank's silver hair thinned.
His jowls thickened. His neck grew puffy. And his midsection no
longer resembled *Body & Soul*'s eerily sleek author's photograph—
although, as yet, he didn't rely on a cane to support his arthritic
joints. Meanwhile, from playing basketball, I'd become muscular. I
wore reading glasses. And my beard had faded to white. But, invis-
ibly, our affection deepened. And we saw no need to acknowledge it.

At sunset, the play ended. In separate cars, we drove to Frank
and Maggie's house. Several window lamps glowed and illuminated
patches of lawn. Knowing Jody and I wouldn't spend the summer
there made me melancholy. Also, I'd hoped to explain my paranoia
to Frank, but two poets arrived. One had a bottle of tequila, and
every few minutes he raised it overhead and shouted, "Hecho en
Mexico!" The other lit a joint, took a hit, and then offered it to me.
I passed. I didn't throw back shots, either. I drank beer, judiciously,

to Frank's surprise. Soon he began to play the piano, and blues filled the living room. Over the din, Maggie said she hadn't seen Frank so animated in months. Yet, he had less energy; that was clear to me. He'd also stopped closing the Foxhead three nights a week, in part because he'd outgrown his need for its atmosphere. The students were younger, the anxiety he felt while writing *Body & Soul* had dissipated, and his disappointment over the novel's reception had sapped his strength. He resembled a boxer who, after his best punch failed to knock down his opponent, returned to his corner psychologically defeated. As for me, had Frank noticed my emotional vulnerability, he would have asked about it.

But we didn't reveal our secrets. Instead, we squandered the evening. The next day Frank left town, and three years passed before I returned to Iowa City.

* * *

Two months after Frank headed for Nantucket, W. W. Norton & Co. published *City of God*. Before the novel reached bookstore shelves, *Publishers Weekly* called it a "clichéd, disappointing yarn."

Charlie's blurb described the novel as "funny, smart, dreamy, brilliant, exact and surreal." *Kirkus* countered with a "starred" review, which began: "Pungent with the lunatic language of consumer-driven tabloid America, this horrifying prophecy of a book . . . seems closer to social commentary than satire." It ended: "Grimes makes a quantum leap into DeLillo land."

The novel received six reviews. Total. Most positive, some ecstatic. But the *New York Times Book Review* ignored the book, and four thousand copies sold before my once again never-paper-backed novel vanished.

But in the United Kingdom, the prestigious house Picador published the novel. And in France, Gallimard issued it. According to London's newspaper, the *Guardian*, Gallimard had the "best back-list in the world." The firm had published Proust, Camus, Sartre,

Hemingway, Faulkner, Kafka, Joyce, and Roth. Its authors had won eighteen Nobel Prizes, twenty-seven Goncourt Prizes (the French equivalent of the Pulitzer), and eighteen Grand Prizes for the Novel awarded by the French Academy. Gallimard's reputation exceeded FSG's, and its name now graced my novel's cover.

So, was I a success, or a failure? That's the wrong question to ask. While revising this book I've had to press the language more firmly. As Frank repeatedly said, a reader must always feel the pressure of the writer's soul behind the words. What he meant by soul I would call one's deepest sense of self. My psychiatrist claims that whenever I'm not writing I don't know who I am. But I know exactly who I am. I'm a writer, and despite my failures, rejections, and minor successes I've never questioned my longing to be a great writer. Now, I've nearly run out of time and I may never become one. Yet all along I've known so deeply who I am that, until now, I've been ashamed to admit it, even to myself.

* * *

In addition to keeping my literary ambitions to myself, I also deftly masked my shattered state of mind. But this is what a writer does: creates and wears masks. So no one I worked with sensed, or at least never asked me about, my paranoia, although after reading *City of God* someone did say to me, with regard to the dialogue of various characters, "You must hear voices in your head." I answered, "You have no idea."

Late one Friday afternoon, the English department's chair summoned me to her office. I was certain that she planned to fire me. Instead, she asked me to direct the MFA Program in Creative Writing, and as its reputation developed Frank enjoyed taking partial credit for the program's growing national stature. His son Will once told me, "Dad would shout, 'That's my boy down there!'" Then, after a slight pause, Will added, "Whenever your success reflected well on him, of course."

"Befriend your dean," Frank told me. "It also wouldn't hurt if you knew your university's president."

"I play basketball with him three times a week."

"Well, if you guard him," Frank said, "let him score."

I was afraid the job would steal my writing time, and it did. Still, the quickness with which the five-year-old program developed was due, in part, to good fortune. I was allowed to hire two well-published writers, and within a year secured an Endowed Chair in Creative Writing position, which, to my astonishment, I began to fill with my literary idols: Tim O'Brien, Barry Hannah, Denis Johnson, and Robert Stone. My bad luck as a writer had been transformed inexplicably to good luck as the program's director. Writers who were once my heroes were now my friends, and I found myself having conversations I'd never expected to have. But we understand one another. As writers, we each strive for perfection. I've known Tim, who continues to teach in the program, for ten years now. And he's so modest that occasionally I have to remind him that *he* wrote *The Things They Carried*, a book he revises each time a new paperback edition is issued. He says, "I can always make the book a little bit better." We also understand that our next novel will be as hard or even harder to write than those we've already put on a shelf and forgotten, and we often doubt ourselves, and our purpose. "I don't know if I even believe in the efficacy of words any longer," Barry said to me one day. For years, he struggled with an unfinished novel. "There's a lot of Christ in it," he'd announce from time to time, hoping to make the book make sense to him, the writer writing it, who's completely lost. One evening in workshop, he read the Twenty-third Psalm to his students. "Aspire to create language of that power and beauty," he told them. We treat students as young writers. Most of them enter Tim's workshop expecting to hear about blood, war, and metaphysics. Instead, he lectures them about proper pronoun and comma usage. "Meaning, sense, clarity": Frank's mantra, repeated endlessly.

I no longer write Frank's words on my classroom's blackboard as frequently as I did. Instead I say, "Every good story contains a clock, a period of time during which all dramatic events must begin and end. After Holden Caulfield is kicked out of Pencey Prep, he has three days to get home for Christmas. Nick Carraway rents a cottage beside Gatsby's. Summer begins when he arrives; fall arrives when he departs. The seasons contain the story. Understanding how time operates in your story will help you write it." As I speak, I see students jotting down what I've just said, making notes. It's taken me thirty-five years, but, in my idiosyncratic way, I can now talk to young writers. And, as the program's director, I've matured the way Frank must have matured, by learning that we are all simply writers who travel in the same literary universe.

Two years after I became the program's director, a colleague at work told me that Katherine Anne Porter's childhood home, located ten miles from the university, had been put up for sale. Many critics consider Porter one of the twentieth century's greatest writers. She won the Pulitzer Prize and the National Book Award for her fiction, but I hardly knew her work. Nevertheless, I felt obligated to do what I could to keep the house she'd lived in from vanishing.

The small, nineteenth-century building stood on a corner lot in Kyle, Texas, ten miles from campus. The town's population: 2,000. The town: nothing more than a central Texas railroad line's way station. I'd made an appointment to look at the house. Carroll Wiley, a fund-raiser for the university, accompanied me. Standing on the street, we saw a weather-stained clapboard shack listing on the brittle stone foundation beneath it. In her fiction, Porter describes the house as a Southern mansion, a kind of Tara.

A pecan tree shaded the weedy backyard, and a rotting lean-to had fallen onto a pile of rusted gardening equipment. The porch's roof and floor were soggy; a torn, decaying sofa, covered with dog hair and damp to its core, sat near the rear door. Cobwebs from the low eaves brushed my head as I stepped inside. The small kitchen had been remodeled in the 1950s with tin cabinets, a yellow Formica countertop, and a porcelain sink. I scanned the dining room's maple floors and its casement windows. The room gave off a serene vibration. With sunlight and some white curtains, it could be pleasant. Off the parlor was a sitting room; through that a small bedroom with an unattractive built-in closet, but a surprisingly spacious bathroom, which I later discovered had been the bedroom Porter had shared with her three siblings, as, back then, everyone in the family had used an outhouse.

Carroll stood next to me, waiting. "Well, what do you think?"

"It's a mess," I said. Then, with a comic sense of hope, I added, "Let's save it."

I said this quixotically, but perhaps karma guided me because Sam Lawrence had been Katherine Anne Porter's publisher. In the same way he convinced Frank to write *Body & Soul*, he'd convinced Porter to finish her only novel, *Ship of Fools*.

But preserving the house—which she described, in a letter to a friend, as a "dreary little place, empty, full of dust, even smaller than I remembered it"—would be expensive. So, Carroll, I, and a few Kyle residents formed a committee and announced our preservation efforts. Between April and September, we raised $35,000. As the house alone cost $75,000, we decided to have a fund-raiser in the backyard. In ninety-degree heat, I outlined my vision to twenty people seated on folding chairs. I explained that I saw the house as a writer's residence and a place to bring visiting authors. "Let them use Katherine Anne Porter's childhood home," I said, "to extend literature." After I finished speaking, a tall gentleman approached me and said, "I'm very interested in this." Then he left.

He was Bill Johnson. During the Great Depression, his father had purchased Kyle ranchland for nine dollars an acre. Through the thirty-five-hundred-acre ranch ran the Blanco River, where Porter had swum and fished in a deep green pool called "Halifax Hole." Later, she wrote about the place in her novella *Noon Wine*. By the time I met Bill, he ran his family's multimillion-dollar foundation. Wanting to do something for Kyle, he wrote a check to buy the house. Then we began to restore it.

We replicated historical detail as best we could. We agreed that the front porch had not originally rested on concrete, so we jettisoned the cement and set the porch on wooden posts. Then we balanced the house on a new foundation and screened in the back porch. At that point, I estimated that we needed another $400,000 to complete the renovation and $1,000,000 to operate it and fund a visiting writers series. I was hesitant to proceed until we had money to cover both.

One evening in his office, where we'd been meeting, Bill said to me, "Don't worry, I'll take care of it." He'd contribute $400,000. Then, if we needed $25,000 a year to cover initial operating expenses, he'd handle that as well. Bill had discovered personal, cultural, and historical threads he didn't wish to see broken. By preserving the house, we were weaving these threads, and then the weave grew more intricate.

Curt Engelhorn, the fourteenth-richest man in the world, was the son of Porter's childhood friend Erna, who had lived across the street from the house. At seventy-one, he lived in Switzerland, but his sister Elizabeth owned a ranch in west Texas. Her close friend, Mary Giberson, said to me, "You know, Curt's coming through town. I think he might like to see the house where his mother played." Three months later, Curt arrived. As he walked through the rooms of the small house he, like Bill, may have sensed the thread stitching us all together, because, after I wrote him a letter requesting a gift, he gave us $1,200,000.

Two years later, the house was designated a national literary landmark. At the ceremony, Tim spoke about Katherine Anne Porter. As I listened and contemplated the improbable story of preserving her house, I thought of Frank, Sam Lawrence, and me, and how mysteriously all of our lives had been woven together. And how the weave continues to add new colors as writers come to read their work, hold classes for MFA students, and pay homage to Katherine Anne Porter's ghost.

CHAPTER TWENTY-ONE

Publishing a fiction anthology by Iowa graduates was Leigh Haber's idea. She was an editor at Hyperion, the firm owned by Disney to which Pat Mulcahy had defected when she left Little, Brown. Leigh called Henry and asked him to recommend an editor. When he named me, Leigh agreed. I was certain I could do a good job, yet I'm still shocked whenever I see my name below the anthology's title. But I told Henry and Leigh I wouldn't edit the book without Frank's approval. So Henry contacted Frank to ask for it.

"At first," Henry told me, "Frank thought I was asking him to edit the book."

Frank explained that he couldn't take on the project as he was already editing an essay collection by Iowa grads called *The Eleventh Draft*.

Henry said, "There was an awkward silence when I told him I was asking for his blessing for you to edit the anthology."

Briefly flustered, Frank answered, "Oh. Of course, Tom. Absolutely." Then he gave Hyperion permission to use the workshop's name "in connection with the sale, advertising and promotion of the book."

I decided to select stories from 1930 to 1999, write a foreword, and add a brief overview of the workshop's seventy-year history. Every writer or writer's estate would receive the same compensation for reprint rights, $500, and every living author would contribute a three- to five-hundred-word preface to his or her story. All profits would be donated to provide scholarships to workshop students. I wanted Frank to write an introduction, too, but I didn't know what would be a reasonable fee. So I called and asked "How much?" thinking Frank would say $1,500.

He answered, "For you, my friend, $3,000," which was the exact amount he'd paid me for my *The Eleventh Draft* essay. He'd simply taken back my money. Plus, I gave him five thousand words, and he returned twelve hundred.

"Bastard," I said, while Frank laughed, softly.

I knew he'd write a succinct, graceful introduction. Elegant brevity defined Frank's nonfiction. But, at the time, I didn't know that anxiety also accounted for his concision. Several years later, he described his feelings in, ironically, an essay entitled "Observations Now" that begins:

"I think most people who attempt to write with a degree of seriousness are curious about others doing the same thing. Writing is a lonely enterprise, after all. Some seem comfortable in the mental solitude."

But, Frank admitted:

I am uncomfortable writing, and I know a number of writers (although I won't mention them) who feel the same way. The isolation, self-doubt, perfectionism and other idiosyncratic impediments to action—some completely irrational, almost like superstitions—mix in various ways in various people to create something close to dread at the sinister urgency of the blank page. For myself, once I'm up and moving, if not running, through the lines, I zip back and forth between feeling okay and feeling terrified. Once in a while I am exhilarated, but more often it is as if my inner self, my sense of myself, is at risk. Something like the tension one might feel watching the ivory ball circumnavigate the roulette wheel after having made a large, foolish, impulsive bet.

Given this, it's odd that Frank chose to become a writer, but, as he said, a writer's life is irrational. True, elation sometimes makes its way from a writer's fingertips to his or her heart and, for a moment, the writer believes that he or she has fashioned a chain of perfectly conjoined words. But the feeling recedes. Then the sublime seems trite, the harmonious dissonant, and perfection imperfect. Writing's daily difficulties humble a writer; few writers earn a living from their work; fewer still receive accolades; and, at best, two dozen a century are remembered. So what compels us to do it: a naïve but persistent hope for transcendence through art?

In his anthology introduction, Frank wrote:

> When I was a kid of eighteen I went to Paris. I had very little money, lived in an Algerian slum, ate so badly I lost half the hair on the back of my head from a vitamin deficiency, got robbed, got beaten up, and endured various other hardships. Nevertheless, I stayed, because I had read about prewar Paris—about Hemingway, Fitzgerald, Joyce, and all the others who used to hang out in "Boul Miche" at The Dome or The Select. Surely it would all start up again now that the war was over. I wanted to meet artists, I wanted to connect with the literary ex-pats I assumed must be there. But of course I was too late. There was no doubt an artistic community, but it was no longer open and welcoming, if indeed it had ever been as open as I imagined.

Dejected, Frank returned to the States, but he never forgot his youthful literary longing. Concluding his introduction, he added, "It has never surprised me that young American writers want to come to the Iowa Workshop. A place to read, write, and talk, a place to test ideas and to experiment. A literary community of some sophistication. Of course they want to come."

By the time I entered the program, twenty-four new students came each August. Many of us published, many didn't. Of those who did, I could choose very few to represent each decade. Between June and October of 1998, I read eighty story collections (having decided that novel excerpts would be less satisfying to readers). I wanted to present a variety of voices, subjects, styles, and sensibilities to refute the widespread notion that a formulaic "workshop story" existed. Tacitly, the anthology asked readers to decide whether Denis Johnson's work differed from Jane Smiley's work, or if Jayne Anne Phillips mimicked Raymond Carver.

Also, I felt the anthology needed to give the reader a sense of time, place, and student experiences, rather than simply being another soulless compilation of stories. So, I solicited recollections from graduates. Some had hated the workshop. A few griped about being overlooked. A famous Latina author accused the workshop of racism, which I asked her to write about, believing her remembrance would provide a unique perspective on the late 1970s; she politely refused. Pulitzer Prize winner Michael Cunningham recalled "a fellow student slapping a story of mine down on the table and announcing to the members of our workshop, 'This is just *pornography*.'" James Hynes wrote that, "In many ways, being at the Writers' Workshop was like being in high school again. It was a cliquish, judgmental place, where your reputation could be decided in a moment. You weren't judged on your hair or clothes, however, but on the contents of your bookshelf." Despite these comments, though, a singular theme emerged. "What I loved best about the Workshop," Tom Barbash wrote, "was that it was, and still is, a place where writing is sacred, paramount." Cunningham added, "I actually walked around at night sometimes and stood for a while under certain lighted windows, knowing that inside someone I admired was struggling to put something down on paper, and that what was getting put onto paper might, in fact, be extraordinary." Occasionally, something was. Flannery O'Connor's classmate, Jean Wylder, remembered that "On the opening day of class, Flannery was sitting alone in the front row, over against the wall. She was wearing what I was soon to think of as her 'uniform' for that year: plain gray skirt and neatly ironed silkish blouse, nylon stockings, and brown penny loafers. Her only makeup was a trace of lipstick. [The writer] Elizabeth Hardwick once described her as a 'quiet puritanical convent girl from the harsh provinces of Canada.'" But, several weeks later, "after Flannery finished reading her story, we sat there until Andrew Lytle gave meaning to our silence by saying Workshop was over for the day. For once, there was not going to be any critical dissecting." Later that day, Wylder and a classmate went around Iowa City, picking flowers from people's front yards. Then they walked across town and carried them to the cramped, second-floor apartment where O'Connor lived.

* * *

That fall, before I wrote the anthology's foreword, I flew to Iowa City, hoping that a Proustian memory rush would close the nine-year gap between my arrival in Iowa and the workshop's current incarnation. But the trip had the opposite effect; it made the era when I was a student seem geologically remote.

Frank had convinced the university's administration to give the workshop the two-story, 150-year-old Dey House. It overlooked the Iowa River, had white clapboard siding, and jade green paint trimmed every windowsill, eave, and porch column. As I approached, walking along a curved cement path bordered by neatly clipped lawns, yellow leaves fell from the front yard's tree. Inside, students sat in a spacious lounge, its walls painted a subdued, oaky color. And, although the fire-place didn't work, upholstered couches surrounded a plush rug that lay on the polished wood floor. By contrast, our EPB lounge had had buzzing overhead lights, a plastic couch, a coffee-stained table, and a gray tile floor tattooed by crushed cigarettes. But more than the house, the students disoriented me: most of them appeared to be fifteen.

Once I'd entered Connie's large office and hugged her, I said, "I know I've gotten older, but have these guys gotten younger?"

Connie nodded and said, "Yeah, a little bit." A hundred e-mail messages striped her computer screen, and papers seemingly scattered in a tornado's wake covered her desk. But once we took our seats, she ignored it all, leaned forward and said, "So tell me everything," by which she meant my program, my writing, and the anthology.

"I want a 1999 graduate's story to end it," I said. "Whose work should I read?"

Without hesitating, Connie said, "ZZ Packer." Then she gave me ZZ's number.

After I left Connie's office, I walked down the hall and knocked on Frank's partially opened door. He positioned it this way, intentionally. The slim crevice created an illusory passageway between his world and the world outside that made him seem omnipresent, yet unavailable, except to Connie. When I stepped inside and saw his personal fireplace and the long, antique mahogany table around which he and his students gathered for workshop, I said, "Nice digs. You couldn't have done this ten years earlier?"

He smiled. Then he said, "Sometimes you have to suffer for your art, Tom." Knowing my eye would follow his, Frank scanned the room, as if to say, "Pretty sweet, no?" He wasn't quite boasting. But, clearly, acquiring the coveted Dey House pleased him.

I lowered myself onto a cushioned armchair and its pillow's soft exhalation whispered that, in a tangible way, the luxurious surroundings matched Frank's age and stature. The workshop's EPB offices and classrooms had been cramped and grim. But Frank had been leaner, then, and had no laurels to rest on. Now, his jowls bulged, he was sixty-two, and, the previous year, *U.S. News & World Report* had ranked Iowa number one among the nation's three hundred creative writing programs. "It's harder to get into the workshop than it is to get into Harvard medical school," he told journalists, repeatedly.

"What's up with the teenagers in the program?" I said.

Frank shrugged. "The MFA degree's culturally acceptable. Most students earn a BFA and come straight here after college." Then he pointed a finger at me and added, "But just because they're young doesn't mean they're not incredibly talented. Read their stuff. Some of it's terrific."

"I have. I'm anthologizing Brady Udall's 'Buckeye the Elder.'"

"Great story," Frank said.

In Brady's preface, he admits:

> Frank had dismissed my first offering as the worst kind of amateurish yearnings, so I wasn't hopeful about the reception "Buckeye" would get. For the first fifteen minutes of class, Frank allowed my fellow writers to do what comes natural in a Workshop class—they tore the story to bits. Frank fidgeted, shook his head sadly, and finally, when he could take no more, held up his hands to halt the proceedings and announced that "Buckeye the Elder" was a perfect story, there was not a flaw or blemish in it, not even a comma out of place, and no amount of second-guessing and nit-picking would change that. Send this story off right away, he urged me, and it will certainly be published.

The story won *Playboy*'s college fiction competition.

Frank said, "Come by the house for dinner tomorrow night. We'll raise a glass."

From my hotel, I called ZZ and asked her to meet me the next morning to talk about contributing an anthology story. After hesitating and dodging my request, she said she'd be at a downtown coffee shop around eleven.

"How will I recognize you?" I said.

"I'll be the black one."

I laughed. "Come on, ZZ. It's not that bad." But it was.

At first, she resisted my request for a story. To an extent, ZZ distrusted the swift, clamorous interest her work had generated. Before coming to Iowa, in her late twenties, she'd been a high school teacher, an SAT tutor, a coffee shop barista, and a barmaid. Given that I'd been a waiter when Frank accepted me, I understood her uneasiness. Good things were happening too fast; the effect could be disorienting.

But she had that inexplicable aura of literary confidence. The instant I spotted her, I thought, *writer*. Despite this, ZZ and I had a problem: all of her stories were either published or unfinished. The only material she had was a novel excerpt that needed editing. "So send it to me," I said. "We'll edit it together." And, by FedExing envelopes to each other over a period of two months, we did.

* * *

That evening, I brought a six-pack of Guinness to dinner, but Frank, I learned, no longer drank bourbon and beer. His internist had ordered him to begin a regimen of fast walking at the gym and to quit smoking—for good. He had also limited Frank's daily alcohol consumption to two glasses of red wine, since red wine supposedly contains antioxidants that may prevent heart disease. Standing in his living room, Frank carefully tapped his huge, brimming glass against my bottle's neck. Lowering his voice so Maggie couldn't hear, he said, "The doctor specified 'two glasses,' but he didn't specify what size." Frank's "two glasses" emptied a bottle of cabernet.

An hour later, Tim, who was eleven, and Frank topped off dinner with vanilla ice cream. "And pour some chocolate syrup over it," Frank yelled to Maggie, who, from the kitchen, yelled back, "Great diet for a diabetic, Frank." He merely glanced at me and grinned.

The following fall, when the anthology was published, I traveled to Iowa City to participate in a panel discussion. Onstage, Frank, two other writers, and I sat behind a long table and looked out at two hundred people. As Frank introduced me, he told everyone that if they hadn't read *City of God*, they should. I was stunned. I thought he'd forgotten my existence as a writer. After the discussion ended, Frank, clearly exhausted, stooped forward, headed for an exit, and I couldn't make my way through the crowd to catch him.

* * *

The next day, I had lunch with Fritz McDonald and two other workshop friends. Although of the four of us I was the only one who had published and continued to write, it wasn't a source of tension among us. Still, we represented a typical workshop graduating class: three out of four hadn't survived as writers. So I concluded the anthology with Fritz's recollection, which, to me, captured how not surviving felt.

He wrote:

> I was most haunted by the Workshop the year I graduated. Like the last guest at a party, I lingered in Iowa City. I hung out with the new crop of students, religiously attended readings, drifted around the cramped, smoky pall of the Foxhead. In the afternoons, light slanted dully through my apartment window while I labored to transform a short story into a novel, the one story that had earned a positive reaction from my classmates. Evenings, I applied for teaching jobs in the worst academic job market in decades.
>
> I was numb. I'd come to Iowa to be elevated into a literary world I'd fantasized about since I'd first read *A Moveable Feast*. For two years, I brushed up against it—the heightened talk about fictional craft; the late nights drinking with famous writers; the odd rhythm of days liberated from having to make a living. Literary fame seemed plausible. Close. A visiting eminence would save me from the sorrow of an ordinary life.
>
> But it hadn't, and now I spent hours in Prairie Lights investigating dust jackets and *The Best American Short Stories* for evidence of other graduates' success. One by one, friends went off to careers, marriages, other places. I spent more time alone. I went out of my way to avoid people I knew on the streets of Iowa City, even those who, like me, had been unable to let go of the dream. One day, I slipped into EPB, the building where our classes were held, and in a dark hall, listened to the articulate voices of a workshop in progress.
>
> My apartment overlooked the Oakland Cemetery, and each day, long ruminative walks among the gravestones led me to the

Black Angel, a life-sized statue memorializing an anonymous citizen. Legend had it that touching the Angel brings death; I stroked its outstretched palm and my novel died. I piled up draft after draft of the same two chapters—false starts, dead ends, revised revisions.

Eventually, I ran out of money. I took a part-time job teaching freshman composition to indifferent students at a local community college. I moved away from the graveyard and Iowa City. I boxed the novel and put away Workshop voices, and in time, the last of my illusions about the literary life faded. In a wet Iowa summer, I married the best person I've known and everything changed.

What did I learn? That life goes on with or without fiction. I work for a marketing firm these days and write fiction when I can steal the minutes. Under trying circumstances, sentence by sentence, I progress. And this is how it should be. As the first act in my writing life, the Workshop allowed me to confront my most destructive habit—getting lost in the lifestyle and not the work.

I have a photograph of us back in our heyday at the Mill, and whenever I look at it I feel lucky and blessed. On the long list of students who have attended the Workshop, many do not survive, their faith extinguished. Frank Conroy had said over and over that "the writing life is hard," and I'd resented him for it. Now, I owe him a debt of gratitude and I think I understand him. How difficult it must be to pass judgment on so much hope.

A year ago, a prominent literary journal sent me a postcard; it had just published one of Fritz's stories.

* * *

After lunch, we wandered through used bookstores, skimming long out-of-print novels and story collections. When I checked, the time was three o'clock. Frank had told me to come to his house that afternoon; I thought he meant late afternoon. So I waited. But when I called at four, he said, "I thought you were coming this afternoon." Then he paused, and he must have glanced at a clock, because he added, "Well, I guess four o'clock still is the afternoon."

I'd misunderstood him; and today, I wish I had arrived an hour earlier. At three o'clock, autumn's blue sky seemed eternal. By four, dusk began to fall, and a dull gray light covered the rooftops and the river. Uncharacteristically eager for me to arrive, Frank stared out a foyer window and watched the lawn darken. Soon, he turned on a lamp. Pacing through the rooms, he tapped a piano key and, briefly, a despondent, minor note reverberated. I've imagined this, of course. But Maggie was out; and down the street, Tim was playing with his friends. So when Frank answered the phone and asked where I was, I immediately felt his loneliness and regretted stealing the hour I hadn't known he'd wanted.

At first, I didn't understand Frank's urgency. But sometime earlier he'd begun to suffer from depression. When he told me, I admitted that I'd been paranoid for a year and I sent him excerpts from my journals, which, he said, riveted him. Now he wanted to talk about our experiences.

Angry with myself for making him wait, I ran through campus, then sprinted across the bridge. Breathless, I hustled up the long hill. Frank opened the front door before I rang the bell, and, as he shook my hand, I leaned forward and half hugged him. Still winded, I removed my coat. Frank poured two drinks, which we carried into the living room. As we sat opposite each other, logs burned in the fireplace, warming my skin. By then, we'd ceased to be teacher and pupil, or surrogate father and dutiful son. We were equals, trying to answer unanswerable questions. Frank got straight to the point. "That paragraph you wrote, about seeing an apparition of yourself crawling along the floor, begging you to kill it," he said. "Why does the mind begin to attack itself?"

I confessed that, after puzzling over the same question, I didn't know. "Terror?" I guessed. "Pain? Maybe the mind wants to eradicate what it hates, which is its own projection."

"But the process contradicts the impulse for self-preservation. So the instinct can't be hardwired into the brain."

"I don't think it is. I think it's learned, or nurtured."

I told Frank that another writer had explained to me that the brain has a "switch" connected to our "fight or flee" instinct, and its accompanying rush of fear. If the switch is flipped too many times, it can't be turned off. So our fear never subsides, and after a while the brain can't hold itself together.

I added, "Writing a book changes you." Frank nodded. "When you're finished, if you're lucky, you remain whole; if you're not, you shatter."

Or "crack," as F. Scott Fitzgerald put it. In 1936, *Esquire* magazine published his essay "The Crack-Up," in which he wrote, "There is another sort of blow that comes from within—that you don't feel until it's too late to do anything about it, until you realize with finality that you will never be as good a man again."

Sixty years later, in a *GQ* essay, Frank wrote, "I imagine F. Scott Fitzgerald as a kindred soul. I'm not thinking of the quality of his work . . . but of what I take to be his underlying state of mind—a tense mixture of manic energy and deep unease. I believe it was there long before his breakdown."

To read Fitzgerald's confessional essays, Frank claimed, "is to understand not the etiology but the subjective reality, the pain, the darkness, the confusion, of a man hitting bottom."

"Such an experience," he added, "puts an end to innocence. One is violently changed by such trouble. For most people, a nervous breakdown, whatever the causes, constitutes the most profound event in their lives, creating such deep changes in their understanding of themselves and of the world that they are forced in many ways to begin all over again."

"Have you come all the way back?" Frank asked me. "After the paranoia, I mean."

"No."

"Not even with the pills?"

I shook my head.

"Sorry," he said.

We talked for another hour and, although I can't recollect what we said, I believe our conversation may have shaped what Frank wrote two years later. He'd collected his essays—forty years' worth—and published them as a book titled *Dogs Bark, but the Caravan Rolls On*. To link them, Frank composed "observations" and, in 2001, he finally admits:

> The term 'nervous breakdown' is currently out of fashion, but I allow myself to use it because that is what I used, several years after the fact, to describe to myself what happened to me as I finished my autobiography thirty-five years ago. I've never written about it, in part because I don't think I can adequately describe it. Indirection is the best I can do. A fear of consciousness itself, fear of myself, beginning on a single afternoon when the sky fell (Chicken Little was right!) and continuing for a number of years of panic and struggle. My condition became my life, and in those days there were neither pills nor any appropriate theoretical models of brain function to help explain what was going on. I could only, out of shame and great effort, hide the inner turmoil, put on a mask of normalcy and soldier through one day at a time. It was a close thing, a very close thing.

Long past dark, Tim returned. Then Frank and I took our drinks into the kitchen, where I helped him prepare dinner, slicing whatever vegetables he slid my way on the countertop, as we stood side by side. The three of us ate in the small, single-windowed breakfast nook, our plates, glasses, and silverware set on an old metal table with a glazed white surface. Pretending to be completely absorbed by his food, and displaying a young boy's guile, Tim said, apropos of nothing, "You know, I think a Mercedes would be a nice gift for the family." Not for him, but for his parents, to whom the idea obviously had never occurred. As a meaningless aside he added, "X's dad has one." Having offered his father advice, rather than requesting a present, Tim returned to eating, seemingly unconcerned with his father's response. Frank and I smiled. Then he said to Tim, gently, "Well, X's dad is a doctor, and he makes more money than I do." Tim asked how much more. "Not a lot," Frank said, "but enough to make a difference." Staring at a piece of meat before placing it in his mouth, Tim said, "Well, it's just something for you to think about."

After we had cleared the table and laid our dishes in the sink, Frank said, "Come on, I'll drive you to the hotel. I go to bed now at nine thirty."

With Tim and Gracie, their golden Labrador retriever, occupying the van's backseat, Frank stopped outside the hotel doors. Then he looked at me and said, "I'll see you."

* * *

Figuratively, Frank hadn't "seen" me when we first met. I was a ghost he walked past in an auditorium's lobby. Now he didn't question the fact that he'd see me again. But had he wanted a cigarette rather than a cup of tea and walked out another door that morning—it was so bright and warm then in Key West, and so dark and cold in Iowa when I stepped out of his van—I never would have seen him. Instead, after waiting for twenty minutes, I would have pedaled home on my bike, not in a rush, simply disappointed, rather than enraged to the point where I tore *Stop-Time* in half and told Jody that Frank Conroy could go fuck himself. I was even angry the day he called, thinking I'd be asked to cover another waiter's shift. But Frank's voice had surprised me, and what he said directed me toward the life I'd hoped to lead. I didn't get everything I longed for, but I got more than enough. True, nothing will quell my chronic doubt or fill my depthless emptiness, and I'm not ungrateful for all I have. I simply don't know how to love it because I don't know how to love me. But I've escaped my father's mockery and earned Frank's admiration. Yet had Frank not driven me that morning to the heart of my anger, which led to me shredding what he'd made and what I longed to make—a book—his opinion of me may not have mattered. (I never told him I'd ripped up a copy of *Stop-Time*, although his reaction likely would have been, "So you had to buy another copy. I'm a buck richer!" before adding, in a low voice, "But you know, Tom, Nazis destroyed books, too. Consider your company, my friend.") In the end, I may have been no more than another student with some talent. Of course, what my other life might have been like is unknowable. But I know this: if I hadn't met him, I wouldn't be typing these words, hoping to marry meaning, clarity, and sense to memory in order to keep him alive.

CHAPTER TWENTY-TWO

C ollecting Frank's essays and publishing them in book form
was Maggie's idea. Frank consented, with a caveat: her idea,
her task. Hunting through unmarked cartons, searching
for yellowed newspapers and wrinkled magazines that contained
his work, would have bored Frank before he opened box one. So,
with his blessing, Maggie became his official archivist. "Miss Lee,"
he called her, affectionately, referring to Truman Capote's devoted
assistant, Nelle Harper Lee, author of *To Kill a Mockingbird*. Maggie
enjoyed finding essays and articles Frank had written after he'd finished *Stop-Time*. He wrote strictly to make money, then. "Not very
much money, to be sure," he notes, in one of his "observations," "but
I did it occasionally. *Stop-Time* had been a critical success, but had
brought in next to nothing." However, the *New Yorker* had printed
chapters of his memoir and the magazine's legendary and eccentric
editor, Mr. William Shawn, who lunched every day at the Algonquin
Hotel on a dry English muffin, urged Frank to write Notes and
Comments columns. Over the next two years, Frank composed a

dozen pieces. But, he said, "I finally stopped because I overreacted to rejection. Whenever [Mr. Shawn] turned one down, even with good reason, it broke my heart." (Frank later counseled students not to be "weakened by rejection"; handle it, or you'll never be a writer.) Despite Frank's *New Yorker* experience, he accepted magazine assignments. Between the late 1960s and 2001, he wrote about sex, shooting pool, music, his father, becoming a father—in his thirties, and then again at age fifty-two—the workshop, the jazz trumpet virtuoso Winton Marsalis, Charles Manson, and the Rolling Stones. "Who are they?" he asked his girlfriend. Believing that Frank was putting her on —he wasn't—she said, "You haven't heard the name Mick Jagger?" Frank answered, "He's in the group, right? He sings?" (After meeting Jagger, Frank described him in the article as a "narcissistic egomaniac.") Frank's literary pittance, combined with tips he earned playing the piano at various Nantucket bars, kept him from starving, but not from collecting unemployment. During the island's off-season, almost no work existed; hence, little shame was involved. His neighbors accepted government handouts, too. Frank decided that "the cliché is true: when you don't really need money, it's easy to get, and when you absolutely must have it, it's hard to come by."

His literary friends asked him why he didn't write another memoir. "A lot of people expected me to continue the story of my life," he later wrote, "but I was determined not to write that kind of book again. *Stop-Time* stands alone, and I'm glad of that. I did not think of the book as the start of a career, I thought of it as a thing unto itself, and was astonished that I'd been able to make it."

Yet, one year after publishing his essay collection, he unexpectedly began another memoir, then hoped he'd live long enough to finish it.

＊　＊　＊

A malignant tumor in his colon had metastasized. By the time his physician detected it, Frank's cancer had reached stage four. There is no stage five. In four to six months, he'd be dead.

I hadn't seen Frank since we'd had dinner, three and a half years earlier. We spoke often, of course. But my identity had been shaped so deeply by him that his physical absence no longer mattered. In my life, he was ever present.

When I called one evening, Maggie answered. Frank now spoke to few people. He wanted to say only what was necessary, I imagine.

After Maggie handed Frank the phone, he and I were momentarily silent. I remember lying on the couch in the room where I wrote, floor-to-ceiling bookshelves behind and before me, his books beside mine. We'd each written four and edited one connected to Iowa. 2,200 pages, 600,000 words, our lives converging like the letter *V*, moving through time from the moment we each said, "I want to be a writer." Six words then, and six different words now. Midway through our conversation, Frank's voice began to quake, and he said, "You know I love you, right?"

He wanted to be certain I understood, and he was asking me to release him. "Right?" he said.

Softly, but unequivocally, I said, "Yes, I know."

Then, beginning to cry, he said, "I have to go," and the receiver rattled as his trembling hand dropped it into its cradle.

He didn't even hear me say, "Okay." But then, he didn't need to.

* * *

While writing this memoir, I believed I knew Frank completely. The illusion was necessary. But the truth is: like all of us, Frank was a mosaic. We know a person not only by what we observe and what he or she says or tells us but also by what we infer, imagine, and are told by others. Toward the end of his life, the latter is how I knew Frank.

A few weeks ago, I e-mailed Frank's son Will to ask if I had certain dates right—the date Frank learned he had cancer, and the date Frank flew to Washington DC. The reason for his trip was simple. The news headline read, "Iowa Writers' Workshop Wins National Humanities Medal":

The University of Iowa Writers' Workshop has been selected to receive the National Humanities Medal, presented by the U.S. government to honor America's leaders in the humanities. Only one organization has been honored in the past—all the other honorees have been individuals—and the Iowa Writers' Workshop is the first university-based organization to be honored.

President George W. Bush will present the medal to Frank Conroy, director of the Writers' Workshop, in a White House ceremony today (Thursday, Feb. 27) in Washington, D.C.

"The Iowa Workshop was the first in the country, and I am accepting this award for all the people who have built it over its 67-year history," Conroy said. "We are deeply grateful for this national recognition."

Will answered:

Dad was diagnosed shortly (like a week or two) before he took that trip to Washington. The trip happened between the diagnosis and the surgery, actually. A weird, dark time. When I asked Dad about that DC event I remember him saying it was surreal and that the various characters—Bushes, Lynne Cheney, Clarence Thomas, et al,. looked somehow like cardboard cutouts.

My favorite story about that—which Maggie told me and which, to me, is pure Dad—had to do with the after party held in some White House room near the Oval Office—people mingling and sipping white wine, etc. There was a small military brass band on a little stage beside a roped-off piano that had been a gift from some king or sultan or someone—a piano not meant to be played, just displayed. But of course it was a nice instrument and Dad removed the velvet rope and walked to it and started to sit down. One of the band, a black guy, a bit startled, leaned over and informed Dad that he was not allowed to play the piano. Dad just nodded and said, "It's cool, babe," and got himself set and started to play. Probably "Autumn

Leaves" or one of the standards he could swing through so well,
or maybe a twelve-bar blues—I don't know. But the surprised
band checked each other and quickly realized they'd have way
more fun with Dad than with whatever (undoubtedly stiff)
playlist they'd prepared, and so they joined in. I guess it was
a great jam—a real foot stomp in the White House—and it
changed the feel of the whole room and prompted high fives on
stage and smiles all around.

I love that story. Not only could Dad always seem to under-
stand the absurdity of the velvet rope/display piano kind of
bullshit, he also had a quietly disarming way of making everyone
else see the absurdity of it too. And as a result those guys just dug
in and swung hard. How cool is that? But I'm only repeating this
secondhand—Maggie was there. I wish I had been.

Had I paraphrased Will's e-mail, you would have experienced the
episode thirdhand, and Frank would not have become "Dad." After all,
Frank had three biological sons. He wasn't simply my surrogate father.

Also, I got certain facts wrong; or not facts, exactly, but inter-
pretations and perceptions. I'd mailed a published excerpt of this
memoir to Maggie, Will, Tim, and Frank's oldest son, Dan, offering them my version of "Frank." But what if it didn't conform to
their version, or versions? Would Maggie hate her husband's por-
trayal? Would his sons loathe their father's depiction? Would they
despise what I'd written, and me as well? I realized that Frank
didn't belong solely to me, and I worried about what they'd think.
But Will's e-mail relieved me:

Hey Tom!
*   This is an excellent piece—really first rate, and I happily*
learned a few things I didn't know about Dad.
And his e-mail surprised me:
*   Also—and because I can't be any kind of fair critic of my*
father's work I've appropriately kept my mouth shut about it—I

really love Body & Soul and I was glad to read your thoughts
about it. My dirty little family secret is that I love B&S even
more than Stop-Time. . . . Body & Soul seemed to me to be
as honest a book as Stop-Time, but it came mostly from love
rather than anger. Needless to say I'm very glad Dad got to a
point where he could write from such a place.

And my perception about Frank's hands, as described in the essay, was wrong. I'd written, "His hands were large, his fingers long, ideal for a piano player." But, by e-mail, Maggie corrected me:

> *I had to smile because actually, Frank had small hands. He*
> *was secretly proud that he couldn't reach an octave but came*
> *up with a way to do it if required.*

In a sense, I was also wrong about the amount of time Frank spent with his sons after his divorce. It "would be limited to three months each summer," I'd written. "Otherwise, he was absent, mimicking his own fatherless childhood."

Which was not entirely true. Will wrote:

> *One thing I need to say—although you're absolutely right*
> *that Dad's time with Dan and me was essentially limited to*
> *three months a year after the divorce, and technically it's true*
> *that he was 'absent from our lives,' as you write, I promise you*
> *it didn't really feel that way. We spoke on the phone all the time*
> *and wrote letters and he was always very carefully attentive*
> *and respectful and helpful with regard to any of our little wor-*
> *ries or problems. He was great about that—made it feel like*
> *he was there, still, in Brooklyn. It always seemed like he was*
> *coming to NY for a visit within the next few weeks or we were*
> *visiting him somewhere or meeting for Thanksgiving or some-*
> *thing like that. I missed him sometimes, of course, but it always*
> *felt, every day, as if he was very present and accessible. In fact a*

joke I had with Dad was that, in contrast to his own situation in which that wall of books became (replaced) his father, I had such a great father that I never had to read a single book (!).

Our feelings, perceptions, and imaginations create the constantly changing mosaic of those we know, but know incompletely.

* * *

Once cancer reaches stage four, nothing, not chemo, not an operation, will halt its metastasizing. Yet, after reconsidering the test results, Frank's oncologist changed his opinion. "Now he says I'm a three," Frank told me, "or more like a three and a half."

The operation, on a late-winter afternoon, lasted four hours, maybe five. Frank's entire colon and all malignant tissue surrounding it were removed. Before Frank had fully recovered, he began chemo treatments. "And let me tell you," he said, "they're no fun."

Before his diagnosis, he had signed a contract to write *Time and Tide* for Crown, which published a line of "walk" books in which famous writers described the places where they lived, at least part of the time. When Frank's agent, Neil, broached the idea, Frank immediately said, "Nantucket." Like other "walk" books, Frank's paperback-sized volume would be short—140 pages—and it would blend the island's history with Frank's history. It's a somber book, at times, and its audio version, read by Frank, weakened by chemotherapy, is haunting. A sense of letting go—of his work, of his family, of his life—permeates the memoir. And, after thirty-five years, certain regrets remain vivid. "I don't have much nostalgia for Nantucket in the seventies," he writes. "Personally, it was a tough time both emotionally and economically. I was a writer, after all, and, to make it worse, a literary writer. I left Brooklyn with three hundred dollars, no job prospects, and an unheated, unfinished barn on a remote island as my only possession." He scraped by, "living on the cheap," as he put it. "I installed electric heaters in

the bedroom and kitchen, but the barn hadn't been built with winter in mind and I spent a lot of time in the crawl space underneath
working on frozen pipes with a propane torch, or installing new
ones with an instruction book lying open in the dirt in front of me.
My mortgage was $600. I discovered anew how claustrophobic and
narrowing it is to live with little money. (I'd known it in my childhood, too, although in a different way.)" But he noted the farcical,
as well. During the nineteenth century, when most of Nantucket's
male population was out to sea, whaling, lonely women managed
the island. Frank unearthed a newspaper ad that read: "Nervous?
I will spend the night with thee. 25 cents." He also discovered that
"a type of ceramic dildo imported from Asia called 'He's at Home'
was a common domestic item." Wanting the fullest sense of Frank's
mood while he worked on the book, I asked Neil for his impressions.
By e-mail he replied: *The diagnosis threw him, and he talked about
canceling the contract, or not taking the money until he was done. But
in fact writing was a joy for him (not common to writers, as you know),
and I think it gave him a pleasurable task to distract his mind.* Frank
didn't overlook other treasures, either. "The kids discover the joys of
clamming," he writes, "and of the fact that you can bring something
back for dinner even if you're seven years old, let's say. We always
went out to a tidal flat near the entrance to Polpis Harbor in our boat,
with the dog. Maggie and I might swim while Tim, my youngest,
went off with a bucket for an hour. We could see him in the distance,
hunkered down, his small form bright in the stark sunlight, elbows
akimbo, digging with purpose. Or on a foggy day, he would simply
disappear as the sound of buoy bells rang muffled in the air. We call
it Tim's Point, and we go there often."

*   *   *

Eighteen months later, the *New York Times* announced Frank's semi-
retirement. He would continue to teach but resign as the workshop's
director in August 2005. Asked to "reveal the secret to his success" as

director, Frank answered, "I wing it." He didn't discuss cancer or chemotherapy. Instead, "he said now it was time for him to get on with
his own writing." Then, as if this were more important than his health
or his work, I can hear him saying, "*And* I've found an 'angel' who
has offered to give the workshop $1 million for its own library," add-
ing, as a casual aside, "if I can match the funds," which Frank blew
off as a minor inconvenience. The important thing was, he'd won
another game. "A *million* bucks!" he would have told me. But when
the reporter asked Frank about his new book, he reiterated advice he'd
given me years earlier. "If you talk about it," he said, "it will disappear."

But Frank and I knew he'd never write another book. From the
day he finished *Time and Tide*, his relation to books would simply
be to read them like a boy "seeking only to escape from [his] own
life through the imaginative plunge into another." And his temperament changed. "He was so gentle with everyone," Maggie said,
referring to his sons and grandchildren. No matter how trifling
their questions or concerns, they had his full attention. After all,
how long would he be able to offer it? Frank knew he'd cheated
time. He should have been dead a year earlier. So, regardless of his
treatment's continued success, he expected to die soon. For the
moment, though, being surrounded by his family constituted a
miracle, and he lived exclusively for them. Once, Maggie said to
me, "I told Frank I thought chemo agreed with him."

* * *

Which seemed to be the case. Whenever we spoke, he was buoyant.
But, despite his upbeat mood, I decided not to visit. Sitting beside
each other would have wrapped us in a funereal cocoon, and I didn't
want to face the fact that we'd never see each other again. Instead,
I needed *my* image of Frank to remain intact. But he was already
becoming a memory. Like a magic wand, his cane irrevocably separated the past from the present. Frank had been in my life for fifteen
years, and when he died my past died, too. Without him I can no

longer be the boy seeking his approval, and worrying that I might not receive it. Instead, I was forced to decide who I am. And I have. I'm the man who wrote this book. I can't ask Frank if he thinks it's good, but I don't have to; this book is one thing alone: necessary.

Late one November afternoon, I called to ask about his health. Astonishingly, he sounded lighthearted, his voice strong and clear. He'd quit smoking, and his speech was silky and soothing. Happy that I'd called, he seemed carefree. We talked about Charlie's recently published *New Yorker* story. "Did you read that?" he said. "I mean, the language, holy shit. How's he doing, by the way?" Good, I said. "Well, send him my love."

We discussed books until Frank said, "You understand, the day I can't read, it's all over. And between us, if it weren't for these chemo treatments, I'd keep directing. But let's not kid ourselves, this is going to kill me."

Then, imagining our futures, he added, "You know, running this place will be easier than running your place in Texas. We both know that Connie does everything." True, some people expected me to succeed Frank, but he and I had never discussed the matter and I thought we had a tacit understanding that we never would.

Surprised, I said, "They need someone with a big name, and that's not me."

Frank disagreed. But I directed an MFA program and I knew that if I were running the search, I wouldn't hire me, either.

I had other concerns, though. To inherit Frank's job, his office, and his desk would have been like inheriting his ghost. I loved him. But attempting to extend his literary legacy would have diminished it. And Frank's career deserved a full stop, not an ellipsis.

Shortly after New Year's, Frank's new regimen of chemo treatments began, and I called to see how they were progressing. Frank answered, but I was no longer Tom! or Professor Grimes! Those words were already memories. I detected no fear in his voice, no grief or despair, only exhaustion. We spoke for less than a minute. I told him to take the fall semester off, stay on Nantucket, and then drive Tim to Wheaton in September to watch him enter college. "We'll see." Frank said. "We'll see." He lacked the strength to say good-bye, and I wouldn't say it for us both.

On February 8, 2005, he walked into Connie's office and said he had to leave. He never saw the Dey House again.

* * *

Frank had arranged to die at home, not in a hospital. "He planned it all," Maggie said. Frank spent his days in the upstairs bedroom in which I'd spent two hundred nights. He permitted few visitors. James Salter, his closest friend and the workshop's visiting writer the semester I entered the program, traveled to Iowa City to have a final lunch with Frank. A photograph shows them smiling, their arms around each other's shoulders, each holding a glass, Frank's filled with clear liquid and curiously resembling one used for drinking a martini. Otherwise, only his sons and grandchildren came and went whenever they could.

As for Dad's last days and the hospice care, Will wrote to me, *I'll say two quick things about what I experienced firsthand*:

> First, Dad stayed cool. And he didn't ever complain to me (nor, to my knowledge, to anyone else) about his fate, and in fact when the end was near he once quietly mentioned to me— as far as longevity—that he appreciated his 69 years. I'll always remember how well he handled himself in his last days, and I'll always be grateful to him for it.
>
> Second, there was only one time I saw him discouraged. They were still saying he had a couple months left, and since he'd been beating their projections for a few years there was no reason to think it would be less. I was visiting him in Iowa City. Late one afternoon I jogged upstairs to ask some little question and I found him sitting on the edge of his bed, looking ashen and staring out the window at nothing in particular. I understood

right away that something new was wrong. "I can't read," he said, sounding sort of amazed by the fact. I guess he and Maggie had thought maybe there was something wrong with his glasses or something, but Dad had quickly realized it was his mind. The meds, the illness, whatever, he could no longer process words on a page. That was a hard moment, I'd say. He didn't apparently dwell on it, but he put down whatever book he was reading and from then on I think he just wanted to get things over with.

Frank couldn't read the card I mailed to him; Maggie had to. I remember writing, *You changed my life and I hope that in some small, happy way I've changed yours. After that, there's nothing I can say or send but love, love, love.* When he heard what I'd written, Maggie said, "Frank gave a little smile." It was his final gift to me.

In early April, he asked the hospice staff to stop his morphine. For three days, his body curled and twisted, spastically, like a helpless infant's, as his organs died. Then his heart stopped, and he no longer belonged to time.

*   *   *

I spent sixty hours writing and revising what became my 1,019-word eulogy. I printed pages, spread them across my dining room table, circled sentences I wanted to keep, and struck those I didn't. Jody assembled the survivors. And Charlie said, "You have to say something about a public man who was also your friend, so which side of that do you address for such an occasion? Both, I guess. You don't have to sum him up for all time, though. Just stick with what you feel is truest and you'll do great. Go the Whitman route—what is true for you will also be true for the rest of us. I think you can trust that."

When I finished writing the eulogy, I read it aloud until I'd numbed my emotions so I would be able to read it to others.

*   *   *

For Frank's memorial service seven hundred people packed a campus auditorium, and a three-page program was printed. A photograph of Frank, taken when he was in his mid-fifties, appeared in the center. Below it, his name and the span of his life, 1936–2005.

To Frank's right was a photocopy of a handwritten manuscript page of *Stop-Time*. Three paragraphs described his decision to leave his New York high school and return to Florida. His first draft began: *It might have been the thought of school that crystallized me.* Frank scratched that. *It might have been the thought of school that changed me, the impossible prospect of another day inside that soul-destroying prison.* Frank blacked out several words, then wrote, *That might have been what did it—the stillness inside me, the thanatoid silence frightening me into a last-ditch effort. Or the thought of school, the prospect of another day in prison crystallizing my formless mind as the pencil tap crystallizes a super-saturated solution.* The paragraph ended: *I turned from the window, walked down the hall and went out the door. It was as simple as that.* Then he blotted a phrase and added, *I disregarded the pounding of my heart.*

To Frank's left, a list of his memorial speakers' names. Marilynne Robinson and I would offer "Reflections." Then John Irving and T. C. Boyle would read from their work. I'd taken two milligrams of a tranquilizer, but my hands still shook. Five feet from the podium, I sat in the first row beside Marilynne, who stood up to speak. She hadn't written what she wanted to say and, at one point, her eyes moistened and her voice faltered. Terrified, I don't remember a word she said. Once she finished, I walked to the podium and adjusted the microphone. I saw Maggie and the three boys seated in the second row, behind T.C. and John Irving, and, for a disorienting moment, I was a waiter again, watching writers gathered on Sam Lawrence's deck. My life's arc, from waiter to writer, and from cursing Frank to reading my eulogy at his memorial service, seemed improbable, and, in that respect, utterly like Frank's. Returning to the present, I cleared my throat and said, "I dedicated my second novel to Frank. This is my final dedication to him." Then I slipped on my glasses, looked down at my typed pages, and said:

> *Literature was Frank's school, his salvation, and his joy. One can't separate Frank the writer, from Frank the reader, from Frank the teacher. Each aspect of his personality was of a piece. Forget for a moment any one of them and you'll remember and cherish him incompletely.*
>
> *As a boy Frank read his manic-depressive father's entire library, which became his refuge. "Safe in my room with milk and cookies," he wrote in Stop-Time, "I disappeared into inner space. The real world dissolved and I was free to drift in fantasy, living a thousand lives, each one more powerful and more real than my own."*
>
> *Ultimately, reading turned him into a writer. As a genre, the memoir barely existed before Frank published Stop-Time, which, he once told me, was completely out of sync with its era. Yet the book became a classic because the purity of Frank's perfect prose not only stops time, but renders time timeless.*
>
> *Writing the book exorcised and, at the same time, celebrated his childhood; and by age thirty Frank had fulfilled what Susan Sontag deemed to be the sole responsibility of a writer—to write a masterpiece.*

I paused for a moment, then continued:

> *People speak of great writers, but few people speak of great readers, and Frank was one of them, perhaps the best reader I've ever known. He took genuine pleasure in the act of reading and somehow he was able to retain his complete innocence as a reader, to read as the boy he once was, alone in his bedroom, keeping his anxiety about his complicated childhood at bay by turning the pages of a novel.*

Yet for all of Frank's innocence, he never failed to pluck from each great book a master's lesson, which he then selflessly passed along to his students. Frank read great writers without any fear. He didn't worry about imitating them; he didn't worry about being overwhelmed by them. Instead he took pleasure in them and learned from them, and by doing so he elevated reading to the level of art, which Picasso described as "serious play," a phrase that captures Frank's relationship to reading literature and to teaching it.

Frank was also a generous reader. Recognizing that his escape from his own Dickensian childhood had depended on chance, unexpected benefactors, and good fortune, he repaid the pleasure and enlightenment Dickens had given him by writing Body & Soul, a novel that astonishes us because it's a truly happy book. For a second time, Frank had composed a work that was completely out of sync with its age. Not a single word in the novel is tainted by cynicism, postmodern game-playing, or lyrical pyrotechnics. Over all of Frank's prose, from the books right down to his essays, there hovers an Olympian calm. He could even write about seven days on a cruise ship and make the experience seem somehow sacred.

Yet the boy in Frank never entirely vanished. Last fall, when I called to ask him how his summer had been, he said, "I read a book a day. It was heaven."

I turned a page.

His other heaven was Maggie and his three boys. In his life as a husband and a father, Frank composed yet another masterpiece.

"How odd it is," he said to me in his car one morning, "to find the perfect woman just when you think the possibility is gone forever." Wistful as he could sometimes be about the great bliss Maggie brought into his life, he was also proud of the fact that he'd *picked her up on Nantucket while he was headed to the garbage dump. "Her face seemed to radiate vitality," he wrote, "an almost shocking kind of aliveness that laser-beamed its way through the dirty windshield and my gloom-obsessed, three-quarters shutdown consciousness." "Dickensian coincidence!" he gleefully shouted when he told me the story. But he was somewhat cooler on the page when he wrote about it. "She got in and sat in the backseat. 'Hi,' she said cheerfully" (using an adverb that in workshop he likely would have told one of us to cut). "I accelerated and glanced in the rearview mirror, tilting it." (Good detail, the tilting it, he would have said.) "Yes indeed, I thought. Most particularly her eyes. Hope—like some glaciated mammoth slowly stirring in the heat of a miraculous arctic thaw—revived." (I'd watch the "slowly stirring," he would have warned the writer. "It's a bit . . ."). And then he wouldn't say anymore, yet every student in the room would know exactly what he meant, just as I knew exactly what he meant when, late one night, Frank and I were leaving his house, bound for the Foxhead, and he reached down and shook one of Maggie's bare toes as she sat with her feet up on the couch, reading. I knew in an instant, by that simple gesture, how deeply he loved her.*

In each of his boys, Frank was reborn, and the pleasure he took in each of them overflowed until their simple presence became for him a palpable joy.

One day, while Frank and I were talking on the phone, he said, "Tim just came into the room; he's beautiful." I told him that Tim had always been good-looking, and Frank said, "No, I don't mean looks. I'm mean, he's beautiful. Just him being there makes my heart leap."

Silence.

Everything, by this point in Frank's life, had become a gift, and through the final days all the gifts he'd been given were transmuted into an unexpected and unbidden sweetness. The disquiet Frank had carried in his heart ever since childhood had been stilled by the birth of his oldest son, Dan. Afterward, it was impossible for him to let his love for his boys remain unspoken.

Years ago, Frank and I were standing on the front lawn outside of his and Maggie's old house. His son Will had just left, and we watched Will's car drive away until it disappeared. Then Frank looked at me and said, "You know, it's amazing when they're here, unfathomable when they leave, and unbelievable how much you miss them once they're gone."

CODA

Last night in the woods, at dusk, as I walked through a dim, gray light, I knew I would finish the book tomorrow. I needed one or two more sentences and I realized that I would type them on August 28, the day Frank and I first met at Iowa, when he was fifty-four as I am now. I hadn't expected to write this book, but, in a way, our memoirs form bookends. His about childhood, adolescence, and a lost father; mine about writing, teaching, and a father found. Our story has come full circle. The story's meaning mystifies me, yet if Frank were alive he'd agree that neither of us would choose to live in a world that was unmarked by the passage of time, and anything other than inscrutable.

ACKNOWLEDGMENTS

Deepest thanks to Jody Grimes, Charles D'Ambrosio, Connie Brothers, Janet Silver, and Lee Montgomery, who suggested that I write this book when I didn't know there was a book about Frank Conroy and me waiting to be written, and to all the great people at Tin House Books—Deborah Jayne, Nanci McCloskey, Janet Parker, Tony Perez, and Meg Storey.